KU-572-498

The Dance

◆

A HANDBOOK FOR THE APPRECIATION OF THE CHOREOGRAPHIC EXPERIENCE

by Joan Cass

1767562

LIBRARY

ACC. No. 3602G188	DEPT.
CLASS No. 792.8 CAS	
UNIVERSITY OF CHESTER	

McFarland & Company, Inc., Publishers
Jefferson, North Carolina, and London

The present work is a reprint of the library bound
edition of The Dance : A Handbook for the
Appreciation of the Choreographic Experience,
first published in 1999 by McFarland.

LIBRARY OF CONGRESS CATALOGUING-IN-PUBLICATION DATA

Cass, Joan
    The dance : a handbook for the appreciation of the
choreographic experience / by Joan Cass.
        p.   cm.
    Includes bibliographical references and index.

    ISBN 0-7864-2231-9 (softcover : 50# alkaline paper) ∞

    1. Dance—Philosophy.   2. Choreography.   I. Title.
GV1588.C37   2005
792.8—dc21   99-39737

British Library cataloguing data are available

©1999 Joan Cass. All rights reserved

No part of this book may be reproduced or transmitted in any form
or by any means, electronic or mechanical, including photocopying
or recording, or by any information storage and retrieval system,
without permission in writing from the publisher.

On the cover: Paul Taylor company dancers Christopher Gillis and
Monica Morris in Taylor's Private Domain. Photograph © Jack
Vartoogian, courtesy Paul Taylor.

Manufactured in the United States of America

McFarland & Company, Inc., Publishers
    Box 611, Jefferson, North Carolina 28640
    www.mcfarlandpub.com

This book is dedicated to the memory of George Cass,
who encouraged me to write

Table of Contents

Preface

There is an eternal triangle in the art of dance: choreographer-performer-viewer. The choreographer creates, the dancer interprets and performs, the viewer observes and receives impressions. Although the first two initiate the experience to which the third reacts, and although sometimes the same person may occupy more than one side, all three are necessary for the completion of a dance event.

This book is addressed to those who sit on the third side of the triangle. It is not a substitute for viewing, nor does it claim to tell viewers how to react. Its purpose is to heighten their appreciation, and make dance events more approachable, with a body of background information and ideas concerning various facets of the art form.

This study constantly refers readers to examples of the works themselves. Choreographers, dancers and compositions whose names appear in each chapter were selected because of their importance to the dance art. The context will, I hope, make the references clear. More detailed clarification is available in the histories, encyclopedias and videotapes listed in the Bibliography.

The text opens with a presentation of the central thesis: that the inner life of choreographers is transformed into the framework of dance imagery, thus creating art objects for perception. Next, the topic of choreographic

1

style is introduced. Although the viewers addressed and the repertory discussed loosely fit into the category of "western theatrical dance," worldwide cultural variations are very important and receive due consideration.

The next five chapters discuss the components of all choreographic works. These are body language and content, structure, the contributions of music and design, and the interpretive power of performers. Lastly, thoughts are presented on the development of repertory and questions of aesthetics.

The material for this survey has grown out of a long career of taking classes, reviewing performances, interviewing artists, reading, researching, writing, and teaching criticism and history. I also studied videotapes that Michael Blackwood kindly sent me of butoh and postmodern dance, and films from the extensive collection of the University of Indiana.

As far as possible, my use of the words and ideas of dance artists and writers is indicated in the text and notes, although undoubtedly through so many years in the field, I have absorbed many insightful remarks that are not credited.

I would also like to express my gratitude to a number of people who were directly involved in producing this book. Photographers Martha Swope and Herbert Migdoll, as well as dance artists Paul Taylor, Murray Louis, Gerald Arpino and Tina Ramirez, were generous in supplying the photographs which help bring the repertory to life. Linda Piette and Madeline Strosberg patiently edited the text for clarity. Computer expert David Cass contributed his unfailing technical support. Thank you all.

Please note: Balanchine is a trademark of the George Balanchine Trust.

1

Life,
Art and Dance

At the height of the "Happening" craze in 1968, a work of art walked into my newspaper office. It was a young man in turtleneck shirt and blue jeans wearing a picture frame around his head. With a perfectly straight face he announced, "This is my frame of reference."

He got what he came for: publicity for his dance troupe. In return, the young man left behind an unforgettable image of art as something fenced off from the everyday world, something selected and arranged for our attention. His frame became a symbol of the stage—an enclosure for moving art works.

Choreographer Paul Taylor expressed a related thought in his autobiography. He wrote that when he was a child, "a proscenium had been stamped in me, a frame, a door that was to swing back and forth between a private and a public domain."[1]

That phrase "between a private and a public domain" is a key to unlock the door to dance appreciation. Taylor's—and every other choreographer's—output consists of objective dance works framed for our perception. But their expression is deeply connected to inner, private sources.

Aesthetic philosopher Susanne K. Langer elaborated on this point in a description of our art form: "A dance ... expresses the nature of human feeling—the rhythms and connections, crises and breaks, the complexity and richness of what is sometimes called man's 'inner life', the stream of direct experience, life as it feels to the living...."[2]

During the period in which I met the framed young man, my own frame of reference in trying to understand dance was general art theory. It seemed to me logical to begin with a long view of the nature of art, and then zoom in for a close-up on dance.

The first thing I learned was an unpleasant truth, not about the philosophy of art, but about the philosophers themselves—those academics who are labeled "aestheticians." While they freely draw examples from music, literature, painting and sculpture to illustrate their theories, only a small minority ever refer to dance. Indeed, many academicians turn up their noses at the specialty. Uncomfortable with the medium of bodily movement, they won't rank it with the "fine" arts, but limit its place in the college curriculum to women's physical education.

Fortunately, Susanne K. Langer is an outstanding exception to this group. Not only do her art books clarify many difficult questions, they provide insightful comments on dance, like the statement quoted above.

Dance as an Image of Behavior

What makes dance able to bear such an impressive burden as Langer describes? The answer lies in its very nature: the fact that the medium of this art form is movement. Movement, which is the raw material of the dance art, is much more than physical activity. Our language is clear on this point. "Motive," "motion" and "movement" have the same root. To move is to progress; to excite feelings and passions; to impel someone to action. In other words, movement is connected to a person's deepest intellectual and emotional being, and often functions as speech without words. Recently, psychologists have been studying nonverbal communication—the ideas and emotions expressed by bodily movement alone, in social relationships.

Because all human behavior involves movement, there is, conversely, no such thing as a dance motion or action that does not have some behavioral connotations. A leap conveys a kind of youthful excitement, or soaring free; kneeling implies weariness, subjugation, or prayer; an arm lift may be a greeting, or a reaching; a head turn may indicate looking or rejecting; a head bend can show despair.

However, choreography does not recreate concrete experiences or events of life. What is actually presented in a dance is a semblance—a reflection— of behavior and emotions.

John Cranko put it this way: "Suppose somebody gets lifted up—it gives you at once an image of flying. When Juliet gets carried through the air, she's not really flying—but you see her flying, you feel as if she is: it becomes an image of ecstasy."[3]

In short, a dance is made up of experiences transformed into images. Cranko, who choreographed many literary works like *Romeo and Juliet*, *Taming of the Shrew* and *Eugene Onegin*, clarified the question of dance imagery:

> You can make your movement poetry, so to speak. You find a movement image to illuminate the idea. Take something very simple, like falling. You see someone sink to the stage and you respond, "Ah, he's fallen." In *Onegin* at the end, when Tatiana sends him away, there's a rather tortured *pas de deux*, with a movement where they sink to the floor, all sort of knotted up together. You know, if you looked at it realistically, well—a woman in Victorian times would never sink to the floor like that. It becomes an abstract image. It's like a diamond that has no color of its own. But if you turn the diamond in the light it can be pink, or green, depending on how you view it.

When we feel sad, we may slump ¼ of an inch. A mime would imitate this posture exactly, and the explicit meaning of the sequence would be immediately clear to the viewer. A dancer however, may magnify this slump 2,304 times to a drop of 6 feet, from a relevé (standing on the toes) to a prone position on the floor. This abstract expansion of a downward droop can only be grasped in the context of a given work.

Merce Cunningham, although he is cited as a dance artist whose interest is confined to movement as movement with *no* emotional associations, recognizes the connection between movement and feeling. Tucked into the middle of Cunningham's scribbles and notes are a few general observations: "joy, love, fear, anger, humor, all can be 'made clear' by images familiar to our eyes. and all are grand or meager depending on the eye of the beholder.... the sense of human emotion that a dance can give is governed by familiarity with the language, and the elements that act with the language; here those would be music, costume, space, together with which the dance happens."[4]

Implicit versus Explicit Communication

An image is an impression, a reflection, a portrait. To understand the nature of dance imagery, we return to a comparison between words and movement. Words are used for the ordinary business of life; yet they can also take off on flights of poetic fancy. A poet may compare a beloved woman to a summer day. A dramatist may present life as a birthday party in which one is alternately delighted and disappointed by gifts. In the same way a choreographer transposes events and feelings of life into a language of dance.

When we say that a dance expresses something in language, we are talking about communication. The purpose of the artist, however, is not to deliver information or directives. Notwithstanding the fact that artworks are frequently used in the service of propaganda, moral uplift, or therapy (or publicity, like the young man wearing a frame!), their essential function lies elsewhere. Artworks are unique expressions of feelings.

Because of this special nature, art expressions do not easily lend themselves to rational explanations. Despite the fact that they may include some intellectual content, the communication is basically nonverbal. In other words, what is created in an artwork is primarily implicit, not explicit. Even in a poem, whose medium is words, the meaning is not explained in the words, but emerges from them.

In dance, it works like this: Performers in motion, accompanied by sounds and designs, create images which become the stuff of a dance work. Whatever "meaning" there is in a dance is embodied implicitly in these images. A dance work presents an overall image; at the same time, however, within that work are many minor images. These can be as brief as a single phrase, or they can run to a scene of any length.

We will now consider specific illustrations of this thesis. As we proceed, please keep in mind that words can only "talk around" a dance. They do not stand in its stead.

Public and Private Domains

Our first examples take us back to Paul Taylor, who created public and private domains in choreography long before he expressed the idea in his autobiography. *Public Domain*, a grab bag of ideas that make fun of various bits of dance and music, premiered in 1967. The title refers to musical scores that are in the public domain, either because they were never copyrighted or because the copyright has expired. Accordingly, the dance accompaniment (arranged on commission by John Herbert McDowell) is a mixture of excerpts from works for which no permission or payment of royalties is needed, like Tchaikovsky's *Swan Lake*, Gregorian chants, Elizabethan music, and folk tunes. The piece is a bizarre mixture of movement scenes, many of them spoofs of dance clichés—which because of their overuse can be thought of as in the "public domain." Two couples do a series of combinations in unison with a third male who partners an invisible girl, while ignoring a real one who reclines on the floor. A figure enclosed in a cube scurries across the stage. A male dancer leans on a crutch, then uses it to pole-vault. A female performs a slow meditation on the state of her soul while waving a small flag, accompanied by a lively folk song. A male rolls over on the floor and lies there helplessly stuck on his back. Two ballerinas, competing to show off their technical prowess, smash into each other. Their limbs become so completely entangled that they are forced to hop off the stage as a single monstrosity. Someone calls out, "Medea beware!" and a large white ball rolls onstage, pursued by a smaller one. Finally, as the company starts to build a grand climax to Brahms' "Variations on a Theme of Haydn," the curtain drops abruptly. Finish.

In contrast, there is nothing lighthearted about *Private Domain* (1969), which is fixated on sex. It presents people in sexual couplings that are like callous, sleazy games, played for the blatant satisfaction of lust. Integral to the choreographic conception is Alex Katz's décor, which consists of an opaque drop curtain hanging up front across the footlights and split by three open archways. The dance action takes place mostly behind the drop. But as the five women and three men reach out to caress and clutch at each other, various parts of their bodies are revealed and others hidden by the abstract drapery. This creates a peephole effect, forcing audience members into the voyeuristic position of watching hips, heads, hands and feet, thrusting into view in a dispassionate sex cruise. The placing of a curtain so close to the footlights also serves to flatten out the stage in a manner appropriate

Paul Taylor and Bettie deJong in Taylor's *Public Domain*. Photograph © Jack Mitchell, courtesy of Jack Mitchell.

Paul Taylor company dancers Christopher Gillis and Monica Morris in Taylor's *Private Domain*. **Photograph © Jack Vartoogian, courtesy Paul Taylor.**

to the superficial actions of the dance figures. Critic Marcia Siegel wrote: "The proscenium barrier in *Private Domain* is in a way simply an actualization of the aura of privacy that veils all Taylor's works. Here he encourages us to speculate about what may be behind the screen."[5]

In his autobiography, Taylor related a series of trashy sexual liaisons that preoccupied him during the period before he created *Private Domain*. In no way, however, are these episodes represented in the dance, and it is completely unnecessary to know such factual details in order to appreciate the work.

As Judith Jamison wrote: "When you get onstage it is an arena, and that arena is a reflection of what is going on in life. Whether you're performing a ballet that is abstract or a dance that has a story to tell, the audience should have a mirror held up before them."[6]

That is to say, the images in a dance reflect both the choreographer's and the audience's inner life. It is this reflection that makes communication possible. Years before Taylor's autobiography was published (1987), the reviewers of *Private Domain* had no trouble getting the idea. They, like most people in the audience, had enough direct or vicarious knowledge of sordid sexual situations to grasp the spirit of the work. It is the universal quality of experiences and feelings that allows subjective private life to be mirrored in objective choreography. Taylor told interviewer Nancy Dalva: "I just don't think of my work as an autobiographic form. I try to think of a different kind of scale—more, sort of, international. Larger."[7] In turn, Dalva commented on the artist: "Fact or fancy? It doesn't matter. In the territory of the subconscious, wishes and lies, truths and half-truths intermix and are interchangeable; and all are signifiers. Taylor's dances have a dream logic and they tell dream truth. They relate to strong emotional experiences. You can trust them with all your heart."

Heartfelt Emotional Extremes

If any choreographer dealt with the most excessive, dramatic emotions, it was Martha Graham. Her art displays images of women in the throes of emotional transport and trauma. Martha Graham's choreography is frankly filtered through the psyche of a woman, a being who reveals every nuance of feeling and behavior. In her few light works, the starring woman is coy, silly, submissive or vain. In the far more numerous dark works she is lustful, passionate, enraged, jealous, or exultant. Graham's heroines are not well-rounded individuals. On the contrary, each heroine is the embodiment of a single major emotion or characteristic, and each work explores this particular quality carried to its ultimate.

Graham was not concerned with the sorrows of daily living that preoccupy most of us. Particularly in the tragedies, her characters struggle with boulders in a world of grand scale, an effect the artist achieved by combining psychological insight with myth and legend.

Consider *Cave of the Heart*, which portrays jealousy. This emotion attacks most of us at one time or another, but Graham magnified the feeling one hundred fold, to create an image of evil jealousy etched in acid. To personify the theme she chose Medea, a legendary aging queen. The tale goes that when Medea was displaced in her husband Jason's affections by a young princess, she murdered her rival (and her own children, but not in this dance) most horribly. The use of the story lends the dance theme all the heroic vibrations of Greek tragedy.

Cave of the Heart has only four characters: Sorceress (Medea), Adventurer (Jason), Victim (the young princess) and a one-figure Chorus. Its tone is primitive grandeur. Jason, the triumphant hero of the golden fleece, preens in his hour of victory and woos the princess as the Chorus warns of impending doom. The princess cherishes the returning hero while trying to evade his vicious wife.

But it is the malevolent Medea figure who mesmerizes the viewer. The scorned Sorceress lurches around the stage, her middle sucked in and her back curved like an animal's, coiled for a deadly spring. Shivering in a fever of rage, she crawls upright on her knees. In a graceless squat, she opens and closes her knees like a predatory insect. She extracts from her mouth a long, venomous, red ribbon. She causes the princess to writhe in the poisonous agonies of a savage death, and arranges vile suffering for Jason. When her vengeance is complete, it is Medea's turn to wallow in a victorious orgy. But in the end she is imprisoned by her own overwhelming rage.

Using the barbaric Medea story offered opportunities for forceful design, a crucial factor in Graham's theater pieces. (Writer Leroy Leatherman referred to Graham's works as outright "plays."[8]) Isamu Noguchi came up with scenery and costumes splendidly suited to the powerful mythic import of *Cave of the Heart*. The Sorceress wears a spiraling headdress that suggests snake fangs, and a black silk robe decorated with a winding snake motif that is echoed in the sinuous movements of the Sorceress's hips and pelvis. There is a marvelous spikey arch—part prop, part costume—that this Medea figure can crawl through, wear like an evil mantle, and finally be enclosed in, as though she too is a victim of her heart's corrosive evil.

Symbolism and Flight

A hallmark of Graham's choreography is richness of symbolism. She used the device more consciously than other dance artists had in the past (or have since) to bring home theatrical imagery. A symbol can be a prop or a costume, like Medea's wiry arch, the serpentine figure on her skirt, or the red ribbon she draws out of herself as a reptilian symbol of her blood-red fury. More significantly, dance itself can be symbolic.

Graham clearly understood the power of symbolic movement. She once told a gathering of students: "No movement is completely represen-tational that a dancer makes. There is a very old symbolism behind move-ment. The arabesque is not to show off a girl's or a man's body in flight. It goes to the meaning of flight—anything cleaving through space. The audi-ence does not have to be aware of the symbolism. What the spectator has to be aware of, is something within his own body. He does not have to ana-lyze what flight means, but he should have the feeling or sensation of flight."[9]

It was stated earlier that all movement acts as a semblance of behav-ior. The words "semblance," "image" and "symbol" reach towards the same concept. In the next chapter we shall examine the ways in which dance movement achieves symbolic meaning.

Here we return to the idea that objective dance works mirror subjec-tive inner sources. Just as there was a connection between dance theme and personal life in Paul Taylor's *Private Domain*, so it was with Martha Gra-ham's *Cave of the Heart*. Graham biographers suggest that *Cave of the Heart* grew directly out of the artist's desperate, destructive difficulties with her partner and husband Erick Hawkins who, like Jason, was attracted by a younger woman. However, when she choreographed the piece and repeat-edly gave her dramatically convincing interpretation of the vicious queen, Graham could not have been consumed with jealous fury any more than Taylor could have made *Private Domain* while gripped with burning lust.

Self-Expression

Giving vent to an emotion—letting off steam—is self-expression, not dance. Self-expression takes place in private, or in certain kinds of therapy. While dance artists make movements based on feelings, the actual feelings are not present. As Susanne K. Langer wrote: "No one, to my knowledge, has ever maintained that Pavlova's rendering of slowly ebbing life in *The Dying Swan* was most successful when she actually felt faint and sick, or proposed to put Mary Wigman into the proper mood for her tragic *Evening Dances* by giving her a piece of terrible news a few minutes before she entered the stage."[10]

You can understand that artistic creation is not possible for dancers in the throes of extreme emotion. After the fact, rather, they cast remembered or imagined feelings into movement images. Langer wrote, "An artist expresses feelings, but not in the way a politician blows off steam or a baby laughs and cries.... He objectifies the subjective realm. What he expresses is, therefore, not his own actual feelings, but what he knows about human feelings."[11]

To do this, artists consciously make use of all the choreographic devices at their disposal. And don't forget the role of the subconscious. No matter how closely we observe the artist at work, the process of creation remains a mystery.

It doesn't really matter to us in the audience whether or not biographical facts inspire a choreographer to choose a theme. In any case, the staged image to which we react is abstracted from its lived context.

Abstraction versus Representation

This is as good a time as any to nail down the word "abstract," which has been a stumbling block for many. "Abstract" has several meanings in art.

First of all, "abstract" stands in opposition to "representational," which refers to those artistic works that display objectively recognizable (some would say "realistic") subject matter. Abstract is nonobjective, that is, the use of art materials is divorced from situation and emotion, solely for the pleasure of their perception. Abstract dance is movement presented only for its physical properties: actions used to explore rhythms, spatial designs, and dynamic qualities for their own sake. Most dance works contain at least some passages in this category, sometimes developing representational material, sometimes alternating with it, according to the needs of the composition. In this sense also the overall approach to movement by avant-garde dancers led by Alwin Nikolais and Merce Cunningham is abstract, as is the balletic method developed by George Balanchine.

Secondly, *all* dance is abstract, even the most representational, because the very act of "framing" it for the viewer's perception makes it unnatural. For example, when a scene clearly shows a person drinking, the action is exaggerated in size or rhythm—treated in some way to focus it. This serves to distance it—abstract it—from life.

The third meaning of abstract is the very essence of something. In dance, it is a treatment of natural gesture to reveal its essence, to arrive at the kernel of emotional experience. It is like the "abstract" of a report, which succinctly states the contents. Doris Humphrey and Martha Graham were the foremost creators of this kind of abstraction. As Graham repeatedly said, "Every time you drink a glass of orange juice, you're drinking the abstraction of an orange. That's an abstraction to me: the whole effect."[12]

Animals and Other Symbols

Symbolic dance images are abstract. They extract the essence of a dance character or event and match it up with the essence of an animal, or a natural phenomenon, or a manmade object. Thus choreographers create similes and metaphors in movement, for example representing Medea as a snake.

Remembering Graham's talk on the meaning of flight, it is interesting to note the frequent appearance in choreography of images of flight. Traditional ballets have often used the bird or otherworldly flying creatures (like sylphs and wilis) to symbolize graceful feminine beauty, ecstatic flights of freedom, or ideal female forms floating—elusive, unattainable—above mortal men.

Of course the symbolism of animals goes back thousands of years before the appearance of ballet. In tribal hunting rituals, performers were masked and painted to represent certain animals, whose behavior they would mimic. The object was to win the power to kill the animals, and after a successful hunt, to propitiate their dead spirits, so that these spirits would then intercede for the tribe in controlling natural forces like the rain and the sun. Our study is focused on western dance, starting with the development of ballet as a theatrical art form, separated from magic and religion. Inevitably, however, connections continue to exist between the arts and the human spiritual concerns from which they originated.

Fokine made this point about his ballet *The Dying Swan*: "A high degree of technical perfection is necessary for the correct interpretation of *The Dying Swan*. But ... the perfection of technique serves only as the means of creating a poetic image, a symbol of the perpetual longing for life by all mortals.... This dance aims, not so much at the eyes of the spectator, but at his soul, at his emotions."[13]

Similarly, when Fokine's *Firebird* is imprisoned in the arms of Prince Ivan, her frantically beating, darting attempts to escape remain in one's memory as an image of fear and frustration. We experience real relief when the bird is allowed to fly away. "Live free or die" is an old, deep-rooted impulse.

We identify as well with other, earthbound, animals. A popular ballet, *The Duel*, is built on the movements of horses. The one-act piece is based on Tasso's *Jerusalem Delivered* by William Dollar (1949, music by R. de Banfield). It portrays the Christian crusader Tancred dueling with an unknown Saracen warrior. Throughout the ballet, the dancers prance and paw and dash around the stage like spirited horses. The lead couple and their cohorts are dressed in armor and high-plumed helmets with visors that conceal their faces. Tancred strikes a fatal blow. Too late, his dying opponent removes her helmet, revealing herself to be Clorinda, a dark-haired beauty who had previously won his heart. The horselike action serves both as a literal representation of trained thoroughbreds in battle and a symbolic portrait of proud, arrogant warriors who ride them, glorying in their fighting skills.

Unlike horses, insects inspire in most of us negative feelings ranging from irritation to disgust and fear. In *The Cage* (1951, score by Stravinsky), Jerome Robbins drew on repulsive mating habits of certain insects like the praying mantis to present a tribe of female creatures who trap males, use them sexually, then mutilate and kill them. The women in turn scuttle like beetles; make angular, spidery, contorted motions of their arms and torsos; and use their hands like claws and the points of their toe shoes like knives. They teach a novice to straddle a helpless male; they crack his neck between their knees. The horror of these predatory actions is relieved by a romantic interlude when a handsome male overpowers the novice and she succumbs willingly to his embrace. But in the end the monstrous tribe reclaims their temporarily tender defector, who strangles this male, too, after the vicious females climb over him, devour his limbs, and render him passive.

A less extreme view of the insect world (and by implication the human one) is contained in Paul Taylor's *Insects and Heroes* (1961, music by John Herbert). The piece has comic overtones as a large insect figure, garnished with floppy, shiny spikes, moves with small quick steps and menaces a number of men and women. When one man bravely reaches out to confront the monstrous stranger, he becomes entangled with another man instead, and the two humans take on an insect look as they flap their elbows in and out. Later the creature throws the whole group into spasms of twitching and contorted grappling. Finally, when one man and then the group defy the creature, it sheds its spiky cocoon and peacefully joins the others.

There are innumerable other instances of animal motion treated symbolically in choreography. Several occur in *The Sleeping Beauty*.

Communication and Ballet

Basic differences exist in the way entire dance forms communicate. Ballet, for example, is less directly concerned with inner life and more focused on outward appearance and form than is modern dance. Now we take a look at *The Sleeping Beauty*, to illustrate, first, that all dances, including classical ballets, express feelings; and second, that the kinds of feelings expressed in a classical ballet have a certain formal character, regardless of the specific theme.

The opposite number of the evil, decadent Medea is the lovely princess

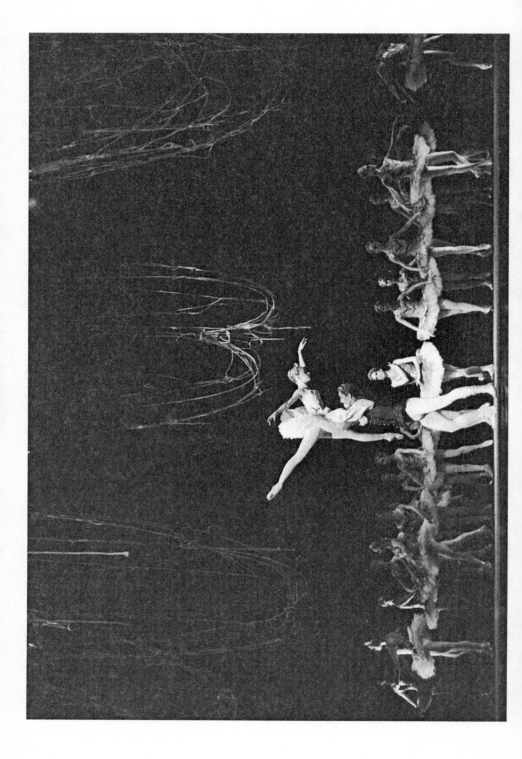

in *The Sleeping Beauty*, who exemplifies the purity and innocence of dreamy girlhood, and whose very name, Aurora, refers to light and the Roman goddess of dawn. Although this ballet is commonly classed as representational and is surely never considered in the same category as works by Nikolais, Cunningham or Graham, its movements too are abstract.

The Sleeping Beauty presents a beautiful girl, put under a spell, from which she awakens to love and happiness. The seed that germinated into the 1890 *Sleeping Beauty* was sown by Ivan Vsevolojsky, director of the Russian Imperial Theaters. In admiration of the court of seventeenth century France, and aware of its similarities to the court of his Russian tsar, he based a scenario on a Mother Goose tale by Perrault, a Frenchman who lived during the reign of Louis XIV and wrote for his court circles. Vsevolojsky decided, too, that the setting should be a palace of Louis XIV, which allowed for palatial splendor and courtly, "civilized" ceremony in choreography. He also designed elaborate costumes, for example dressing the men in seventeenth century plumed hats.

Such a setting assured an image magnified to heroic visual scale, the same scale that Martha Graham would later seek for *Cave of the Heart*. Here, however, the décor projects an effect that is completely the opposite of the primitive brutality required for the Medea legend.

The director's final contribution—the one that was to ensure artistic greatness—was his approach to Tchaikowsky. The composer responded enthusiastically to Vsevolojsky's outline of the action and agreed to work on the music. Tchaikowsky, too, took advantage of the setting in the court of Louis XIV to use for his model the music of Lully, who was the opera and ballet music director for the so-called Sun King. The result was an excellent dance score.

Now choreographer Marius Petipa entered the scene, to correspond with Tchaikowsky on details of the scenario. The music contains two major leitmotifs (melodic themes that always accompany the same character). One is an angry theme for the wicked, spell-casting Carabosse, and the other is a pleasant theme for the good Lilac Fairy. Recurrence of these two motifs turns the score (and the ballet) into a running conflict between good and evil.

In addition to working out the scenario with Vsevolojsky and making suggestions to Tchaikowsky about the music, Petipa's main contribution to *The Sleeping Beauty* of course was the choreography, which is characterized by a number of magnificent processions. Here's a brief summary of the plot and how some of Petipa's ideas carried it forward:

OPPOSITE: **American Ballet Theater dancers in Petipa's** *Sleeping Beauty*. **Photograph by Martha Swope, © Time Inc.**

The king and queen arrange a regal party to celebrate the birth of their daughter, Princess Aurora. The choreography offers a grand procession of the royal parents, their courtiers, six fairy godmothers and attendants. Each fairy presents a gift to the new princess in the form of a special solo dance. Petipa introduced a bit of symbolism here in his invention of the Bread Crumb Fairy, who called to mind the Russian custom of breaking bread over a new baby's cradle. Suddenly the wicked fairy Carabosse crashes in. Angry at not being invited to the party, she pronounces a dreadful curse: One day the princess shall prick her finger on a spindle and die.

The good Lilac Fairy has not yet presented her gift. She is not powerful enough to remove the curse completely, but she can modify it: The princess shall not die, but fall into a deep sleep, until a prince kisses her awake. This episode is staged with dramatic pantomime, contrasting the horrid old Carabosse (traditionally played by a man) with the loving Lilac Fairy.

Time passes to Princess Aurora's sixteenth birthday party. Again we see an impressive procession of royal guests, joined by peasants who waltz with flower garlands. The high point of the party scene is the famous "Rose Adagio," danced by Princess Aurora and the princes who have come to seek her hand in marriage. Grandeur is again the mode as not one, not two, not three, but each of four suitors presents a rose to the beautiful princess and takes a turn supporting her as she continues slowly to revolve, balanced on the tip of one foot. But the festivities are suddenly interrupted as Carabosse's dreadful curse is carried out, with Aurora pricking her finger on a spindle and collapsing. The Lilac Fairy gently waves her wand, and everyone in the palace falls asleep.

One hundred years go by. The next procession is at a royal hunt, led by a handsome Prince Charming. The young prince is moody and wanders alone in the forest as night falls. Into the moonlight glides the Lilac Fairy, to lead the melancholy youth to a vision of the sleeping Princess Aurora. Instantly smitten, the prince pursues the vision of Aurora.

Finally Prince Charming gets to the palace, which is suitably covered with weeds and spider webs. He enters the room where Aurora is peacefully sleeping and kisses her. As she awakens, everybody in the palace comes to life. Their wedding gives yet another opportunity to stage a splendid procession. The royal family and the courtiers parade pompously. Among the guests are Perrault's other Mother Goose characters, who take turns performing for the court.

Outstanding in the entertainment are two duets: The brilliant soaring Blue Bird *pas de deux*, a symbol of happiness, and the White Cat flirting coyly with Puss in Boots. Symbolically, the cats represent a human love game, as described by critic Vera Krasovskaya: "The White Kitten lazily stretched herself and preened, flirting sweetly with Puss in Boots. The game changed into a quarrel; the soft jumps became resilient as the woman rose on point, folded her arms and drew her head into her shoulders. But, having received an answering solid slap, she again coquettishly brushed him with a soft paw and enticed him across the stage to continue the amorous game-quarrel there."[14]

The loving climax is the appearance of Aurora and Prince Charming in a *pas de deux* that is gracious and technically magnificent. Finally the whole court joins in a spirited mazurka, which ends with a flourishing pose.

Then, as if there weren't yet enough courtly ceremony, the choreographer offers one last tribute to royalty: The god Apollo, dressed up as King Louis XIV, appears surrounded by the fairies and lit by the rays of the sun. Thus overall *The Sleeping Beauty* presents a sumptuous image of an environment where harmonious grandeur reigns supreme.

A God Comes of Age

Balanchine choreographed *Apollo*, considered to be one of the most important ballets of the twentieth century, for the Ballets Russes in 1928, after the music and scenario were already written by Stravinsky. If Stravinsky wasn't the only modern composer—or even the first—to be used for dance, he was probably the most influential. This was partly due to his own great talent, and partly to his association with Sergei Diaghilev. In the creation of *Apollo*, Balanchine credited Stravinsky with pointing the way towards his own groundbreaking neoclassicism: "This score, with its discipline and restraint, with its sustained oneness of tone and feeling, was a great revelation to me. It was then that I began to realize that to create means, first of all, to eliminate."[15]

Apollo is based on the Greek myth about Leta, a human woman who is impregnated by Zeus. The work begins with Leta giving birth to Apollo, a male infant, who unwinds himself from swaddling clothes to step about clumsily and try (without success) to play the lute. Gradually this hesitant youth, sired by a god, grows in confidence and strength towards a mature nobility. Three muses appear and bestow on him gifts of poetic rhythm, dramatic mimesis, and dance. Apollo partners the muses, separately and together, entwining himself in graceful poses with all three until, with a surge of masculine virtuosity, he drives the trio like a master charioteer. At the end Apollo, conscious of himself as a god, leads the muses in an ascent of Mt. Parnassus, the home of the gods.

The movement patterns in the ballet are cast in the classical mode, but they are restrained and pared down. Instead of the flourishes of a grand ballet spectacular, here are purity of line, a small cast of soloists, and a shortened duration (under thirty minutes as compared to a full evening).

Balletic Intimacy

Images that portray emotions in a more intimate fashion, in tune with the feelings of ordinary people, are to be found both in modern dances (by Doris Humphrey, Anna Sokolow, Paul Taylor, etc.) and in modern ballets. In this respect, Michel Fokine was perhaps the first "modern ballet" choreographer. His *Petrouchka*, like Graham's *Cave of the Heart*, portrays a love triangle leading to a murder. But how differently the theme is worked out! Where the Graham work embodies barbaric cruelty on a heroic scale, Fokine's image of three puppets portrays the pathos of naive simplicity.

Each of the artists who, along with Fokine, took part in the conception of *Petrouchka* was to have a major influence on the development of ballet: composer Igor Stravinsky, impresario Sergei Diaghilev (producer of the groundbreaking Ballets Russes), and painters Alexander Benois and Léon Bakst. Fokine entered the process only after the others had done their part. With all these great artists involved, to whom does one attribute the ballet? Fokine put it this way: "When I say 'my' ballet *Petrouchka* ... I feel that I am perfectly justified.... One could call it a musico-dramatic composition by Stravinsky which assumed an exceptionally important place in the field of modern music; and one could say that it was one of the greatest works of Benois. One could also classify *Petrouchka* as a Fokine production.... Each of us, in his own language, told about Petrouchka's suffering."[16]

The genesis of this ballet reminds us that a dance production is a collaborative affair. Stravinsky first composed *Petrouchka's Cry* and the fragment of a Russian dance. His inspiration came from the clown-puppet called Petrouchka, familiar to the Russian people from traveling shows that were staged at village fairs—like the Punch and Judy shows in England and the *commedia dell'arte* in Italy. Sergei Diaghilev heard in Stravinsky's two pieces the possibilities for a ballet about the Russian carnival—a perfect subject for his company to show the Paris public. He immediately called on Benois, who had always loved Russian street theater, to come up with a story, and on Bakst to create designs for the setting.

The ballet opens in a large public square during a carnival, where the crowd is entertained by a puppet show. In Acts II and III the puppet characters come to life: the poet Petrouchka; the Ballerina, a frivolous Columbine-doll whom Petrouchka adores; and the Moor, a powerful figure of black magic with whom the Ballerina is in love.

Bakst had the ingenious idea of creating a stage within a stage, so that

Nureyev performs the title role in Fokine's *Petrouchka*. Photograph by Martha Swope, © Time Inc.

the ballet conveys a double life: the outer, public happenings at a Russian street fair, and the inner, private life of the entertainers. The central ballet action occurs among the puppet characters, but always against the "reality" of people in a town square. Bakst's set and costumes were noisy with color, unconventionally combining folksy designs and tones in the manner of a children's picture book.

The puppeteer, called the Charlatan, who controls the onstage behavior of Petrouchka, Ballerina and the Moor, also controls their offstage destinies. After the show he shuts them up in their boxes, which become the rooms where they play out their private drama. Petrouchka performs tricks for the Ballerina, who is not impressed. She leaves, and the poor fool pounds the walls of his box in frustration. When the Ballerina and the Moor make love, Petrouchka rushes in, wild with jealousy, and tries to separate them. The Moor first pushes Petrouchka away and then chases after him with a sword and kills him.

An odd twist occurs at the end. Act IV takes place back outside at the fair. People in the crowd hear noises of a struggle and the cries of a dying puppet (not a puppet but a person?). But then the Charlatan picks up the lifeless clown and shows the crowd: See, it is just a puppet! A final turnabout occurs, however, with the sad appearance of Petrouchka's ghost, which frightens the Charlatan himself. So maybe the fool was human after all?

Fokine's choreography for the title character features sunken gestures and turned-in poses: head hanging, arms drooping, hunched over torso, knees and toes turned in, sometimes actually touching, to express his pathetic introversion. After Petrouchka is killed by the Moor, the unfortunate clown character slumps into the total relaxation of lifelessness, as though the puppeteer put down his strings. In contrast, the choreography for the Moor includes widely spread legs, hand resting on well turned-out knee, head high, chest out, to express his cruel self-confidence. Even as they display these personality gestures, Petrouchka and the Moor must at all times keep a mechanical, puppet-like attitude. In the case of the Ballerina, Fokine's idea was simply "an attractive, stupid doll" (a parody of the classical ballerina who is capable only of doing tricks on cue). Fokine's jerky movements for the three puppets, which may be said to symbolize the reduction of persons to objects, caught the fancy of other choreographers and were widely imitated.

As a clear and interesting foil for the puppets, Fokine tried to make the crowd as alive as possible. He peopled the scene with a variety of characters: coachmen, organ-grinders, soldiers, ladies, gentlemen, children, policemen, drunken peasants and so on. This was a nod at traditional balletic spectacle, but instead of copying Petipa's symmetrical ensembles, moving in unison, Fokine pointed the way to a modern approach. He gave each type suitable motions, the way a play director would stage a scene in a realistic drama. (It is through this ballet that western audiences made the acquaintance of the wet-nurses employed by noble families. These women, the most spectacular persons to be seen on the streets of St. Petersburg, were gorgeously attired in theatrically brocaded peasant costumes with gold buttons and balloon sleeves.)

The premiere of *Petrouchka* in 1911 made a brilliant impression largely through the dance-acting of Nijinsky as Petrouchka and Karsavina as the Ballerina. Less impressive was the crowd scene. Fokine complained that he had only a two-hour rehearsal to set it. But the problem of uniting about 100 passersby, each one a unique, vivid character, into a lively, well-designed dance scene, was a problem that continued to plague Fokine when he restaged *Petrouchka* as he was to do many times for other companies. (Chapter 6, which discusses music, will reveal how Stravinsky both helped and hindered the choreographer.)

The music also presented problems for the touring Ballets Russes. At the opera house in Vienna, Diaghilev was confronted by an orchestra that simply refused to perform the music, which they labeled "pig swill." When forced by their contract to perform, according to one critic they engaged in deliberate sabotage.[17] Thus for our purposes, *Petrouchka* serves as an illustration of the complexities that surround the creation and performance of a dance work—demanding as it does the willing and able cooperation of so many individuals.

The Nature of Dance Imagery

In each of the above examples, the dance is more than it seems. *Apollo* is not just a coming-of-age scene. It stands as a metaphor, or representation of the idea, of the development of the creative imagination. The uncoordinated youth, who gains in discipline, nobility, and vigor, stands for the glorification of civilized man.

Petrouchka is not really about a lifeless puppet. Rather it is a meditation on suffering, with the title character representing a victimized person.

In the musical motifs and the dance action of *The Sleeping Beauty*, a world is presented nearer to our heart's desire than the one we know. It is an allegory of a noble, well-ordered universe in which good and evil are forces that battle over our fates—and good emerges triumphant.

Cave of the Heart is not the enactment of a historical legend. It is a revelation of psychological truth, using an ancient queen to stand for the evil, corroding jealousy that lies waiting to be awakened in each human heart.

Even when a work seems to mirror "reality" it is a selected reality that expresses viewpoints of the creator, such as Paul Taylor's irreverently humorous outlook on the dance world in his *Public Domain. Private Domain* is not a peek at a burlesque show, but a mirror of Taylor's disgust at the dreariness of loveless lust. At a rehearsal, the choreographer told his company to think of themselves as icons (religious symbols), "but icons who don't deserve their standing and have just been given an aphrodisiac."[18]

The dance examples cited in this chapter all have something in common: They present images that give us flight. They lift us from the mundane gravity of daily life into a more significant awareness. As passage through space evokes the sensation of being alive, all dance is flight for the dancer and the viewer.

At the same time however, the dances are very different from one another. These differences reside in their choreographic style, which is our next topic.

2

Styles in Review:
Ethnic and Ballet

—

Dance works exist in a style. Style, which can be equated with personality, refers to qualities like grace, harmony, angularity, or distortion. Choreographic style emerges from the way the choreographer treats movements, and is further affected by music and design. In creating, however, choreographers do not start from scratch. Instead, they apply their individual talents and vision within an already existing tradition.

We distinguish among the following stylistic categories: ethnic or folk; ballet (itself divided into classical, romantic, modern, and neoclassical); modern dance (separated into expressive modern and nonobjective or concept dance); jazz (including swing, ragtime, tap and hiphop); and avant-garde or postmodern.

As in any art form, each style comes from a particular time and place, and "is a manifestation of the culture as a whole, the visible sign of its unity."[1]

But while we all use this language, we must recognize that it is inexact. Art is not science, and human variables do not allow the elements of artworks to be isolated and studied like chemical compounds. Stylistic differences appear within a single culture according to geographical factors. They may also be due to social or religious philosophy and the amount of free choice accorded to individuals. Further, decisive changes in style are frequently associated with original works of outstanding quality. Then the psychology and the gender of a single artist and her or his growth from year to year play their parts in stylistic variations. All in all, a term like "modern ballet" may have opposite implications from one time to the next.

The whole question of style is particularly appropriate for the current age, a time of eclecticism and restless ambivalence. A great many styles exist today in preservation, revivals and fresh versions of traditional works; in borrowings, influences and attempts at authentic stagings of ethnic forms; and most of all in new creative efforts. Ours is a catch-all age, perhaps a transitional period in which nothing from the human past or present is considered alien.

Taking all these factors into consideration, we will now embark on a tour through time and across space, to map dominant dance styles. Such a survey touches only on a few selected high points, but it should serve our purpose, which is to provide a general context for appreciation.

Ethnic Dance

We start with ethnic dance because its forms predate the other styles that concern us. With the dictionary, we define "ethnic" as pertaining to a particular racial or cultural division of humanity. Folk dancing also belongs to a specific human group, the difference being that folk dances are done by any members of a community for recreation, while ethnic dances, designed to be seen by an audience, are performed by trained specialists.

Ethnic dance forms bear clear movement personalities, as has been documented by filmmakers who applied techniques of anthropology and movement analysis to films of Polynesians, Iroquois Indians, West Europeans, and others. The overall findings of this branch of study, called "choreometrics," were summarized by one of their adherents:

> Choreometrics affirms the existence of a very few large and very old style traditions: 1) the primitive Pacific, 2) black Africa with Melanesia and Polynesia, 3) high culture Eurasia and 4) Europe.... These continental distributions of movement styles point to the existence of communication styles which are extremely stable across time and whose life spans extend for hundreds, perhaps thousands of years. Apparently every human group has found a pattern of rhythmic art to match its life style, carrying it everywhere and employing it in all fresh creations.[2]

La Meri, a student of ethnic forms worldwide, made these observations: "The most sensuous part of the Japanese feminine body is the back of the neck, but the Spanish woman lifts her breasts proudly upward.... Feminine thighs cling, masculine spread in nearly all forms of ethnic dance."[3]

The traditional techniques of ethnic dance were developed over centuries. They acquired specific forms both from the mother culture, with its ideals of beauty and strength, and from the muscular structure of the bodies within a racial grouping. The origins of danced rituals and legends were lost in misty beginnings of age-old cultures.

Inevitably, due to the invasion of outside forces like religious missionaries and militarily stronger nations seeking raw materials, ancient traditional cultures have fallen by the wayside. Such losses, however, in time have led to resurgent national and ethnic pride, along with attempts to revive and preserve age-old traditions by artists like Uday Shankar of India and Argentina and José Greco of Spain. To accomplish their goal, they assembled companies to showcase their dances at home and abroad, incidentally providing a good source of needed currency.

But such enterprises have a built-in problem. No matter how skillful the performers, ethnic dances do not lend themselves to be viewed in foreign theaters. They developed as activities that marked important occasions and lasted sometimes for days at a time. Even cut to a two-hour length, the repetitive patterns that characterize ethnic forms may strike viewers as monotonous.

The result is that as often as not, folk and ethnic dance programs we see do not consist of age-old works, lovingly treasured and passed along from generation to generation. Instead, they may include works that were created recently, maybe even specifically for the festival we are attending. Does this mean they are not "genuine"? Not at all. If they are built on folk materials—the basic themes, the steps, the body carriage, the rhythms, and the native gestures and byplay—then they are surely a genuine expression of a people's culture.

Asian dance evolved in close connection with religious content. To this day, Asians look on dance as a form of spiritual communication, which adheres to ancient myths and legends, with god and demon characters. Asian bodily stance is fluid. The spine undulates; the hips, ribcage and head shift from side to side; the shoulders ripple and shake. Knees are most commonly bent. With the feet and legs held in fixed positions, the dancer lunges, springs, stamps and turns.

Movements of Asian dance glide low over the ground and often sink down altogether, until the dance is performed in a seated position. Arms, hands, fingers and head perform the most subtle and expressive motions. Stylized gestures of the eyes, brows, nose, cheeks, mouth and chin are part of the choreography. In Asian dance, there is a sharp distinction between the broad and vigorous movements of the males, who spread their legs in wide lunges, and the females, whose gestures are more subtle and who keep their bent knees modestly close.

Hindu dance is the oldest of the world's developed dance forms. Hindu dance depicts a serene and ordered universe. Gracefully intricate hand gestures and subtle facial motions tell a ritualized story from the storehouse of religious legend. There are also Hindu dances that proceed in complex rhythms whose intent is solely the offering of a prescribed pattern of motion for contemplation as a spiritual experience.

All Southeast Asian dance styles have a common origin in Hindu dance. At the same time, each Asian nation has expressed its unique personality in its own ethnic forms.

Take Bali, for example, a tiny island nation to the east of Java. Bali's dances are not centered at court, as are the Javanese. The style of Balinese movement and music is more impetuous and vigorous, at times jerky. The mastery of the quick and difficult movements of Balinese dance requires rigorous training. Not only must every part of the body be worked independently of every other, the limbs are painfully forced into extremely unnatural positions. This approach to movement creates an impression of continuous, frantic energy.

Dancers and musicians of Bali appeared in the United States in the spring of 1996. Reviewers were impressed by the gamelan—a mostly metallic orchestra of clanging gongs, chimes and cymbals, whose sounds range from gentle and silvery to a cacophonous clangor. Then there was *Kecak* or

Monkey Dance, in which the musicians, stripped to the waist, abandoned their instruments and gathered on center stage. A priestly figure in white blessed them, and they began a low, rhythmic chant in accompaniment to a singer. Two maidens danced, to be chased off by large, shaggy, evil spirits, wailing and crying. In another piece, a witch danced with a king and suddenly cried out, "I love you!" (In English!) Hardly authentic, that bit was a frankly good-humored salute to American audiences.

Along with theatrical interest as a motivation for revising ethnic choreography, there is also the artist's ever-present need to communicate fresh ideas, feelings and attitudes. To serve this purpose, choreographers do not hesitate to move outside the boundaries of their traditional dance.

Hindu dance artist Chandralekha was renowned in the 1960s as a performer of *bharata natyam*. This is a female solo dance practiced originally in the temples. The content of the dance is variations on the theme of the heroine's bliss, achieved through sexual surrender to her lord. While the sexual meaning is symbolic, standing for the perfect union of humanity and God, it also reflects the subjugation of females in male-dominated Indian society.

Chandralekha's interests were not confined to Hindu dance, however. As a woman, she lived very much in the modern world, and for a period, she left the theater to campaign for human rights. In the 1990s she returned to dance with pieces that used traditional Hindu movements to express new ideas: Females could be powerful, while males could reveal their feminine side.[4]

Tina Ramirez founded the Ballet Hispanico in 1970. One goal of this company is to present the richness of a heritage that includes classical Spanish dance along with Puerto Rican, Columbian, and Argentinean variations; another goal is to continually expand and develop the choreographic art. In 1994, Ramirez invited modern dancer Susan Marshall to add *Solo* to the company's repertory. The piece, accompanied by guitar music from Victor Cavini's *Fiesta Andalusa*, opens with the male dancer seated on a high-backed Spanish chair, placed at the top of a ramp. He holds a large bowl on his knee. Rising slowly, the dancer lifts the bowl to his head and begins the fierce, rhythmical heel work of flamenco dance—while water splashes out from the bowl, drenching the performer! As he moves down the slippery wet ramp (at times ascending backwards!) he must focus intensely to keep his balance. Kisselgoff insisted that *Solo* was not gimmicky, but "an exploration in risk and concentration." She wrote that at the premiere, the audience went wild when José Costas completed *Solo* by swinging the bowl up "like a matador taking his hat off to salute a crowd.... Mr. Costas's triumph was no less real than that of a bullfighter."[5]

The oldest extant European dance art comes from Spain. Due to the

Poema Infinito, choreographed by Maria Rovira for the Ballet Hispanico. Photograph by Bruce Laurance, courtesy of Ballet Hispanico.

eighth century Moorish invasion, Spanish dance is also a point of contact between eastern and western dance. With its proud, intense or joyful manner and its themes of pride, passion and the imminent arrival of death, it is a complex art of spectacle and tradition.

For hundreds of years, Spanish dance has been a consistently popular style throughout Europe. The high point was reached at the beginning of the twentieth century, with the emergence of the flamenco from the hidden caves of gypsies onto stages of the world. The best flamenco dancing is still not available to the public, because it is a form that entails improvisation, with the dancers letting themselves go into transports of ecstasy— a state not achieved on demand in a theater.[6]

In flamenco dances, a tension is established between the arched back and sensuously curving arms straining upward, away from beating feet and legs pounding into the earth. The heel work, *taconeo*, is a male specialty.

Ethnic dance requires long exposure and specialized knowledge for appreciation of its choice of dance themes, music, scenery and costumes, as well as movement. On the other hand, the very foreignness of an ethnic style has an exotic appeal for western choreographers and their viewers. All through western dance history, old ethnic and folk forms have frequently been incorporated into ballets and modern dances for their exotic novelty. A sensationally popular piece that comes to mind is Fanny Elssler's *Cachucha* (1836), a tempestuous Spanish solo inserted into a long ballet at the height of the Romantic age.

A groundbreaking example of ethnic adoption is Léonide Massine's *Le Tricorne* (*The Three-Cornered Hat*) (1919). Massine was both a sensational dancer and an outstanding choreographer in the *Ballets Russes*. When the company visited Spain in 1916, he fell in love with the country. It helped that the Spanish composer Manuel de Falla became the group's tour guide and immediately introduced them to the best native dancing.

Diaghilev hired Felix García to dance in the Spanish ballets that he was planning with the enthusiastic Massine and de Falla. García taught Massine flamenco and arranged lessons for him in the intricate technique of *zapateado*. A scenario was worked out by de Falla, together with the playwright Martínez Sierra, after a traditional Spanish romance about a loving village couple: the miller and his wife. The villain, a doddering provincial governor in a pretentious three-cornered hat, guarded by his soldiers, chases after the pretty woman. She pushes off the clumsy attacker, who falls into a stream. To support their good-hearted miller and his wife, the villagers rise up against the foolish governor, who flees with his soldiers. The ballet ends with the peasants dancing a happy *jota*.

Somewhere during the ballet's gestation of more than two years, two significant changes occurred. Massine stepped in to replace Felix Bell in the leading role of the Miller, and the choreography evolved from Spanish dancing to a synthesis of modern ballet and the basic Spanish style. At its premiere in London, the ballet was a smash hit, particularly Massine's solo, a *farruca*, which "drove audiences into a delirious frenzy."

The choreographer described his *farruca*: "Throughout the dance my movements were slow and contorted, and to the style and rhythm which I had learned from Felix I added many twisted and broken gestures of my own. I felt instinctively that something more than perfect technique was needed here.... The mental image of an enraged bull going in to the attack unleashed some inner force which generated power within me."[7]

A sad footnote to the first change: Felix García, a sacrificial lamb to the Diaghilev-Massine conception, went literally mad with disappointment at losing his promised role, and spent the rest of his life in an insane asylum. The second change had a much happier result. Clive Bell, a famous critic, declared that Massine's greatest achievement had been to take ballet out of the class of a mere "theatrical" form and put it "on the level of literature, music and the graphic arts."

Other ethnic accents occur in the Chinese dance in *The Nutcracker* and the Japanese marriage ritual in Balanchine's *Bugaku*. Modern dance offers Martha Graham's *El Penitente*, based on a Mexican religious ritual, and Alvin Ailey's African-inspired *Masekela Language*. Nevertheless, these pieces are not themselves ethnic works. When Graham used a Mexican legend she translated it into her personal movement vocabulary, and Balanchine's *Bugaku* is a lot more American balletic than it is Japanese.

Classical Ballet

Ballet, the dominant form of western theatrical dance, can be seen as ethnic, in the sense that its techniques reflect the spirit of the time and place of its origin. Ballets started out as elaborate court entertainments in honor of special occasions or important persons. Ballets themselves had developed from a combination of medieval morality plays, the offerings of singers, dancers, poets and musicians (troubadours) who wandered from one village square to another, and masked balls. Certainly in the medieval period, the people involved in these shows were anonymous. And indeed, the first dance steps taken by courtiers were refined versions of folk steps.

We date the birth of ballet arbitrarily in the 1500s, from Renaissance spectacles produced at Italian courts. These featured richly costumed noblemen who sang, spoke, mimed and executed simple dance steps among magnificently constructed sets, including props that simulated clouds or chariots moving through space. The performers portrayed mythological characters who sometimes represented contemporary royal figures. Spectacles were loosely tied together by themes from Greek and Roman mythology, which allowed ample opportunity for diversions, interludes and pageants.

Members of court society were trained for this activity by dancing masters, whose lessons stressed courtly etiquette and dignified demeanor. Dance entertainments took place in palace ballrooms. The spectators were seated on three sides, above the performers. The choreography consisted of mimed passages and changing floor designs that could best be viewed from on high.

From the dancing masters' emphasis on noble bearing sprang the elegant manners and the formality, that centuries later are still the hallmarks of classical ballet as a system of movement training.[8]

Academic Foundation

Louis XIV, who was himself a polished dancer, established the world's first ballet academy in 1661, under the joint direction of his teacher Pierre Beauchamps and his leading music master (also a dancer), Jean Baptiste Lully. Beauchamps codified the techniques that were then practiced, including the turnout, the five positions of the feet, and the formal révérence, and Lully collaborated with Molière in stage productions of comedy drama. Before Beauchamps and Lully were through, ballet was well on its way towards professionalism.

Balletic style has altered considerably from time to time and place to place. Only in respect to technical training has there been real continuity through the centuries. True, the sixteenth century courtier would not be able to do properly even those exercises that the contemporary student performs well after a year's study. Nevertheless, there is a line of development traceable back to the teachings of Beauchamps and even earlier dancing masters, with every generation adding poses and steps of more demanding virtuosity.

Choreographic imagery is another matter. When in the Renaissance the focus of philosophy and scholarly inquiry shifted from God to man as an individual, there was already a foretaste of the search for novelty that is today so evident. Characteristics opposite to dignified nobility could be found in the earliest ballet sequences—with the appearance of grotesque low-comedy buffoons, for example, to provide comic relief and variety.

Dance Technique

There is an intimate relationship between dance technique and choreographic style. A dance technique is a method of studying dance. It is concerned with mastering physical skills like body alignment, strength, coordination, balance, leaping, jumping, turning, falling, moving together with a partner and with a group. However, there are many ways to dance, which means that there are many systems of studying it. As a method, every technique includes a series of exercises with distinctly stylized spatial and rhythmic patterns. After thousands of hours of repeating these patterns day after day, the dancer's body becomes an instrument that can move with skill and control. Beyond the physical ability, however, the trained dance instrument has a characteristic stance or body attitude—an overall look that comes from the parts of the body held or stretched, the posture alignment, and even the facial expression. This look makes a statement about human identity that is different in each technique, the way a violin produces different sounds from an oboe even when they play the same notes.

Choreographers, who are themselves dancers, have been trained in this way, and they create within a specific technique. At some point, however, great dance artists go on to fashion their own personal movement language. Like George Balanchine, they may build upon an established technique. Like Martha Graham, they may develop a completely new technique. Like Twyla Tharp, they may combine a number of techniques in a totally individual manner.

Our main interest, for purposes of the present discussion, lies in the periods that gave birth to the ballets that survive in one form or another in today's repertory. A ballet period that is most appealing to contemporary audiences is the Romantic era, with *Giselle* its most popular example. Before we escape into romanticism, however, we will take a short detour back to the eighteenth century.

Around 1760, Jean Georges Noverre introduced the *ballet d'action*, which means a work of unified drama. Noverre's intention was to infuse ballet with expressive truth, in contrast to the superficial character of light entertainment it retained from the days of Louis XIV. The philosophical split initiated by Noverre continues to the present. Theatrical dancing can be said to possess two faces: a side which emphasizes spectacle and virtuosity, and a side which attempts to communicate dramatic human emotions.

Noverre's influence was widespread during the eighteenth century. A ballet that survives from that period is *La Fille Mal Gardée*, by his pupil Jean Dauberval. During the early years of the nineteenth century, however, technical displays predominated—particularly in Italy. Male dancers figured out how to do multiple pirouettes until they could practically spin by the hour. At the same time, female dancers learned to rise and step *en pointe*. Since the blocked toe shoe was not yet devised, when they did the new toe-dancing they held themselves very stiffly. It was quite a gymnastic stunt to stay in that position.

Too much of a good thing got boring. The reaction came with Marie Taglioni and the Romantic ballet. Taglioni transformed ballet from a display of circus type acrobatics to a presentation of grace and poetic beauty. Although this ballerina, too, had to manage without the blocked toe shoe, using cotton wool padding and darning the points of her slippers for stability, she danced on her toes like an otherworldly creature, as ballerinas do today—gliding, appearing to float. When Marie Taglioni came along with her lovely feminine style, the audience was delighted at the change and embraced it wholeheartedly.

The Romantic Era

"Romantic" refers generally to the spirit of all arts in the 1800s. Romanticism was fantasy that stemmed from a sense of dissatisfaction with the here and now; a longing for distance in either time or space; a wish to escape from present reality. Its favorite themes were poetic love that could never be real; spiritual creatures that resembled people but couldn't be grasped by ordinary men; and sentimental views of peasants merrily folk dancing.

The dreamy image of an ethereal dancer as an ideal of feminine perfection (her sexual area hidden by yards of tulle) originated in the Romantic era, as did the position of the female as the center of the ballet art. Both men and women still needed great strength and precise technique, but the overall emphasis shifted to poetic artistry, in which the females excelled. For the next fifty years or so, the female dancers dominated ballet. The ballerina's movements were soft in attack and round in line, designed to express feelings. Males were present to escort the females and to elevate them onto pedestals.

The outstanding masterpiece of the period, *Giselle* (1841, music by Adolphe Adam, choreography by Jean Coralli and Jules Perrot), combines the themes of happy village innocence and female, otherworldly spirituality. *Giselle* is a "classic" ballet in a "romantic" manner. Classic here means that *Giselle* has enjoyed countless repetitions, revivals and new versions, having appeared and appealed innumerable times since its birth. Classic also means that it was based on academic (classic) ballet techniques. It is about an innocent village maiden whose heart is doubly threatened: first, because she loves to dance, even though the activity endangers her weak heart; and second, because she harbors love for Prince Albrecht, who playfully courts her disguised as a commoner. Their love is forbidden by their differences in status. When Prince Albrecht's true identity is revealed, Giselle's heart breaks, her reason fails, and she drops dead at his feet.

It is *Giselle's* Act II moonlit forest scene whose imagery embodies the true spirit of romanticism. Here Giselle appears with the Wilis, a mystic band of ghostly female creatures—spirits of maidens who, deceived by ruthless men, died before they were wed. Garbed in filmy, dead-white, calf-length tutus, the Wilis go through a nightly dance ritual, avenging themselves against the male sex. Any hapless man who wanders into the forest ballroom is doomed to dance with them—and dance and dance until he drops dead of exhaustion. Giselle joins their cruel sorority, and when Albrecht, overwhelmed with guilty grief, visits her tomb, he is trapped into their pitiless dance of death. But the macabre plan is foiled by Giselle, whose love is so strong that even now she uses her own body to give him moments of rest, and pleads with the relentless Myrtha, queen of the Wilis, to let Albrecht go. The climax of this act is a *pas de deux* for Albrecht and Giselle in which he dances himself almost to death, ending exhausted on the floor. Finally he is saved by the dawning day, which sends the Wilis floating away into the mist. The viewer receives unforgettable images: of Albrecht trying vainly to grasp Giselle's flitting spirit; of the cruel queen of the Wilis coldly rejecting Giselle's pleas for mercy; of Giselle's love reaching beyond her mortality.[9]

As mentioned earlier, ballet of the Romantic era was dominated by female dancers. Male dancers were essentially porters, their main job being to carry exalted ballerinas from place to place. Women even took the parts of soldiers and sailors, and in the premiere production of *Coppélia*, the "male" lead of Franz was danced by a female.

But through a French choreographer, male ballet dancers got a boost in Denmark. August Bournonville, who moved to Denmark from Paris, created dozens of compositions that became the basis of the contemporary Danish repertory. While these were based both on the academic technique and the Romantic style then current in Paris, they included personal variations that are taught to this day as the Bournonville technique, forming the style of the Royal Danish School and company. The influence of the Danish character and folk dances clearly mark this gentle, lighthearted style which features lilting, gliding patterns and small quick steps, and which gives the men as much dancing prominence as the women—maybe more.

Russian Academic Classicism

Choreographer Petipa would have been very much at home in Louis XIV's court. He would have fit right in with Beauchamps and Lully. With every ballet, Petipa added steps, poses and new rhythmic variations to the ballet vocabulary, but his spirit was royally academic.

Petipa's groupings were arranged to set off a central star (royal) figure. A dominant couple flanked by dancers on each side, focusing towards the soloist(s), was the final pose of many of his ballets. He always arranged the limbs of the ballet body in harmonious lines, geometrically placed in relation to the stage space and to the lines of the other dancers, so that the eye was directed to a middle point. This approach descended from the theory of perspective, which originated with Renaissance painters.

Since one never turns one's back on a royal audience, Petipa's orientation was always frontal. Since there are no sudden surprises in courtly ceremony, Petipa's balletic rhythms fell into in eight-bar phrases of 4/4, 2/4 or 3/4 meter (according with molds of court music). Balletic arms framed the face like elaborate crowns and collars. The angle of the head denoted the superiority of the performing noble courtiers.

Classical ballet teaches its dancers to deny the pull of gravity, an impression achieved by seemingly effortless control of the body. In practical terms this means that the ballet body has a fixed torso and fluid arm motions that draw attention from ferocious energy applied to knowledgeably flexed and stretched high-powered legs.

In contrast to Bournonville, Petipa brought dance literally to new heights with his emphasis on virtuosity. Russian ballet stars were ready to shoot across the firmament when, in 1848, Marius Petipa moved from Paris to join the staff of the Russian Imperial Ballet in St. Petersburg to exploit their talents. Petipa is credited with polishing both the movement and choreographic techniques of classical ballet to a standard never before achieved. He laid the foundation for the current style and repertory of classic ballet.

Petipa classicism goes like this: 1) Ballets are made up of three or more spectacular acts designed to supply a full evening's entertainment. 2) Scenarios keep the otherworldly and melodramatic elements of Romantic ballet, but use them only as a line on which to hang pieces of dance that spotlight the virtuosity of the ballerina. 3) The manner of movement is no longer lyrical, but sharp, geometrical, polished and majestic. Perfection of form is the ideal. 4) Each act is made up of numerous passages called *pas*: *pas d'action* (a mimetic bit or whole scene to carry the action forward); *pas caractère* (a passage of dance with a folk or ethnic flavor); *pas de deux* (a duet for the two main characters which comes at the climax of the ballet, generally near the end of the last act); and passages for a very large *corps de ballet*

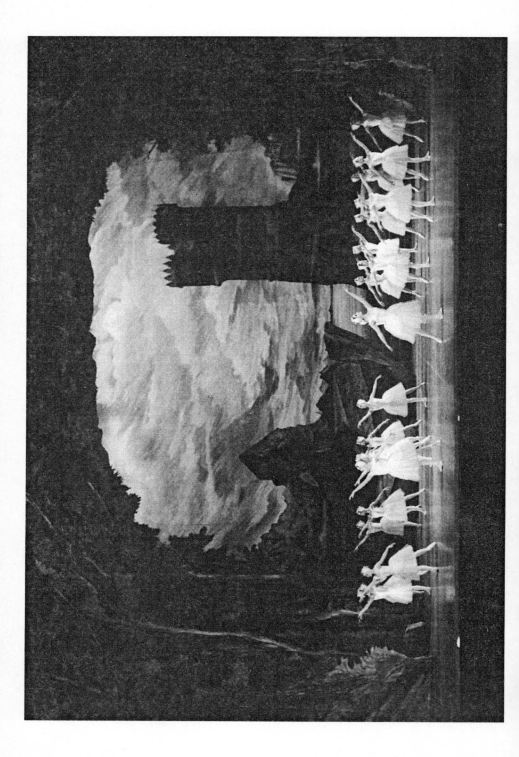

(ensemble). Petipa's ensemble is not a collection of individuals, but a series of impressive massed shapes that serve as a kind of grand scenic design in motion.

A performance by Margot Fonteyn and Rudolf Nureyev of the grand *pas de deux* from *Le Corsaire*, to music by Richard Drigo, was preserved on film in 1965. A look at this piece illuminates the classical style. Nureyev runs on stage, his arm bent at the elbow, his chest arched more fully than is usual for the *danseur noble*. The arch and the sharply bent arm pose, along with the costume—tights and a bare chest—are visual concessions to the particular role. He is after all a corsair (a pirate), as indicated by the title and program notes.

Shortly after the male runs on stage, Fonteyn enters, wearing a classical, short tutu. She steps slowly in a steady 4/4 rhythm, conforming to the measures in Drigo's music, and takes a stately pose. His and her entrances are both designed to tell us: The stars have arrived! (Sort of an applause sign.) The female's leisurely procession takes two measures. Her partner approaches. She lifts her right arm. He takes the hand and supports her in a slow turn, at the climax of the music phrase. The turn has what might be called a breath rhythm, that is, a suspended, sustained motion, unlike the metrical steps of the entrances. The two bodies are positioned in a harmonic, geometrically proportioned relationship: The legs, arms and torsos are either parallel or at clear, open angles. While turning, Margot Fonteyn holds her raised arm in a curve, one leg bent at a right angle, lifted behind her (in what is called an *attitude* position), and her standing leg fully stretched and balanced *en pointe*. Nureyev's stance while supporting her is similarly formal: He stands at attention, focused courteously on his partner.

The couple's demeanor is gracious. The arms are lifted lightly and smoothly—not limply relaxed, but certainly not taut or heavy. The turn is completely calm, and the effort needed for it is supplied by the man who firmly supports and propels the ballerina. Because she is poised and held in fully collected control, he does not need much strength either to hold her in balance or to turn her, but without his support it would be anatomically impossible for her to execute this sustained revolution on the tip of one foot. The *pas de deux* continues with splendid technical feats: leaps and turns for the man, intricate footwork for the woman, and difficult balances for both.

The behavioral associations are exclusively the courtesy and courtliness of a classical ballet show piece. We do not see, hear or feel any of the terror

OPPOSITE: **American Ballet Theater dancers perform the symmetrical poses of Petipa's** *Swan Lake*. **Photograph by Martha Swope, © Time Inc.**

and passion of Byron's poetry which served as the initial scenario: A Greek girl about to be sold into slavery is saved by a pirate, who almost loses her again while men are stabbed and drugged and the hero is nearly executed; the couple escapes on a ship, which is explosively wrecked at sea. We get nothing even so piratical as the swashbuckling romanticism of *The Three Musketeers!*

In the annoying way of art, which always refuses to be pinned down categorically, the finest masterpieces of Russian classicism reveal more than a few traces of the so-called opposite, romanticism. That's because the severe brilliance of Petipa's choreography was modified by his longtime assistant Lev Ivanov, who brought to his work a talent for emotional imagery that his master lacked. Thus the three most magnificent works from the age of Petipa—*The Sleeping Beauty*, *Swan Lake*, and *The Nutcracker*—continue to win audiences by combining all the best features of nineteenth century ballet.

Other famous works choreographed by Petipa and his assistant Ivanov include *Don Quixote* and *La Bayadère* (music by Minkus), *Raymonda* and *Les Saisons* (music by Glazounov), *Cinderella* (music by Baron Shell), and *Le Corsaire* (originally produced in 1856, but rechoreographed by Petipa in 1899).

Modern Ballet

Finally, however, by the turn of the century, more than fifty ballet shows in the grand Petipa manner wore out the audience's fascination with classicism. Audience boredom was hastened by the artistic deterioration of productions to the point where ballerinas' technical tricks and acrobatics in search of applause were the main focus of performances.

The end of the nineteenth century saw far-reaching cultural upheaval. A changed world outlook was reflected in the new ideas and techniques explored by modern painters like Van Gogh and Cezanne, modern composers like Debussy and Ravel, modern writers like Walt Whitman, Emile Zola and August Strindberg. The brilliant artists who created Diaghilev's Ballets Russes introduced modern ballet to the West.

Sergei Diaghilev was not a dancer, but as an enthusiast of exciting new art works, he became an impresario-producer of ballets. Diaghilev restored fine art and craftsmanship to the ballet stage. He saw to it that scene design, music and libretto as well as choreography were created by first-class artists of the day. Further, under his rule, first-rank male soloists and choreographers appeared on the scene. The breakup of the female monopoly on dance imagery opened the door to many interesting choreographic possibilities like Nijinsky's *Afternoon of a Faun (L'Après Midi d'un Faune)* and Balan-chine's *The Prodigal Son*, in which the respective central characters are a sen-suous male animal and a youth who rejects the path of righteousness.

In style, "reformer" Michel Fokine vociferously protested that the clas-sic ballet was "correct but ugly." He reinstated the *ballet d'action* both with ballets like *Petrouchka* and *The Firebird* and with declarations such as "The dance pantomime and gestures should not be of the conventional style established in the old Ballet 'once and for all,' but should be of a kind that best fits the style of the period portrayed."[10]

Balanchine's Neoclassicism

Trained in Russian classrooms and theaters, where ballet had reached a pinnacle of virtuosity and grandeur, Balanchine exported the excellent Russian traditional classicism to Europe (where it had all started four hun-dred years earlier) and then to the United States (where the art form had no firm roots). Balanchine's central interest remained the ballet form itself, in particular the wide variety of brilliant steps and poses found in the clas-sical academic tradition of Petipa. Once he came to the United States, however, he absorbed the generosity and tempo of new American life. So while his goal was always to present figures clothed in an ideal world of grace, brilliance and respectful dignity, Balanchine himself said he believed in an energetic style, even a "soldierly one." His contribution to the dance form was twofold: He streamlined the style, bringing it in tune with twen-tieth century urban life, and he created singlehandedly a brilliant reper-tory.[11]

On the one hand he toned down the florid, stately exhibitionism that had become the hallmark of nineteenth century ballet. At the same time, he extended the range of ballet movement in time and space. For example, he minimized or altogether eliminated elaborate preparations for pirouettes and aerial steps, as well as the grand entrances of the stars that serve mainly as cues for applause. (For example, a soloist may enter or leave before a pas-sage is complete.) He also cut down the huge Petipa corps to four, eight or sixteen dancers.

The Balanchine corps has more fancy, varied movement. His fast became faster. He increased by many times the number of steps performed within one phrase. He also developed a characteristic linking and entwin-ing use of the arms, where two, three or even four figures hold hands and turn around one another, or around the whole group, or duck under bridg-ing arms. In this way, a male may partner two or three females simulta-neously.

New York City Ballet dancers assume Balanchine's neoclassic poses in *Apollo*.
Photograph by Martha Swope, © Time Inc.

A Balanchine pose (seen in *Apollo* and in many works thereafter) has
a bent leg headed straight front, ending in a pointed foot, with the torso or
hip leaning at an angle. Balanchine frequently took the balletic legs, which
had traditionally turned out at the hips (except in folk or character parts),
and allowed them to turn straight forward—or even inward (pigeon-toed!).
For *Apollo* and others like *Agon* and *The Four Temperaments*, Balanchine also
replaced the standard lightly curved arms and hands with sharply angled
wrists and elbows.

Balanchine's pieces fall into several types: radiant grandeur, romantic lyricism and experimental modernism. Occasionally there are hints of a plot; in a small number there is a forthright story. But for the most part, Balanchine works are plotless, and their beauty lies in the choreographer's poetic vision of classical dance, plus his response to music and to the specific qualities of his favorite dancers. The artist's lifelong fascination with ballet led him to restage many classics. It also led him to include other dance styles in his ballets.

Critic Edwin Denby wrote of the difficulty of analyzing Balanchine's style, but went on to make points that are useful in watching the master's choreography. "A surprise in his ballets, if you watch objectively, is the variety of shapes of steps, the variety of kinds of movement that he manages to make classic." Whether Balanchine uses mime, or ballroom, or square dance slides, he transmutes them into classicism "because of the kind of continuity in motion he calls for. For the continuity in all these pieces is that of which the familiar classroom exercises are the key and remain a touchstone." In other words, Balanchine's style was developed through the special training received by his dancers at his own School of American Ballet.[12]

Whatever themes he chose, Balanchine's output was enormous, comprising almost one hundred ballets from 1920 to 1980. Because so many of these are constantly performed by the New York City Ballet as well as other companies worldwide, his neoclassicism has become a central ballet tradition of the late 1900s.

The story of modern ballet does not end, of course, with Fokine and Balanchine. Great choreographers like Jerome Robbins, Antony Tudor, Agnes de Mille and Frederick Ashton also developed magnificent personal styles. However, none of these artists made basic changes in general philosophy or technique. Their contributions to the art form lay rather in the field of repertory. Some of their works will be taken up as examples of various future topics. At this point we will continue our survey of styles, with the advent of modern dance.

3

*Expressive
Styles and Beyond*

———◆———

LIBRARY, UNIVERSITY OF CHESTER

Modern Dance

Around 1900, led by Isadora Duncan, a group of modern dancers sprang up who, though motivated by the same impulses that drove Diaghilev's artists, responded to those impulses in a different way. Fokine, Nijinsky and Massine ventured into untried territory, but they still arranged their works for dancers trained in ballet technique. The new breed of modern dancers, on the other hand, was defiantly in opposition to balletic traditions. As they spurned the restraints of ready-made dance forms, they shunned classically trained dancers.

To suit their feelings, modern dancers set out to explore free, swinging motions of the whole body with emphasis on the torso. They turned away from virtuoso skills of the legs and used the bare foot. They gave very different spatial and rhythmic shaping to body movements and sought a fuller treatment of space, especially the floor. They replaced symmetry and harmony with distortion and imbalance. They used music with uneven rhythms and dissonant harmonies.

Early modern dancers were serious and idealistic. They looked on their art as a vehicle for expressing feelings and ideas and communicating the deepest truths, concerned with human psychology and social justice. Martha Graham's solo *Deep Song* (1937) symbolized her identification with the sufferings of the Spanish people during their civil war. Helen Tamiris cried out her protest against inhuman treatment of black people in the 1920s and 1930s by dancing to a series of spirituals like *Crucifixion* and *How Long Brethren*. Doris Humphrey created *Inquest* (1944) in memory of an English cobbler who had died of starvation.

Despite the similarities in these works, however, modern dance cannot be regarded as one revolution with common goals. The main characteristic that loosely united these pioneer artists was the way they all looked upon the classic ballet as sterile, restrictive, and not relevant to the spirit of the twentieth century. But they were definitely *not* interested in founding a new "academy." Every major modern dancer was to create a unique system of dance technique suitable to his or her own company, dancing a repertory that expressed a personal vision. In considering their styles, "individualism" is the key word to keep in mind.

We start with Isadora Duncan (born 1878), who had a lifelong goal to tear down the old ballet regime. She longed to substitute dance that would freely express the self. But that wasn't all. Isadora Duncan had a bias against marriage—although not against men or romance—and she called for the equality of women and men in open relationships. She preached for a freer education of children and for the release of the body from tight clothing. Keep in mind that this was the Victorian Age, known for its prudery. In

Isadora's day, women bound their flesh in stiff corsets and covered themselves with layers of material up to their necks and down to their shoes (which is why Victorian women were always fainting).

Isadora danced barefoot and appeared in skimpy, see-through tunics, sometimes with one breast uncovered. She openly took lovers, and as an unmarried woman proudly bore two children. She indulged herself in speechmaking, even among friends, and loudly declared her admiration for Soviet Russia. In a theater she might step up to the footlights, wave a flaming red scarf and shout: "This is red. That is what I am. Don't let them tame you!"[1] For these reasons, she was snubbed by many Americans, at least until she won great success and fame in Europe.

Duncan built her art on simple movements. She devised a natural, graceful way of kneeling, rising, running and swaying, and she relied heavily on pantomimed gestures and facial expressions. Inspired by the culture of ancient Greece, she copied costumes and striking poses from Greek vases. Although she saw to it that her groups of performing children learned patterns and moved in unison, she herself often improvised. Even in front of an audience, Isadora could enter an almost trancelike state and allow famous musical compositions to motivate her to dance with intense feeling. But she did some pieces often enough that their outlines remained the same. Here is a description of one:

> In the *Marche Slav* of Tchaikovsky, Isadora symbolizes her conception of the Russian peasant, rising from slavery to freedom. With her hands bound behind her back, groping, stumbling, head bowed, knees bent, she struggles forward, clad only in a short red garment that barely covers her thighs.
>
> When the strains of "God Save the Czar" are first heard in the orchestra, she falls to her knees and you see the tragic picture of a peasant shuddering under the blows of the whip.
>
> Finally comes the moment of release. Isadora brings her arms forward slowly and we observe with horror that her hands are crushed and bleeding after their long serfdom; they are not hands at all but claws, broken, twisted, hideous claws! The expression of frightened, almost uncomprehending joy with which Isadora concludes the Marche, is a stroke of her imaginative genius.[2]

Because of both her mimetic style and disorganized personal life, Duncan's art did not survive her. However, she was one of those magnetic performers who are capable of stirring an audience deeply. Helped by her own impassioned writing and the words of countless contemporaries, memories of Isadora remain strong to this day. She started a craze for barefoot dancing that swept across Europe and then America. In Tsarist Russia, her dancing affected professionals like Tamara Karsavina and Michel Fokine.

The movements in Fokine's *Daphnis and Chloe* were inspired directly by Duncan's Greek style.

Ruth St. Denis, also born in 1878, started out with ten years in commercial theater as an actress who danced and sang (the way a young woman might work today in musical comedy or television). Then, her spirit fired by images of the exotic Orient, she found her direction as a serious artist. In 1906, she fashioned three pieces: *The Incense*, *The Cobras* and *Radha*, each portraying a scene of life in India. All three remained in her solo repertory for decades.

In *The Incense* St. Denis made a ritual of prayer. Moving about in slow, quiet steps, she held a tray of smoking incense. As the smoke rose into the air, her body mirrored its flow with gentle ripples. A wavelike motion began in the shoulders and passed outward through the arms and the fingers, finally spreading to the torso, which took up the hint of sinuous motion. The high point of the ceremony was reached when the woman lifted the tray slowly, curling it around her body and close to her head, a solid reflection of the rising smoke. Finally, she extended it high upward to the heavens as an offering. This number was theatrically stunning with its dim lighting, the smoking incense stand, and the dancer's grey sari.

In *The Cobras* St. Denis became at once a ragged snake charmer and two reptiles. She stained her body brown, painted her fingers blue, and wore many rings to create snakes' eyes in her angled hands. Her slithering arms became the snakes' bodies and her hands darted and struck out as the snakes' heads.

In *Radha*, she created the part of a goddess receiving homage. She descended from her platform to stroke her own body with flowers. She raised a bowl of wine to her lips. She gave herself over to the ceremony, twirling and reeling in ecstasy until she fell to the ground. At the end she rose to sit serenely in her temple. For *Radha*, St. Denis's brother Buzz invented a cage in which she could sit high up above the stage and change the colors of the spotlights to highlight mood changes. St. Denis wore a great golden skirt which flew outward as she spun into the climax.

When St. Denis's "show biz" sense told her that the momentum was running out on her career as a solo concert dancer, she advertised and came up with Ted Shawn. After an all-night talk session, she invited him to be her partner.

Isadora Duncan, Ruth St. Denis, Ted Shawn—how they loved to talk! They were high on dance, which was for them art, revolution, religion and the meaning of life all in one. They saw themselves as missionaries, practicing a true artistic spiritualism. Within a short time St. Denis and Shawn were dancing together, and then they were married. A year later in Los Angeles they opened the Denishawn School.

Ted Shawn was a well-organized worker with wide ranging abilities. He set up the school's curriculum; he taught stretching exercises, a ballet barre, and free movement. St. Denis taught her personal Oriental techniques, including yoga meditation, and music visualization, which was inspired by Isadora Duncan's work. St. Denis and Shawn attracted the talented dancers of the day and put together a company that toured successfully through the country and abroad. Branches of the school were established all over the United States.

But the strong St. Denis and Shawn egos clashed, and after fifteen years they separated. Miss Ruth, as she was known in the field, went on to practice dance as religious worship well into her eighties. She understood how to uplift audiences with mystical devotions, and the audiences responded fully.

Ted Shawn's solo contribution was to found an all men's group, demonstrating that men had an important part in modern dance. His programs offered themes of American Indians; of European workers; of Japanese warriors; of Negro spirituals. For his men's group rehearsals and performances, Ted acquired Jacob's Pillow, Massachusetts, in 1931. When this group disbanded in 1940, Shawn used Jacob's Pillow to realize another great dream. He founded a summer school and concert series. Jacob's Pillow is to this day an important dance center. Throughout the twentieth century, legions of modern dancers were taught by St. Denis, Ted Shawn or their pupils. Martha Graham, Doris Humphrey, Charles Weidman, Anna Sokolow and José Limón are the best known successors.

In 1916, Martha Graham enrolled in the recently opened Denishawn Los Angeles school and was immediately invited to join the Denishawn company. Graham stayed with Denishawn until 1923, teaching and touring across the United States. In a series of one-night stands she learned to be a trouper. She also learned about costumes and lighting, and about performing on stages of different sizes, in all kinds of weather, for all kinds of audiences. In short, she learned the trade of theater dance.

At Denishawn, Graham also met and had an affair with Louis Horst, Denishawn's musical director. Louis Horst was not a dancer, but he was an important presence on the modern dance scene. When Graham went off on her own in 1926, Horst began his twenty-year role as her adviser on music and choreography. Under Horst's influence, Graham used contemporary music. Like Isadora Duncan, Graham played to the hilt the part of an emancipated artist. But unlike Duncan, Martha was fanatical about discipline where dance was concerned. She demanded that students regard her studio as both theater and temple.

In 1944, Martha Graham choreographed a beautiful portrait of mating: *Appalachian Spring*, with the beloved musical score by Aaron Copland

and a fine set by Isamu Noguchi. In *Appalachian Spring*, a pioneering man and woman marry and move into their new home. The husband (Erick Hawkins in the first cast) does a handstand and slaps his legs joyously, but he also bows formally to villagers and prays quietly. The wife (Martha Graham) adores the husband (Erick Hawkins was, for a brief period, Graham's husband in reality) and walks next to him with obedient little bows. She projects anxiety: Will she be a good wife and mother? But she also looks forward to the future with happy self-possession, and she and her husband greet the community with warm dignity. The humorous side belongs to the preacher (Merce Cunningham). He dances of hellfire and sin, but he is a bounding, light fellow, amusing rather than frightening, especially with his chorus of four adoring little village girls who flutter around him devotedly.

But then Martha Graham began to produce heavier and heavier visions such as *Night Journey* (1947). *Night Journey* unfolds the saga of forbidden incestuous passion between Jocasta and Oedipus, the most famous mother-son duo in Greek literary tradition, later picked up by Freud as a cornerstone of his psychological outlook.

In *Night Journey* the central emotional theme is love between male and female—this time not the gentle awakening of romantic fervor, but incestuous desire that inexorably leads a woman to her doom along with the object of her destructive passion. And since Jocasta and Oedipus are the rulers of a mythic kingdom, the force of their lust brings down their people, too.

Rituals of primitive sex, and myths of ancient Greece and of the Bible that deal with fears, rage and despair, became the content of Graham's work from that time on. Her technique, characterized by movements that dig deep into the dancer's body, was tailored to suit her visions.

The contraction is the foundation of Graham's dance technique. It is a tautly controlled rounding of the entire spine that begins with the hips tucking under and continues upward and outward, with the abdomen pulling way in and the shoulders coming forward. The muscles called into play are stretched and held, and the movement impulse carries out to the tips of the hands and feet. The contraction is usually followed by a stretched, lifted (but *not* relaxed) release. Balance is held by an opposition spiral set up between shoulder girdle and opposite hip. The dancer often jumps sideways, with thighs, knees and feet turned straight forward and the upper body leaning away from the direction of travel. Or the dancer may advance through space in a deep contraction. The arms are taut, and angularly bent. The face is concentrated on some distant, significant focal point. All in all, the attitudes of the Graham technique project a sense of drama and anxious tension.

In the 1930s and 1940s, Martha Graham and Doris Humphrey were the foremost American artists of modern dance. Humphrey's approach to life was the more upbeat of the two. Her technique was built on a gamut of falls and recoveries that expressed a range of ideas between total surrender to gravity (symbolically representing despair or death) and suspended lifts (symbolizing the proud affirmation of human uprightness) .

As an illustration of a modern masterpiece, let's look at Doris Humphrey's *With My Red Fires*, which premiered in 1936 to a score by Wallingford Riegger. *With My Red Fires* exemplifies the goal of early modern dance: dramatic communication of social and psychological insight. The central figure of this work is a grim, vindictive matriarch, inciting the community to tear her daughter from the arms of a lover. The "anywhere" place is set abstractly with long, low platforms and columns. These suggest a village clearing, a temple, a home, a rocky terrain.

A restless opening has women and men of a nameless community, driven by agitated music and cosmic words from William Blake's *Jerusalem II*, to press close or disperse or abruptly arrest their motion in a collective ritual of sexual desire. The focus of the action becomes a pair of lovers, meeting and parting, fearful that they are to be sacrificial victims.

The matriarch is set above and apart from the community by a striking costume that boasts a high-necked bodice, full long sleeves, and a skirt of enormous breadth that emphasizes commanding circular gestures of her legs. Her scowling face is framed by broadly upswept hair. She scolds the young girl, summoning her to respectable domesticity. The girl tries to obey, but, drawn by her lover, she sneaks out and clings to him with helpless passion. The old woman screams an alarm from the housetop. Then she shuts her door firmly, as with virtuous malice people run about, on the "scent" of the couple, whom they hound, pinch, tear, beat, and then abandon on a phallic stone. The group deteriorates from a devotional community to separate petty souls: the moralists pointing accusations; the sentimentalists weeping; the scandalmongers laughing. But in the end, the lovers rise to face the future with composure, and the matriarch is left in defeat, broken by envy of their youthful happiness.

Avant-garde or Postmodern

From 1939 to 1945, Merce Cunningham was an outstanding member of Graham's company. By that time Graham, a woman with a powerful personality onstage and off, had attracted thousands of students and fans and imitators. But Cunningham was not one of them. In fact, he turned against her choreography of emotional turmoil, which struck him as rather silly.

Even before he left Graham's company, Cunningham was experimenting with drier, more objective modern dance. Cunningham himself dated his true artistic beginnings from a 1944 joint concert with John Cage. Although Cage was only seven years older than Cunningham, he already had a name among avant-garde musicians. This man was to be Merce Cunningham's musical director and closest companion for over fifty years.

John Cage was a musician who became better known for his eccentric ideas than for his compositions. For his outlook on life and art, Cage turned to Zen Buddhism, an Eastern philosophy that preaches theories of chance and of nonintervention. Thus in his work, Cage admitted no boundaries between one art and another, or between art and life. He said, "There is no intention when a dance is made." Cage's approach was to treat art as an activity to be arranged by artists according to their own rules, which they could change at random. In his mind, the concept and process of creation were as important, if not more important, than the art product itself. For example, Cage's musical composition *4'33* was four minutes and thirty-three seconds of silence. The idea was to allow any incidental sounds in the concert hall to make up the piece. Of course the audience members were granted the freedom to react as they pleased, and no two audiences are exactly alike. Thus *4'33* was never the same. The spectators' coughing, whispering, rustling programs, laughing or stalking out in protest might be heard; outside noises like the motor of a jet plane sometimes became part of the piece.

Cunningham's working methods did not stem from Zen philosophy, the way Cage's did. He was simply by nature open to all possibilities. He made dances to be seen by people sitting around the performers, instead of just in front of them. At times he did use chance procedures, like Cage. Then Cunningham would spend hours and hours preparing charts of possible dance movements, with spatial and rhythmic variations. He would work out the movement, the time, the direction, how many performers, and other variables for each phrase by tossing a coin. This was a very tedious process. He would toss a coin for movement. Heads might mean jump; tails, turn. Another toss would determine direction. Heads might be front; tails, side. This would have to be repeated for each performer, for each phrase.

It is a waste of time to look for plots in a Cunningham work. Each piece is a development of a movement idea. But there is room for interpretation. In *Antic Meet* (1958), Cunningham danced with a chair strapped to his body; he did a tender duet with a woman who came through a pair of curtains dressed in a nightgown; another woman carried an umbrella across the stage. *Crises* (1960) explored the possibilities of people being joined together by elastics—at their arms, legs, or waists. This piece has been seen as portraying a man's stormy relationships with four women. *Winterbranch* (1964) was made up of bodies falling and of bodies dragged out of the area while lying or sitting down.

How to Pass, Kick, Fall and Run (1965) has people meeting and parting with light, bouncy steps. Poses and technical feats are not "exhibited" to the audience. Instead, arms and legs are flung out, and bodies jump and twirl exuberantly. In shape the limbs are straight or bent in an easy manner, and casual groupings shift constantly. The body is organized and controlled, but not held tightly. The effort element is not an impulse to attack upward or "follow through," but only what is needed to lift an arm or turn the body. Movement patterns do not call attention to themselves for technical difficulty, beautiful line, or emotional meaning. The body jumps to face another way. One sees another shape. The costume of skin-fitting tights and leotard further neutralizes the body. The dancers are on the ready, able to spring into any position or direction. Their manner does not say "I want this" or "I fear that" or "I love him." Rather the image is of play, of people running around in a game of tag, smiling for the pure fun of the movement. In their presence, the viewer feels a peppy spontaneity.

Cunningham's view of a vast universe allows no area of the stage to be more important than another. The artist took his cue from Einstein's assertion: "There are no fixed points in space."[3]

From the point of view of the audience, strong differences among Merce Cunningham's compositions result not from the movement sequences alone, but from the sound accompaniment and the scenic props as well. These are created independently by other artists, in keeping with Cage's approach, which was the reverse of the "total theater" philosophy of Sergei Diaghilev's Ballets Russes and Martha Graham's psychological dramas. Diaghilev and Graham had both looked for reenforcement of choreographic ideas from musicians and designers. Cage held, however, that each artist should work independently, their products merely "co-existing." He questioned the constant search of critics for "relationships" between dance and music (and décor.) He pointed out that when anyone looks around, he or she sees various objects and hears various sounds that have nothing at all to do with one another—except that they exist in the same location at the same time. As it is in life, so it is with art. A dancer moves. A sound is struck. A light is flashed. The observer is free to make connections among these three events. In other words, artworks are completed by the spectator, who is as necessary to the creative process as the choreographer, composer or designer.

Cunningham's *Winterbranch* assaults viewers. Brilliant lights flash on and off at irregular intervals, sometimes turned right into the eyes of the spectators. The accompaniment is an electronic extension of two different sounds, one low and one high, which go on continuously for most of the piece; they rumble and screech at an almost unbearable volume. In Europe, people thought *Winterbranch* was about the Holocaust. In Japan, they said it was the atomic bomb. Some New Yorkers saw terror on a subway train.

Conversely, the accompaniment to *How to Pass, Kick, Fall and Run* is made up of wry anecdotes, written by John Cage, each one read in exactly one minute by one of two men who sit on the side of the stage sipping champagne. The effect is amusing, because the anecdotes are.

Merce Cunningham developed his style by solving problems as they came along. For example, since his company dancers all had different schedules (they had to hold jobs to earn a living), he got into the habit of working alone with any single dancer who showed up at the studio. The artist himself noted that this gave his choreography a sense of "beings in isolation," along with "continuous appearance and vanishing."[4]

He introduced everyday movements into dance at a 1952 Brandeis University concert when, in addition to a few members of his excellent company, he was faced with using untrained college students. He made a dance with two kinds of movement. First, there were difficult phrases he invented for his dancers. Then there were common pantomime gestures like shaking hands, or looking at a wristwatch and hurrying away, for the others. But Cunningham had always been interested in dance that came from ordinary experience. One day he noticed little kids in the street, skipping and running about in their play. He suddenly realized they were dancing. "You could call it dancing, and yet it wasn't dancing. I thought it was marvelous," he observed.[5]

In 1964, while on a European tour, the Cunningham company was invited to perform at a Viennese museum that had no theater. They were going to build a special platform for the appearance. Instead, the ever-practical Cunningham decided that the group would appear in one of the galleries in a specially made piece consisting of excerpts from his repertory, assembled in a new sequence, entitled *Museum Event No. 1*. The choreographer was so pleased with the ideas of recycling his choreography and of performing in non-theatrical spaces, that he has since arranged hundreds of *Events* in museums, gymnasiums and even out of doors.[6] Inventive movement is the keynote of *Events*, which are always different from one another.

In fact, *Events* have by now become a common feature of all company appearances, like the *Joyce Event* held in 1994 in New York's Joyce Theater. On this occasion, to celebrate the thirtieth anniversary of *Events*, Robert Rauschenberg, who had designed the first one, put the cast into purple unitards and created a painted backdrop: "filled with black, white, red, orange and green splotches. In the midst of these bursts of color, the outlines of what appear to be buildings, bodies and a highway stop sign are dimly visible."[7]

In the *Joyce Event*, there was a self-portrait of the choreographer at

Interims by choreographer Murray Louis. Photograph by Tom Caravaglia, courtesy Nikolais/Louis Foundation for Dance.

work, a sequence in which Cunningham, wearing a gray suit, stood beside a dance-studio barre, did a few tentative steps and appeared to ponder their effectiveness.

Although Cunningham departed from most traditions, he never lost respect for well-trained dancers. The object of technical training, he once wrote, is: "to walk magnificently and thereby evoke the spirit of a god.... Not to show off, but to show; not to exhibit, but to transmit the tenderness of the human spirit through the disciplined action of the human body."[8]

Cunningham dancers always perform with control, clarity, and concentration. They are masters of his own technique, a combination of Graham's rounded back and off-center poses with the springy jumps and slow balances of ballet, which Merce perfected at Balanchine's School of American Ballet.

Like Cunningham, and during the same period, Alwin Nikolais turned his back on literal content. He urged viewers to enjoy the sight of moving figures for their sheer beauty. Nikolais excelled in creating brilliant, highly inventive, abstract designs in motion. Added to the beautiful patterns in space made by his dancers' bodies were the fabulous costuming materials and gorgeous lighting effects that he also devised. At the same time, Nikolais wrote electronic scores to accompany his own choreography. The effect of his works, which provided a feast for all the senses, was overwhelming. He was to influence artists of the theater, television and commercial advertising, as well as choreography. Murray Louis, a leading performer of the Nikolais company, was one dancer who went in his masterly direction.

The Cunningham-Cage partners, along with Alwin Nikolais, opened the door to a spirit of experiment that exploded all boundaries. The attention of Western audiences was focused far beyond the confines of ballet.

During the 1960s and 1970s, hundreds of artists followed in the footsteps of Cunningham and Nikolais. In the name of avant-garde art, they retooled every aspect of dance. The idea was to present a fresh orientation to the environment, to explore the nature of our experience of living, to come to terms with the enormous quantity of unrelated stimuli that we confront each hour. Fresh perception was the order of the day: perception of space, of time, of energy, of sound, of behavior, of content, of views of humanity, and of the dance medium itself—all stretched to the limit in every direction. Choreographers no longer had to make decisions alone. They drew on the dancers' ideas, and sometimes allowed them to improvise during the performance.

Experimental dancers played with space. For the same reasons that painters let paint ooze off the canvas onto the floor or even onto the model, so the choreographer asked: Why on a stage? Why don't we do it in the road, or in a gymnasium, or on a beach? So they left the theater. Meredith Monk used a street, Twyla Tharp a museum lobby, Trisha Brown a series of rooftops.

Placing dance figures outside the theater, where buildings, sky, and the distant horizon tended to dwarf them, completely changed the scale of the performers. The outside detracted from their strength, making the imposing presence an impossibility and canceling dramatic communication. Avant-garde choreographers also used inside space unconventionally, climbing the walls or turning the place upside down. In 1976 Trisha Brown had some of her company strapped in harnesses from an overhead trolley walking perpendicularly upright, but along a wall.

The dancers questioned the use of music. They asked, why not take advantage of the sounds of airplane and car motors that often intrude on a concert? Why not go into the street and make a tape recording of all the environmental noises? Why not use passages from several piano selections, joined as you would hear them if you were walking past closed doors of music rehearsal rooms in conservatory? Why not wire the dancers for the noise of their moving bodies, electronically synthesized with other sounds? Straight music was thus eliminated as accompaniment, in exchange for speech or collages of sound—including music.

Experimental choreographers played around with mundane nondance gestures like lighting a cigarette, painting a canvas, or undressing or dressing during a piece. They brought actions directly onto the stage from life outside, sometimes casually, as a throw-away, or sometimes emphasized— perhaps as a fetish, exaggerated enormously and repeated obsessively. In a 1960s performance at the Judson Church, painter Robert Rauschenberg and musician John McDowell, both untrained in dance, took part along with more conventional dancers in performing "everyday" motions such as lying down, drinking coffee, gymnastic cartwheels, walking on the hands, juggling Indian clubs, crying, and climbing the walls.

Some avant-garde dancers rejected not only virtuosity, but dance training itself. Yvonne Rainer sought to make movement like an "object," something stripped of any psychological or formal aspects, simply to be looked at. In *We Shall Run* (1963), a group of twelve people, some dancers and some not, all dressed in everyday clothing, ran around the stage in various patterns. Rainer's idea was not to suggest a situation, or to present a spectacle of virtuoso motion, but to force the audience to pay attention to "running."[9]

Or take Trisha Brown's *Line Up*, as performed at the Brooklyn Academy of Music in 1977. (The time and place are important, because the dance permitted the performers certain choices, and therefore differed from performance to performance.) Dressed plainly in white scoop-necked, long-sleeved shirts and white loose-fitting pants, the performers did various simple things having to do with making lines. In a section called "Sticks" they carried long poles onto the stage. Then they lay down, lined up head to feet, and touched the poles end to end. In another section, advancing with great care from seemingly random motions through a series of about-faces and realignments, they succeeded in marking a neat, squared-off stage space. Later, to a ticking metronome, the dancers, their faces expressionless, lined up quietly one behind the other and placed their hands on their heads with fixed concentration. Their attitude was matter-of-fact, stripped of any hint of personal situation, emotion, rhythmic or dynamic variation, or technical virtuosity.[10] The viewer does not become emotionally involved in a piece like *Line Up* through association of ideas, or through admiration of skilled performers. Rather, the viewer observes such a piece as a process, to see the way a concept is being carried out.

Steve Paxton, who danced in Merce Cunningham's company, is known for his own minimalist choreography. *State* (1968) is a Paxton piece in which 42 performers are instructed to walk to the center of the performing area, where for two three-minute intervals, they stand in random groupings.

During two 15-second blackouts they are allowed to adjust their positions or scratch. Then they exit, walking.[11]

Beginning in 1972, Paxton developed a technique known as contact improvisation. In this technique, movement originates between two people who, through physically lifting and entwining with one another, improvise in "a continuous process of finding and losing balance." There were concert presentations in the form, which remained similar to studio sessions. The idea was to be alert and free and, by building up a relationship of trust with one's partner, to test the limits of balance. It involved much falling and could be frightening to do—or watch. Contact Improvisation spread so widely among avant-garde dancers that its practitioners issued newsletter and held conferences. [12]

Douglas Dunn went so far as to eliminate movement altogether, as Cage had eliminated sound in *4'33*. In *101* (1974), Dunn set up a splintery maze in his studio and lay on top of it for four hours a day (over a period of weeks). The audience was invited to move around his unmoving figure, presented atop the maze like a piece of sculpture.[13]

In the 1990s, the "tradition" of testing choreographic limits remained very much alive. Elizabeth Streb designed hanging ropes and harnesses for *Soaring* and a fifteen-foot-high scaffolding for *Airlines* so that she could place her dancers in mid-air. In her *Rebound* (1990), two plywood walls, eight feet apart, are placed on the stage. The walls are used to provide an external force opposing the dancers' intention to run. The piece has a disturbing aspect, as performers take off at a run, only to slam violently into the plywood set. All Elizabeth Streb's pieces reveal her obsession with the rush of motion to the edge of danger, to the moment of impact. Streb makes motions for her dancers that are as intense as full-speed, straight downhill skiing.

A major change discernible in this later avant-garde is an emphasis placed on meaning, where the earlier period saw a focus on the materials of art. Pina Bausch, whose German troupe frequently visits the United States, absorbs impressions everywhere and anywhere for her theatrical movement and sound collages. As she told reporter Eva Hoffman, "My antennae are out all the time.... When you work on a piece, something comes from the side.... It doesn't fit in with your plans, but you have to follow it."[14]

In 1993, Bausch's troupe brought to Brooklyn the three-hour *Two Cigarettes in the Dark*, to music by a number of composers including Monteverdi and Brahms, along with jazz performed by Ben Webster and Alberta Hunter. The long piece is made up of six women and five men clothed variously in evening dress, bathing suits or underwear. Alone, in twos or together, they move in episodes that are discontinuous and so hard to sum up that Anna Kisselgoff in one review spoke of a "tight structure" and in another of "images are so disconnected that the work as a whole lacks the sureness of tone common to Ms. Bausch's use of collage." [15]

The genesis of *Two Cigarettes in the Dark* helps explain its disunity. It was the result of a six-week workshop in which Bausch posed situations and questions for her troupe of fine dancers, who acted out their responses and came up with plenty of dramatic action. The high point is a sequence of four couples grouped close together on the floor, as though in a lifeboat. To Ravel's *La Valse*, they slide along on their backsides, at times smashing into the walls. Other scenes have a female in a topless gown (cigarette dangling from her lips) stacking bricks, and a male tidying up a female as though she were a dog needing to be housebroken. What unity there is in *Two Cigarettes in the Dark* seems to arise from the grand but austere set designed by Peter Pabst, which Robert Greskovic described as a large white room with three walls that expand to an aquarium with live fish, an exotic terrarium, and a sandy desert planted with large cacti.[16]

Sean Curran performed his own choreography in 1995. In *Lazy Man's Load*, his arms signaled the actions, with the rest of him going along for the ride. They clamped him like a straitjacket, and his fluttering fingers seemed to be driving him nuts. His body responded to the music of *Flexible While Frozen*, "as if to electric shocks." *Am I Dead Yet?* presented him lying like a crucified corpse, and then had him testing his bodily reflexes. At the end he told vivid stories of the moment of his death.[17]

Another significant change is the highly charged, intense virtuosity of contemporary performers. Bebe Miller is one such magnetic dancer. Miller created *Yard Dance* in 1996. Accompanied by music and Miller's own verbal text, the work told of the artist's recent visit to South Africa after apartheid was ended, and the problems she observed. At first, while a group formed, the theatrically magnetic Miller lurked shyly at the side—apprehensive, inquisitive, vulnerable. As the piece progressed, everyone began to move tentatively in unison, to convey a cautiously optimistic message about the troubled society.[18]

Many other pieces that focus on movement quality, without themes that are clearly identifiable, also project a strong undercurrent of feeling—almost always on the disturbed side of the emotional scale.

Jazz and Tap

Alongside ballet and modern dance, there is a third world in American dance. Since the time they were first dragged to this country as slaves, black people have created their own forms of dance and music. They combined their ancient songs and swinging rhythmic movements remembered from Africa with folk and ballroom dance styles that they found in the new world. The result was jazz.

Jazz swings free and easy. Its treatment of the body is opposite to that of ballet. Where the ballet dancer fully extends the legs and feet and holds the torso straight and quiet, the jazz dancer crouches, keeps the spine loose and flexible, and swings the hips. Where the ballet dancer's aim is to move so smoothly that all effort is concealed, the jazz dancer flaunts each movement with a strong attack that begins in the pelvis and spreads outward. Where the ballet style is restrained and pompous, the jazz style is sexual and digs deep into the emotions.

A central aspect of jazz is improvisation. Each dancer is free to add a new twist. The jazz style has immense range. It often speaks the blues, beginning with an expression of painful longing for families and homeland. The uprooted African Americans introduced an element of protest into their style. The jazz dancer may shrug a shoulder or flick a hip in a subtle form of mockery and contempt, directed at the white master and his society. At the same time, jazz can also celebrate the joy of living.

Tap dance, a most appealing Jazz style, is a direct descendant of African tribal drumming and step-dancing. Tap dance developed because slave owners, who feared uprisings by their ill-treated blacks, forbade them to use drums. The ingenious slaves substituted rhythmic clapping, stamping, and shuffling dance patterns. Later, freed blacks were not permitted to dance in theaters and had to make do with performing in low-class dives. There they often encountered another despised minority: the Irish, specialists in clog dancing. (Clog dance is a form that keeps the body and arms quiet, while the feet move fast in wooden shoes.) Together, around 1900, the blacks and the Irish developed the *soft shoe*, an easygoing kind of syncopated footwork in soft-soled shoes, against the sharper tap dance, performed in shoes with metal cleats attached. Tap dance has collected a rich vocabulary of whispered shuffles, exuberant kicks, noisy stamps, acrobatic twirls, backflips, splits, graceful slides, and anything else a soloist might do.

Tap dance continues to climb in popularity. In the 1988 movie *Tap*, Gregory Hines paid tribute to the old tap dance greats who taught him the trade. The film presents, among others, expert hoofers Jimmy Slyde, Harold Nicholas, Bunny Briggs, and Sandman Sims. Hines showed himself to be a worthy follower of those masters.

In the 1990s, the fabulous Savion Glover burst on the scene. At fourteen, he was a sensation on Broadway in *The Tap Dance Kid*. He also appeared for five years as a young teenager on *Sesame Street*. At twenty, Glover starred in the 1994 Broadway and touring show *Jelly's Last Jam*.

Glover excels in recent jazz dance developments like break dancing and hiphop.

In 1995, Glover arranged the dances and starred in *Bring In Da Noise, Bring in Da Funk*, which shows and tells the story of tap dancing in black America. A writer quoted Glover this way:

> "See, it's like we have English, right? English, French, Spanish— and then we got slang. The steps that we usin' now is like slang. There ain't even no name. We can't say 'shuffle step' or 'flap' or something like that. It's just like *vrap-um-ba-boom*." [19]

Savion Glover, always eager to pass on what he knows, doesn't teach a fixed routine, but what he calls learning to "hit." "Hitting" in tap means expressing yourself, having something to say that is yours: how *you* feel, how *you* hear the rhythm. Tap dance is "rapping" with the feet in place of words.

Beginning in the middle of the nineteenth century, white Americans were exposed to some forms of African American dancing in minstrel shows, which were the most popular form of entertainment in the United States from about 1845 to 1900. These minstrel shows borrowed tunes and dances from African Americans, but the performers were all white men in blackface makeup.

In the 1920s, the "high society" of white America became infatuated with naughty, high-kicking, hip-swinging dances like the Charleston, the Lindy Hop and the Bunny Hug. Daring young men and even more daring young women showed them off to the point where the 1920s became known as the Jazz Age. Later, African Americans spun out dozens of variations, such as the rumba, the samba, and jitterbugging, from Spanish folk dances and upper-class European ballroom dances that they observed in the Caribbean and the American South. White Americans responded with enthusiasm to the new dances, performing them in public ballrooms and at private parties.

But while jazz swung back and forth from nightclubs to movies to Broadway shows and television, it did not win full recognition by serious musicians and dancers until late in the twentieth century. Modern dancer Alvin Ailey (1931–1989) gave it a major push toward acceptance.

Ailey, an African American of immense talent, was exploring the emotional depths of his own people. His instincts led him to jazz as the most suitable style for his personal expression. From 1960 to the present, the concerts of Alvin Ailey and his company, starring Judith Jamison (director since Ailey's death), have attracted huge audiences throughout the world. Ailey's works, including *Blues Suite*, *Revelations* and *Cry*, remain great hits. Their choreography is an electrifying blend of modern dance and jazz.

Blues Suite (1958) is a series of separate dances, each expressing the mood of the traditional blues song to which it is set. Among the dances one sees lost innocence, despair, social protest, anger, lost love, and high-stepping honky tonk revels.

Revelations (1960) portrays the experiences of African Americans in the American South of the 1930s, and it is accompanied by spirituals and gospel songs. In "I Been 'Buked," we feel sore burdens in the bent backs and lowered heads of the participants. We watch the men and women huddle close for animal comfort while their arms reach outward and upward for spiritual salvation. They seek the consolations of prayer in the duet "Fix Me, Jesus." Gradually the mood brightens, with a proud procession of figures, dressed up in shining white clothes and parasols, going to church. In the group ceremony of baptism to "Wading in the Water," bodies undulate from head to toe, while long yards of chiffon are waved around them. There is a mournfully repentant interlude in the man's solo "I Want to be Ready."

The last scenes include "Sinner Man," where three men attempt with frenzied shaking to rid themselves of sin, and "The Day Is Past and Gone," in which a group of women enjoy a satisfying exchange of gossip. The smashing finale, "Rocka My Soul in the Bosom of Abraham," takes place inside a church. Women are sitting on stools. Their men arrive. They rock, circle one another, and clap in mounting excitement until the entire community is celebrating religious ecstasy.

In 1971, to take full advantage of Judith Jamison's mighty talent, Alvin Ailey choreographed a solo, *Cry*, to an accompaniment of vocal and instrumental jazz. The dance, a tribute to the spirit of African American women in the face of humiliation and suffering, is strikingly developed in pulsing rhythms. The woman rolls her arched torso with anguish and pride. She poses behind a trailing length of cloth and then uses it as a rag to wipe the floor, as a bunting for a baby, and as a turban to top her own proud beauty. Later, the solo dancer spits out her rage and bends double in the horror of drug captivity. But after all the agony, there is a finale in which the dancer lifts her arms and steps forth proudly in a defiant hymn to life.

One of the first serious ballet choreographers to feature "cool" young people doing movements derived from the African American vernacular was Jerome Robbins. His *Interplay* (1945), to music by Morton Gould, followed the score in presenting bebop and boogie-woogie with a classical form. Four couples (the girls in toe shoes and ponytails, the boys with crew cuts) do "pure ballet technique, with a few syncopations, hip wiggles, and cartwheels.... Their *pas de deux* is a mixture of 'showbiz' and ballet."[20]

In 1958, Robbins did *N.Y. Export: Op. Jazz*, with music by Robert Prince. Again, the dancers relax and show off. They do slides, hip bumps, shoulder shimmies, finger snaps, bouncing backbends. Five boys have a "good time" with one girl and then discard her. A blues *pas de deux* has a couple meet, fool around, and part casually. The last section has the group move in formal dignity, and from there to hope, and finally defiance. Robbins wrote in a program note: "Feeling very much like a minority group in this threatening world, the youth have so identified with the dynamics, kinetic impetus, the drives and 'coolness' of today's jazz steps, that these dances have become an expression of our youths' outlooks and their attitudes."[21]

Today, jazz choreography can be found in productions ranging from the exciting African American repertory of the Alvin Ailey Company and the Dance Theater of Harlem, to the tritest showbiz on MTV, to the most powerful social commentary in a serious work like *Last Supper at Uncle Tom's Cabin/The Promised Land* by Bill T. Jones (1990). Innumerable white dance artists have adapted elements of jazz in their choreography.

We come now, however, to an artist who has done much more than combine jazz steps with ballet and modern movements in the same dance. Twyla Tharp has thoroughly integrated the techniques of the three major fields into a single, unified style.

In her early efforts (from 1965) Tharp, in the experimental mode of her day, threw out everything that was conventionally accepted as dance. Her first piece was *Tank Dive*. It took four minutes and had three scenes, marked off by blackouts: 1) Tharp on stage striking a couple of poses. 2) Two men and two women (non-dancers) exchanging flags. 3) Herself swinging around a pole. But she quickly moved into longer works that dove deep into dance movement, to create a personal style.

Tharp uses every element of dance in her own way, beginning with movement. She draws freely on the flexible torso of modern dance and the technical phrases of its leaders. She takes moves and steps from ballet, tap, ballroom, jitterbugging, karate, and sports like boxing—in short, any physical discipline that seems appropriate to an idea. In fact, the very idea of many Tharp pieces is to dig into one of these dance forms and see what she can make of them.

What she does with all this material is to combine styles in complex phrases that have the dancers moving every part of their bodies in different directions and dynamics. Tharp's method arbitrarily tacks on motions for head, arms and torso, unrelated to what's going on with the legs. This unnatural disjunction of body parts makes for a haphazard, cool style of movement. It is also fantastically complex, varying moment by moment from the most recklessly energetic tension to the most casual floppiness; from bursts of large, free motion, to small, inhibited twitches. For example, a phrase may use large leg movements together with small arm circles or twitches of shoulder or hip, taken at a precarious lean off-center. But this is not always easy to catch, because while one or two dancers do this phrase, other dancers may be doing different sets of movements with entirely different lines and timing. In space, Tharp spreads her figures out so that the eye can't take them all in, or else crowds them in such close-huddled clusters that they hide one another. In either case, no formal design emerges from the spatial elements.

Two unifying factors keep this piling on of diverse elements from disintegrating into total chaos. First, there is a propulsive flowing energy that overlays the whole, expressing Tharp's attitude towards life and art. Second, there is structural organization. True, the structures tend to be so mathematically intricate that it is a rare viewer who can take them in. Nevertheless, one gets a clear sense of order in the repetition and counterpoint of movement themes and rhythms and in the occasional fusion of unison motion.

The Fugue (1970) is a trio made up of short sections arranged in complex contrapuntal phrases, accompanied only by the amplified sounds of the dancers' boots beating on the stage loudly or lightly. As in tap dancing, the performers face front and the emphasis is "on changes of time, the thrust of weight going into the floor and springing out again," while there is a "loose disregard of all but the working body parts."[22]

The following year saw *Eight Jelly Rolls*, in which Tharp explored "the energy, virtuosity, and smooth extroversion of old time jazz ... to music of Jelly Roll Morton.... The movement is eccentric, surprising, impressionistic.... Tharp does an incredible solo where she keeps threatening to fall, just grabs her balance in time, only to throw herself off center again."[23]

1973's *Deuce Coupe* was a turning point for the artist. Made for the Joffrey Ballet, it proved so sensationally popular that it gave Tharp a wide public and brought in its wake commissions from other ballet companies, from films and from Broadway shows. *Deuce Coupe* features a device that Tharp has used many times since. It contrasts dance techniques by having one group of dancers work in one and another group in the second, but by the end synthesizing the movements of both groups. Here the opening of the dance has a soloist give a demonstration of classical ballet steps arranged alphabetically, while around her a "modern" duo moves with free flexibility. As the dance develops, a portrait of 1960s youth in southern California, having one last fling before adulthood claims them, is built up to songs of the Beach Boys. While the ballet soloist goes about her business, the dancers, in constantly shifting moods, show off, joke, argue, act romantic, sexy, and most often are hyperactive. They love speed, danger and disorientation. One scene has six people in a tight group miming slow drags on a marijuana cigarette. One by one they grind their pelvises and travel across the stage faster and faster in an orgy of shudders and shakes. Then, after almost total disintegration, the dancers slowly build into more orderly, conventional patterns. At the end, they freeze, and then drift away, leaving one girl lying still on the floor.[24]

Nine Sinatra Songs (1982) was Tharp's version of classical ballroom—a form for the '80s in which women could lead as well as follow. A series of duets, each to a different song, played out stages of relationships. There was a seduction, a bastardized tango in which man and woman each used the other as a reflection of their own irresistibility. "One More for the Road" was not based on any ballroom form, but implied the sexual premise of all ballroom dance. In this number, an older woman and a babyface man showed that they knew how to get to one another. Other numbers included a duet of innocent infatuation; a part for three couples, suggesting that a successful relationship needs to be worked at ("My Way"); an Apache dance in which the man hurls the woman about and she loves it; and a finale in which seven couples all appear for "a brief second of fulfilled fantasy." [25]

The Little Ballet was Tharp's staging of neoclasssic ballet. Watching this work, we feel the buoyancy of smoothly executed classical techniques. We get the sense of grace from the clean lines of torsos and limbs, and the harmony of lithe bodies in rapport with the lilting music. Instead of ceremonious elegance, however, we find movements that are friendly, free, and arranged with little formality. The central duet of *The Little Ballet* proceeds swiftly and continuously. The male soloist (in trousers, shirt and tie) and his female partner (in a knee-length chiffon gown) glide through a joyful movement pattern. Their demeanor expresses mutual pleasure. They move together in traditional "ballroom" placement, one of his hands holding hers, the other behind her waist. When either of them needs more space to execute splashy leaps or turning jumps, they separate and come together again unobtrusively. Neither is the sole focus of attention.

The viewer senses the motion of *The Little Ballet* as rippling water, rather than the sculptured marble of a conventional *pas de deux* like *Le Corsair*. While the dancers' bodies are totally controlled, the head and arms move freely; the back is arched gracefully; the movements don't stop for ornate preparations and codas to emphasize their technical difficulty; and many transitional steps and arm gestures fill each movement passage. *The Little Ballet* was made in 1983 for Mikhail Baryshnikov and four female soloists of the American Ballet Theater. It is set to music by Glazounov.

Push Comes to Shove was also made for Baryshnikov and the American Ballet Theater. This time, however, Tharp was playing around not only with ballet, but with Baryshnikov himself—his startling virtuosity and even his mannerisms. Recently arrived in New York, the Russian was eager for the latest American-style roles. Tharp gave him ballet movements that were twisted and leaned far back from his base of support, along with jaunty, jazzy moves. She also used his gesture of pushing his hair back. She was after the

athletic hero, the way she saw him: as a ringleader who was also a clown and a womanizer. "I decided to give him his wish: every woman in the company." The last touch was a bowler hat that he wore and tossed all over the place.[26]

Tharp wrote that the two stylistic poles of the twentieth century were represented by Balanchine and Graham. With their passing, "there is no longer a 'modern' dance separate from a 'classical' dance. Now there is just one dance in our past. How to protect and extend the lessons and beauty of that past without burying our own energies and imagination is the challenge for every artist."[27] Tharp has certainly met that challenge head on.

Postmodern Dance

The label "postmodern" dance, like the "modern" label, has developed along with the style to mean many things. In the beginning, it referred to the experiments described above, done in the wake of Cunningham and Cage. Now it is used to refer to choreography that is redefined, or in which elements are put together in new ways. The eclectic approach to styles that characterizes Twyla Tharp's work is considered a quality of postmodern dance.

Bill T. Jones represents a link between early and late postmodern styles. Consider his solo *And the Maiden*, created in 1993 (not for himself). This is a variation on the theme of death, clearly indicated by the stage set, which presents a gleaming skeleton; by the accompaniment of songs beginning with *O Death*; and by the title, which refers to *Death and the Maiden*, well known for its use in (among other things) a string quartet by Franz Shubert. We also have the testimony Jones has given in journalistic interviews about the AIDS death of his beloved partner Arnie Zane and his own HIV-positive state.

But except for the ending of *And the Maiden*, when the dancer goes upstage to bow to the skeleton and extinguish the light that shines on it, the action consists mainly of the soloist woman going through the routine leg exercises of a daily ballet barre—from the waist down. Meanwhile her arms and upper body are flung about—in part to express emotional anguish, but also to demonstrate the technical coordination of modern dance and ballet that makes up the vocabulary of postmodern performers. The message would appear to be that in the face of death the dancer's life goes on,

OPPOSITE: **American Ballet Theater dancers in Twyla Tharp's** *Push Comes to Shove*. **Photograph by Martha Swope, © Time Inc.**

through its unending discipline. This point is made provocatively when the soloist defiantly sticks out her tongue.

Sticking out one's tongue is hardly thought of as a dance movement. Yet its use—and indeed that of any action—is legitimate. In our discussions on style, we have seen how works are created within one or more given dance techniques. Our next topic is the choreography of specific subjects, and the ways in which artists manipulate everyday behavior to suit their ideas.

4

Subject and Body Language

Now we begin our attack on the heart of the matter: choreography. What exactly is it that choreographers do? In most cases, they come up with the concept of a piece. Sometimes they choose music, costume and setting. But whatever else may or may not be in their job description, choreographers always arrange movement to suit subject matter.

This chapter focuses on 1) subjects of interest to choreographers; 2) the function and nature of subjects; 3) the selection of gestures to present ideas; and 4) the manipulation of rhythm, spatial design and effort in creating specific imagery.

Subjects of Interest to Dancers

Where do ideas for dance come from? Certain subjects are of interest to choreographers simply because they are human. Other subjects have particular appeal for dance artists.

Love is a favorite, if not *the* favorite subject for dance. Almost every work focuses at some point on a loving couple, and at one time or another, every kind of love has been shown. A close second to love is death. Characters have died on and off stage in innumerable works. A dance about death always has a comment to make, sometimes expressing cruel injustice and sometimes the inevitability of mortality.

Frequently these two subjects are combined. A treasured source that never loses its appeal is *Romeo and Juliet*, choreographed by over a dozen artists, from the eminent Bronislava Nijinska together with George Balanchine (1926) to the newcomer Massimo Moricone (1992). In its many versions, *Romeo and Juliet* portrays an idealization of love, as well as the tragic deaths of a young, passionately devoted couple, "poor sacrifices" to their families' enmity.

Ninette de Valois's *Checkmate* (1937) portrays life as a chess game, played by Love (red) against Death (black). The end is foretold in the prologue through the ominous music (by Arthur Bliss) and the hopeless position that skeletal Death arranges for Love on the black and white squares of the chessboard stage. Along the way, the eight red pawns have a lighthearted dance, the red knight marches and fights passionately for his beloved, the red queen, the red king totters around, and the black queen sweeps all before her, without mercy: Checkmate.

Murray Louis mourned the loss of Alwin Nikolais with *Alone* (1994), an eloquent solo in which he confined himself to a small area of the stage where, as Jack Anderson wrote, "although he kept turning from side to side, as if expecting someone to enter, no one was ever there."[1] Louis wasn't the only dancer bereft at Nikolais's passing. Company member Beverly

Blossom expressed her grief with *Shards*, in which she presented herself dressed in a black frock coat and top hat, sitting on a battered suitcase, taking apart and putting together a white plastic mannequin.

Murder most foul receives its share of dance attention. Antony Tudor had been wanting for some time to do a ballet about a murder, but until playwright John van Druten came up with an idea (based on a real event, but not suitable for a play) he couldn't hit on a proper plan. The environment portrayed in *Undertow* is not all that distant from the working class neighborhood in which Tudor grew up as William Cook.

The protagonist of *Undertow* is an alienated young man, rejected by his mother. He is unable to fit in with his underprivileged peers. Referred to as the Transgressor, this antihero is a child of the slums who awkwardly and unsuccessfully tries to be part of the shabby life that goes on around him. The ballet proceeds not with passages of dance, but in a series of dramatic vignettes, each one highlighted through most unballetic gestures. The Transgressor enters, holding hands with an innocent little girl clutching a balloon. He makes advances towards a female who exudes lust, only to be rejected in favor of a sleazy old man—picking his nose! The Transgressor stands on the sidelines, his thumb in his mouth, watching the prostitute mistreat an impotent drunk. A trio of swaggering hoodlums pushes through the crowd to rape a silly female. A religious prude tries to organize the rabble into a prayer meeting, but her gaze shifts constantly to the Transgressor, to whom she is irresistibly attracted. As the religious woman tries lecherous seduction, it is the Transgressor's turn to rebuff someone. Finally he has a head-on encounter with Medusa, a viciously predatory creature. Jockeying back and forth between repugnance and lust for this stone cold sorceress, the Transgressor becomes the victim of pent-up emotions. While copulating with Medusa, he orgasmically strangles her.

The sex-murder is designed to echo movements from the opening scene, when the baby Transgressor is taking milk from his mother's breast and she pushes him away so she can lie with a man. The overall image is Freudian: A boy, crippled by his frustrated need for mother love, is rendered unable to survive in his shoddy world. The Transgressor finally matures, but his maturity is no glorious fulfillment; rather it is the resigned acceptance of mortal punishment for his crime.

A nostalgia for past innocence surfaced in 1976, brought on by the American bicentennial year. Donald McKayle's *Album Leaves* plays with old jazz steps and at the same time presents charming little snapshots of America at an earlier period of the twentieth century. The scenes portray, among others, a beach athlete, a self-infatuated belle, and a wild party. Paul Taylor's *Company B* (1991) is tied to the 1940s by its score of songs popular during World War II. Soldiers die on the battlefield while frustrated men and women at home vivaciously dance the Lindy Hop and are unfaithful to loved ones far away. However, according to Taylor this is not a period piece. "There's always some war or other," he said.[2] In fact *Company B* was created while Desert Storm raged on America's television screens.

Function and Nature of Subject Matter

There is an ongoing controversy about the function of subject matter. One side holds that the purpose of a dance is to convey insight about life. Communication of truth is the reason for the creation of a piece, which may embody psychological wisdom, or a glimpse of fate, or a social philosophy. In this type of creation, as with plays, novels, and movies, an important part is played by the mind—both the artist's and the spectator's. Martha Graham represents this group. She said, "Any great art is the condensation of a strong feeling, a perfectly conscious thing."[3]

The other camp holds that the primary function of a dance is to gratify the senses through beautiful movement patterns. If a dance has something to say, its message lies solely in the beauty of the movement. Balanchine, who represents this viewpoint, said, "Some works of art can be appreciated intellectually, but not many good ones."[4]

In theory, the two sides—truth versus beauty—are diametrically opposed. In practice, however, it is a rare choreographer who scorns the search for beauty. As for truth, dance works tend to shade imperceptibly from those that represent the most literal, specific messages and explicit lifelike situations to those that embody moods or vaguely generalized concepts.

In recent years the term "plotless ballet" has come into vogue to describe a piece without a story line or identifiable characters. Like so many terms in our imprecise vocabulary of dance criticism, "plotless" is not a helpful concept. Not every dance has a story line. But every dance does have a plot in the sense of a plan or a scheme.

Beauty or Truth? Plots and Themes

If we want to identify a dance according to whether it has a story line, we must agree that these three do: *The Sleeping Beauty, Pillar of Fire,* and *Don Quixote. The Sleeping Beauty* stages Perrault's fairy tale about the princess who is put to sleep for 100 years by the prick of a spindle tendered by a wicked fairy, to be awakened by the kiss of her Prince Charming. The scenario for Antony Tudor's *Pillar of Fire* is the Richard Dehmel poem which inspired Arnold Schonberg's *Verklarte Nacht.* Tudor used both the poem and the music for his portrayal of Hagar and her desperate fear of losing a chance for love. Balanchine's *Don Quixote* is based on Cervantes's seventeenth century novel about a country gentleman who lands in all kinds of sticky predicaments as he rushes around in mistaken attempts at chivalrous rescues.

Were these choreographers really interested in transposing stories into movement? Or even more to the point, does anybody go to watch these dances to see whether the prince awakens the princess from her spell, or to find out whether Hagar escapes spinsterhood? The answer is emphatically "no!" In every case the artist used the story line to explore the emotional facets of the characters and the nature of these emotions. At all times the movement qualities and patterns were devised to involve us in something larger than a story.

This something larger is the implicit subject of a dance, and may be referred to as the theme.

The Sleeping Beauty concerns a young girl's awakening to love. The roles of both the prince and the princess embody youthful romance and allow the audience full appreciation of these qualities. The Petipa ballet goes further. Russian critic Vera Krasovskaya wrote: "All these central moments of the musical-dance action essentially develop one and the same theme.... This theme speaks of love as the source of life and its chief moving force."[5]

Pillar of Fire is about Hagar, a spinster whose longings for love are thwarted by her own awkward inhibitions. Hagar struggles unsuccessfully with her desires, and finally decides to give herself to a callous seducer. As background to Hagar's story, assorted characters present a gamut of social responses to mating. There are lovers in innocence, lovers in experience, self-righteous disapproving matrons, frozen old maids, and a sister who wins a man with self-assured calculated flirting. At the end, Hagar is redeemed from self-disgust by a compassionate male friend.

Balanchine described the thematic action of his *Don Quixote*: "Don Quixote's anguished search for human perfectibility, the intricate shifts from fantasy to reality that take place in his mind, are vividly expressed through his adventures and the dream of the Lady Dulcinea, who appears in many guises ... and although he gives his whole life for her, he never really sees her."[6]

Thus the stories in which these characters figure are not the real center of the works. They are but points of departure, often spelled out in program notes, to leave the dance free to develop emotional shadings in movement designs. The situations all serve to reveal abstractions of emotions, according to the definition of the word "abstract" that equates it with the basic quality of something—its essence. Sleep-cursed Aurora depicts youthful awakening to love; Hagar represents the determination to live fully despite inner and outer obstacles; Dulcinea is the elusive ideal.

In an earlier chapter, we heard from Suzanne Langer that by nature, a dance expresses human feeling. In other words, no matter what else a subject does, it always yields some scope for emotional interplay. Two choreographers who produced works that deliberately stressed emotions were Martha Graham and Antony Tudor.

Graham's *Errand into the Maze* (1947) uses the Greek legend of Ariadne and the Minotaur to portray an image of a woman confronting deep sexual fears. The curtain opens on a lone female figure, whose motions are subtle, but gripping. Her gaze is hooded. Her torso contracts deeply in slow, gasping spasms. Her hands are crossed at the wrists as a shield in front of her groin. Continuing in this stance, she moves slowly sideways as though magnetized by the stage set: Isamu Noguchi's large sculptured abstraction of a woman's pelvis, from which there trails a sinuous ribbon winding along the stage floor. Almost at the structure she draws away, returning to the starting point. Once again she approaches, this time her feet crisscrossing over the ribbonlike path. She caresses the bony structure and slips inside it, as though trying out the fit—only to scurry away again. Back and forth, the conflict rages. She cannot bear to be at this place, nor can she keep away.

Suddenly a monstrous male figure runs in and stalks her. He jumps inexorably behind and around her. His head is a grimacing mask; his arms are thrust upwards and pinioned by a prop, part bonelike, part phallic. He seizes her and they wrestle. He forces her down, to lie across his thighs. Then he drops her and sinks to the floor, rolling around until he disappears from the stage.

Alone again, she advances and retreats, advances and retreats, frantically agonizing over the symbolic pelvis. Getting up her courage, she pulls in the ribbon, winds it around the prop and ties it.

Once more the monstrous figure stalks onstage, mesmerizing her with his aggressive jumps. She gyrates on the floor while he hurdles her relentlessly again and again until he mounts her body. But she has summoned the strength to fight him. She manages to twist on top of him and then climb on his back. They grapple. She falls and recovers. Again they grapple. He swings her around, but she has gained the upper hand. She throws him off. Exposed as a paper dragon, he collapses and crawls away. Uncertainly at first, and then with increasing assurance, she steps into the structure—claiming it. Drawing deep blessed breaths of relief, she moves up and down on one leg, undulating the other in front. Having faced down her fears, she lifts her arms in triumph.

As Agnes de Mille said of Martha Graham's choreography: "We

realized that what we were watching was revitalized raw emotion made apparent."[7]

From the beginning of his dance studies, Antony Tudor was interested not in pure dancing, nor in dance technique, but in psychological drama. He was to say in later years that his approach to the body had a lot in common with modern dance technique. "We start from the spine and the torso, and we get to the feet later. In ballet school you usually start with the feet."[8] His content, too, was closer to modern dancers than ballet artists. By disposition and by training, he developed the habit of a constant surveillance of human and animal body-language. His memory thereby acquired a large storehouse of revealing gestures on which he drew for his choreography. Once he conceived of his imaginary characters, he would spend hours searching for the exact gestures suitable for disclosing their significant traits.

In 1931 Tudor made his first piece, *Cross-Garter'd*, for Marie Rambert's Ballet Club. He based it on *Twelfth Night*, and as accompaniment he chose music by Frescobaldi, a contemporary of Shakespeare. Tudor himself performed the part of a pompous, foolish Malvolio. He limited the role to walking about in a haughty manner, one arm held out stiffly at the side, carrying the staff of office. His talent for bringing individuals and situations to life through the use of appropriate gestures was immediately recognized.

Tudor's ballet *Jardin aux Lilas* (*Lilac Garden*) (1936) takes place on the occasion of Caroline's engagement to a man she cannot love. It features and interweaves two couples: Caroline and her true love, and Caroline's fiancé and the woman who has been his mistress. The movement phrases are arranged not for courtly or technical display, but to communicate the frustrated longing of Caroline and her lover; the irritation of the fiancé with the mistress he is discarding; and the rejected woman's resentment. Caroline does an arabesque with hands clenched at her sides, her head turned away, to reveal reluctant submission to an unloved fiancé. With a sudden leap, the other woman literally throws herself onto the fiancé. Both couples are constantly interrupted by the need for decorum in the presence of the other guests.

However, we know that a spelled-out story is not necessary for the realization of an emotional theme. We find that a skeletal base—or to shift the analogy from anatomy to sculpture, an armature for modeling—can be provided by such a minimal plot that the term plotless or abstract ballet has been applied to the result.

Fokine's *Les Sylphides* (to selections from Chopin) involves the merest hints of a situation. The choreographer explained: "This ballet contains no plot whatsoever. It was the first abstract ballet. But still I would describe Nijinsky's participation in it as a role and not a part, because it did not consist merely of a series of steps. He was not a 'jumper' in it, but a

personification of a poetic vision. The role calls for youth, a dreamer, attracted to the better things in life."[9]

Fokine went on to say that it was impossible to describe the meaning of this impersonation. However, if we are familiar with ballet history, we recognize the role's origin in *La Sylphide* (Filippo Taglioni, 1832), a Romantic ballet that did have a plot. *La Sylphide* told the story of a young man who, on his wedding day, falls in love with a visionary sylph. He bolts from his fully alive bride-to-be, only to have his soulful sylph snatched from his grip by death.

Biblical stories, psalms and sermons have been an unending source of dance ideas. Ninette de Valois, founder of the classical British Royal Ballet, was a choreographer of modernistic dramas. Her *Job* (to a score by Ralph Vaughan Williams, 1931), was inspired by William Blake's *Illustrations to the Book of Job*. The ballet opens and closes with Job and his family in a pastoral dance of peaceful piety. Through the body of the work, Satan strives to pile misfortunes on Job and turn him against God. In the end of course it is Satan who loses, as Job is lifted up through the intercession of the pure and holy Elihu. The eight dance scenes are staged in a restrained pantomime, with two highly dramatic moments: the fall of the house of Job, after Satan curses them; and the fall of Satan, who tumbles down the heavenly stairs, at God's banishment.

Messages

A message starts out resembling a theme but it is more forceful, at times approaching what we call propaganda. In message works, the choreographer feels so strongly about an issue that he or she wants to persuade the viewer to adopt a given opinion—perhaps even act on it.

Anna Sokolow's works were born of strong emotional necessity, and the goal of her technical approach was the creation of instruments capable of expression. People, poems—life—awaken strong feelings and dramatic images in Anna Sokolow. Honesty has always been her keyword, and she has never hesitated to drive herself or anyone else to get it.

Recurring themes in Anna Sokolow's uncompromising repertory, beginning in 1953 with *Lyric Suite*, are loneliness, alienation and anxiety. Her *Dreams* (1961) is a chilling portrait of Nazi Germany. In 1968 she made *Steps of Silence*, a work about political prisoners, to the accompaniment of a text by Solzhenitsyn.

OPPOSITE: Antony Tudor's *Lilac Garden*. Photograph by Martha Swope, © Time Inc.

Or take Kurt Jooss's *The Green Table*. The burden of the dance is the callousness of international leaders to the suffering they cause through war. Mincing politicians do a delicate, graceful minuet of diplomacy that leads to the very war they pretend to try to prevent, while dexterous profiteers flourish. The victims are ordinary people everywhere. "War is immoral!" the piece proclaims. The only victor is ever-present Death.

In the 1980s, British choreographer Christopher Bruce expressed compassion for the plight of the Chilean people under an oppressive dictatorship in *Ghost Dances*. The ballet, inspired by a letter from the widow of Victor Jara, a victim of a military coup, uses Jara's folksongs to evoke the courageous spirit of a nation that clings to the joy of life in the face of tyranny.

Mark Morris did the choreography for the John Adams opera *Nixon in China*, supplying mordant ballet cartoons about Henry Kissinger and savage beatings of Chinese peasants. He also did *Lovey*, an explicit piece on child abuse, that reviewer Iris Fanger said she couldn't describe in a family newspaper.[10]

The subject matter of Bill T. Jones's *Last Supper at Uncle Tom's Cabin/The Promised Land* (1991) is enormously complicated. It is a three-hour commentary on the meaning of life, suffering, death, artistic creation, the black experience, God, and sexuality. Among other things, it uses various dance styles, masks, athletics, narration, and dramatic dialogue. The ending calls for the company, filled out with forty volunteers, to stand, walk and sing together—totally naked. Jones's idea was to mass together people of all ages, ethnic groups, bodily shapes and sexual preferences, in a plea for tolerance for all the members of one multi-faceted human race.

The Interest and Beauty of Dance

Dancers are unendingly fascinated by movement. It is their very sustenance. In fact some of them are so enchanted with the whole activity that they allow it to define the horizons of their world. Dance becomes not only their medium of expression but also their subject matter. These choreographers play around with chunks of particular styles of movement for their own charm.

Balanchine's *Bugaku*, to a score by Toshiro Mayuzumi, stages a wedding, superimposing gestures of Japanese court dances, angular body lines reminiscent of Japanese prints, and costumes inspired by traditional court dress, onto classical ballet movements. Balanchine wrote: "Just as the composer had transposed the Japanese court music into a Western vocabulary, I attempted in the dances to transpose the classic Western academic Ballet into a style suggested by the music."[11]

Dancers as well as the dance are of interest to choreographers. *Afternoon of a Faun* by Jerome Robbins takes a look at Nijinsky's famous dance from another angle. Instead of showing a narcissistic animal whose desire is awakened by a group of passing nymphs, the piece focuses on a couple of dancers practicing a duet in a dance studio. Each "performs" with total absorption in her or his own image in the mirror, rather than in the partner. Thus the dancer, like the original faun, is portrayed as a limited, self-involved being. Martha Graham composed a work on such a theme entitled *Acrobats of God*. It portrays the arena of the creative artist, goaded by inner drive, and the dedicated performers who jump at the artist's bidding.

Mark Morris paid a tribute to master Merce Cunningham. Although Joan Acocella said that *Behemoth* (1990) was "the coldest, darkest dance"[12] Morris ever made, that quality comes from the accompanying silence and the black, skintight costumes, rather than the impersonality of the phrases. Since neutral movement was in the Cunningham style that Morris admired, he pointed with pride to the machinelike essence of a *Behemoth* section, in which "you've got fourteen people all doing this completely symmetrical and completely complicated thing, and everybody at a different point in it, and nobody bumps into anybody else. That whole movement—it's a perfect system."[13]

Paul Taylor portrayed the dance process in *The Rehearsal* (1980). It was his version of *Rite of Spring*, using a two-piano reduction of Stravinsky's monumental score (that the composer himself had made for Nijinsky's rehearsals of *Rite of Spring*). The work opens with a dance company warming up on stage, and goes on to farcical scenes that parody silent-movie melodramas, as well as the tortured postures of the original Nijinsky choreography.

Mimetic Gesture

Now we will look at the way dance works in any style use body language. The most apparent movement element is mimetic gesture, which is used to convey specific thoughts.

Particular dance forms include certain mimetic conventions. In the classic ballet of Petipa, the hands held over the head and rotating around each other means "to dance"; circling the face and pointing to a woman means "she is beautiful." Spanish flamenco dancing has a form known as the *garrotin* in which the man drags the woman by her hair and threatens her with a long knife. These gestures represent intense sexual passion rather than murderous rage, because the gypsy culture links the two emotional states.

In general, however, formal mimetic patterns are less common in choreography than stylized human behavior. An unending list of ordinary motions are inserted into dances. Their meaning is clear even to the unschooled layman.

At the first appearance of Prince Albrecht, in *Giselle*, for example, the prince knocks on the door of Giselle's cottage. She answers the summons and looks around expectantly for her love. Later, when Giselle grabs Albrecht's sword in her fit of madness, the watching villagers and gentry alike step back in horror. An opposite joyous mood prevails in David Lichine's *Graduation Ball* (1940, music by Johann Strauss), when the young girls at a fashionable school show off their dance steps for the cadets from a neighboring military academy, and the assembled partygoers pat their hands together in applause.

Through most of *Lamentation*, a solo choreographed by Martha Graham (1930, music by Kodály), the dancer remains seated on a bench, completely enshrouded in jersey fabric. She clasps her hands, stretches her arms, bows her head, and sways in anguish. The woman's grief-stricken gestures embody a sense of mourning.

A clumsy lout drags the corpse of his dead sweetheart all around the floor as one might drag an overstuffed bag of dirty laundry. This action in Herbert Ross's *Caprichos* shows up the boor's hypocritical pretense of grief at her death.

Donald Byrd's choreography for *Drastic Cuts* (1993, score by Mio Morales) is filled with obvious sexual gestures, many of them brutal. The evening-length work has men displaying their muscular torsos and grabbing their own crotches. They assault women, stroking their breasts and thighs, stretching their legs apart, flipping them over, passing them back and forth.

A woman fans herself; her husband reads a newspaper; another woman plays the piano in a peaceful scene that opens Frederick Ashton's *A Month in the Country*.

Although Balanchine's works are always thought of as consisting of pure, unadulterated dance, one can also find specific behavior imitated in them. When Leta gives birth to Apollo, the infant god appears wrapped tightly in a swaddling cloth, which two handmaidens unwind. Later Calliope, the muse of poetry, pretends to write with one hand on the palm of the other. A close look at Balanchine's works shows that while his idiom is ballet, he builds at the same time on other movement styles. *Stars and Stripes* (1958), for example, set to music of John Philip Sousa, styles an American Independence Day celebration parade with drum majorettes, marching bands in cadet uniforms, salutes to the flag, all in classical ballet sequences and point work. The theme is further emphasized by the dancers' red, white and blue costumes and the flag décor. One almost expects to find the ushers selling hot dogs in the aisles.

As late as 1980, in *DavidsbÜndlertänze* (to a score by Robert Schumann), Balanchine had a young woman fondle her partner's face as though trying to memorize it.

Implied Gesture

Graham transformed ideas into gestures in a nonliteral manner. For example, concerning *Night Journey*, Graham wrote a note to herself about Jocasta's part: "On high note [dancer] turns—on back—lifts foot as in scream."[14] Now a scream, albeit voiceless, can be represented with the mouth open, the face and neck tensed and straining. Normally one would not convey screaming with a foot. However, by having the Jocasta character hold her body in a deep contraction and shoot out a flexed foot which intensifies the tension, Graham conveyed the emotion of terror. No viewer would describe this gesture as a scream, but she or he would implicitly receive it as such.

Balanchine has certainly done this. In *Serenade*, composed in 1934 to a Tchaikovsky composition, he created a suggestion of fatalism when a female walks behind a boy, guiding him even as her hand covers his eyes.

Dancers repeatedly point fingers up, yearning towards a spiritual heaven, and then sharply down to the contrasting common clay of earthly needs, in Mark Morris's *Grand Duo*.

In studying examples of implicit gesture, the important thing to remember, and the reason why there are many possible connotations in each motion, is that the action by itself doesn't define its import. At times artists use gestures quite literally—pantomimically, as Jones did in *And the Maiden*. At other times they take pains to stylize gestures, keeping the original idea recognizable to a greater or lesser degree. Along with gesture, the elements of spatial shaping, rhythmic timing and application of energy are the keys to expression—the syntax of any body's language. Consciously or unconsciously, choreographers select even pure dance motions with an eye towards their implicit behavioral connotations.

Take the male-female duet, in which he always lifts her. *How* does he do it? Is the timing slow or fast? In shape, are their limbs closely entwined or does he hold her at arm's length? Is the energy applied stiffly, abruptly, with swinging ease or sustained languor? The answers to such questions determine whether the resulting image communicates worship, courtesy, sexual passion, violent anger, or something else. Phrase by phrase, choreography dictates not only motions, but their rhythmic, spatial, and effort qualities.

Now we move from specific choreographic subjects and methods to focus on the elements of movement. How does manipulation of time, space and effort affect the dance image?

Rhythm and Time

An essential rhythmic factor in a dance work is provided by the sound accompaniment, musical or otherwise. The relationship between music and dance will be discussed later on. Almost every dance offers steps in metrical rhythm. Metrical pattern, or meter, denotes the grouping of accented and unaccented beats of dance steps that we also find in musical notation and poetic stanzas. Counting is a pervasive activity in dance. With or without music, the leader or teacher often counts, the voice stressing strong and secondary accents, with the word "and" used for in-between beats or upbeats or preparation for beginning movement. The heaviest stress is usually on the first beat, and the most common arrangements are 2, 3, 4 and 6 counts to a unit (or measure), with 5 next in frequency.

Metrical rhythm in dance is most clear when movements travel through space—in naturalistic steps like walking, running, skipping, hopping; in ballet steps like *jetés, ballonés, pas de bourrées*; or in tap dancing where the performer uses his feet like a drummer's sticks. A particularly satisfying example of metrical rhythm is found in Mark Morris's *Home*, which contains robust Irish style clog dancing. The performers vigorously pound out the beat, facing front in a traditional lineup, their arms held practically motionless as the feet weave their intricate steps. Since passages of the boisterous clog stepping alternate with choreographed ballads that wail of hard times, *Home* communicates the sense that come what may, there is continuity in the community as well as in the individual life.

Tempo, or speed, is the second factor in the rhythmic organization of movement. Just as the human body can survive only in a fairly narrow range of temperature, so most of its movements occupy a limited section of the metronomic scale. Small increases or decreases of speed are appreciably significant in dance. In the finale of Twyla Tharp's *The Catherine Wheel* (1981, score by David Byrne), the dancers outdo themselves in a dazzling exhibition of "fast." *The Catherine Wheel* is a theatrical work that Tharp made in response to devastating events in her personal life—her private domain. Its characters consist of an all too human middle-class family, complete with black housemaid. They are observed by a female who is seeking perfection (like the Catherine of the title, who sought to deny the flesh in a longing to unite with the holy spirit, and was martyred for her pains), and a faceless chorus.

The family members, enmeshed in a world of an unfathomable wheeled contraption, cavort jerkily like figures in an animated cartoon. They vie nastily with one another in their lust after an elusive god (symbolized by a pineapple). Gradually their actions distend to a violent social upheaval, symbolized by piles of plastic garbage tossed around the stage. Now the housemaid expresses rage through a series of contorted grimaces which pull her mouth wide, screw up her nose and forehead, and stretch the muscles and tendons of her face and neck with incredible tension. (Tharp was a pioneer in the introduction of such facial gestures into Western dance. They have always been important in Asia, particularly in Hindu dance.)

In the last "Golden Section" of *The Catherine Wheel*, the dancers and the audience are redeemed in a long, heavenly segment, in which all the performers, now clothed in shimmering gold, move into high gear, shooting across space like meteors. This exhibition brought from reviewers words like "whirlwind," "savagely fast," "plummets," "virtuosic dancing flashes, it spins," "the beat of the music is shattered into twenty intricate motions of legs, body, arms, head." Paradise, for Tharp and her viewers, resides in the outer limits of dance capability.

The other extreme of the tempo scale, the slow-motion register, has had more attention from avant-garde choreographers than top speed, perhaps because slow movement is easier to approach and stay with (for the dancer if not always for the viewer). During the 1970s, Robert Wilson created theater pieces like *Deafman Glance*, in which the performers moved so slowly that they seemed immobile.

Also during the 1970s, Rudy Perez played with the whole scale of speed, alternating between studied, drawn-out, slow motion and bursts of speed. In one piece called *Off Print*, he used small motions, punctuated by pauses, creating the effect of stop-action photography. Critic Marcia Siegel found that in these experiments, a "simple series of actions takes on mystery, persuasiveness, and an entirely unforeseen emotionality."[15]

Phrasing is as important in movement as it is in speech. "Phrases" are the passages that move over and through several measures. Phrases have a rise and a fall like breathing. In dramatic dance, breath rhythm is modified and organized according to an emotional state. It is a waste of time to try to catch emotional breath rhythms in counts. Rather the viewer simply follows the choreographer's lead into the action drama. The measuring standard changes here from a metronome count for steps, to a litmus paper that registers convincing behavior.

The psychological portraits in Anna Sokolow's *Rooms* yield examples of emotional rhythm. Four men and four women are trapped in isolated worlds. One female writhes in desperation. Another sinks into a slow, depressed walk that ends in a standstill. One man starts out optimistically snapping his fingers and stepping in a pulsating, eager rhythm, until he too stops in despair. So it goes, each one expressing in rhythmically stylized movement his or her bleak, individual alienation.

Designs in Space

The next major element of movement is visual shape: design and appearance in space. The art of choreography is very much concerned with lines and areas, with shapes and contours in space, with visual beauty. The passage of time adds a fourth dimension to spatial design. Here, anticipated or preserved as afterimage, the mind perceives contours and lines of spatial trajectories and floor plans. Directional paths traced through space leave a strong impression.

All these forms relate to feelings as do the shapes, lines, contours and colors of paintings and sculptures. Balance and symmetry are stable; asymmetry restless; unbalance disturbing. Straight lines can be plain, or dull, or secure. Curved bodies on rounded spatial paths would be felt to be harmonious or aimlessly meandering. Sharp, jagged and opposing lines tend to project a feeling of attack or anxiety.

Spatial rhythm plays its part. A regular rhythm, with the repetition of identical shapes and lines at even distances, would give rise to a pleasing sense of order or a sterile monotony. Irregular rhythm, with the inclusion in the stage picture of varied or contrasting figures and groupings, might be found exciting or disturbingly chaotic.

Behavioral connotations range from the explicit to the implicit in the arrangement of bodies in pairs or groups. Two people standing back-to-back project shyness or indifference. One dancer towers over another as a dominant or threatening figure. An individual may be encircled with hostility or tenderness.

Alvin Ailey created *In Memoriam* as a moving tribute to a choreographer who had done much for his company. He had a large troupe of dancers link hands and step with grave measure as they encircled a figure representing Joyce Trisler.

Mention has been made of the architectural grandeur of Petipa's ensemble formations, as in the keynote processionals of *The Sleeping Beauty*. How different are the arrangements of groups in works of the 1930s. In Massine's *Choréartium* (1933) to the Fourth Symphony of Brahms, and his visualization of Beethoven's *Seventh Symphony* (1938), bodies are tightly massed in clusters and crowds, in a scale of levels: prone on the floor, kneeling, standing, and held aloft.

The inspiration for dance figures massed in space originated primarily with German modern dancers, led by Rudolf Laban and Mary Wigman. In turn, these artists were infected by the spirit of their time, when European fascists as well as communists held huge popular rallies in which thousands of young people stepped in unison and cried out their solidarity.

To some choreographers, space is palpable. They feel various qualities in it, as though the dance milieu is made in turn of expanding light air, or heavy mercury, or fluid water. Wigman was foremost in proclaiming an intense bond between her body and the live surrounding space. This is how she described the conception of *Death Call*:

> What was it, who was it, who called me and made me stop? A voice? A figure? A thing remembered? Nothing like that at all. But there it was, an opposite pole, a point in space, arresting eye and foot. This probably self-created and self-reflected tension, however, forced the body into a sudden turn and twisted my back down into a deep bend in which the arms spread out again, helpless and hopeless this time.... Thus the dance unfolded in a succession of static, monumental poses and hugely conceived movements through space.[16]

Graham would instruct her students to project an image of what was behind them—not just other dancers, but the very space: to feel it and to make the audience feel it.

Do these qualities of space exist? Yes, but they are not inherent in the space. They are an illusion, a dance projection, created by the dancer's use of the body. As Wigman put it: "Only in its spatial embrace can the dance achieve its final and decisive effect,"[17] and "the dancer [is] ruled by space, which is timeless and visionary."[18]

Other choreographers may deliberately flatten spatial design, treating it like a two-dimensional picture against a backdrop. Take for example Vaslav Nijinsky's *Afternoon of a Faun (L'Après-Midi d'un Faune)* (1912, to music by Debussy), in which the profile lends impersonality to the figure, partially removing the "contact" from its presence. The ballet depicts a line of maidens coming on a faun lazily playing his flute. Attracted to one of the maidens, the male animal dances with her, and after she leaves, the faun makes love to a scarf she left behind. The scene has an abstracted, exotic quality, not only because its protagonist is an animal, symbolizing an indolent youth, but because of the dancers' sideway poses. The faun always moves in profile to the audience, as do the maidens who, poised like figures on an Egyptian frieze, seem to echo another time.

In contrast to profile, full front is direct and open, giving the most ample view of the person and bringing out his facial expressions. Spectators cannot help feeling personally drawn in when dancers standing at the front of the stage gaze directly at their faces. The frontal view is challenging.

Bill T. Jones choreographed a stridently up-to-date message in *Love Defined* (1992). Before the curtain closes, the large cast crowds together shoulder to shoulder, facing the audience in silent community. Because the performers are deliberately chosen to be not only of different shapes, colors, ages, and sizes, but also different in their capability of loving others in innumerable atypical ways, they challenge the audience with Bill T. Jones's definition of humankind: inclusive, tolerant and rich in diversity.

José Limón created *The Moor's Pavane* (1949, music by Purcell), a brilliant work based on Shakespeare's *Othello*. The Moor kills his beloved wife out of unfounded jealousy, deliberately inspired by a courtier and his wife. There are four characters in the dance: the Moor, his wife Desdemona, the envious Iago, and Iago's wife Emilia. At times their movements are the stately steps of a pavane in formal patterns like the circle, crossing diagonal lines, and the wheel, in which all four enact the formality of courtly life. At other times they are jagged encounters, as when Iago almost mounts the Moor's back, to show how he dominates the other man with his evil plotting, or Emilia steals Desdemona's handkerchief and toys with it.

Patterns in Effort

Effort concerns bodily force—the gathering and application of energy to initiate or continue motion. It involves three concepts: power, tension and dynamics. Power is the quantity of strength, force or weight used to attack a given movement. Tension is the quality of energy, the way it is released or constricted in the movement. Dynamics are the ebb and flow of power and tension as movement continues through time.

In spectator sports, great numbers of people experience vicariously the pleasures of physical effort variations. There is genuine satisfaction at a smashing tennis serve, a smooth baseball catch, or a smacking golf stroke. Swimmers in the buoyant support of water; jumpers on a trampoline or diving board; gliding and spinning ice skaters; swooping skiers; floating skydivers—all these athletes thrill the viewer in part because of the physical sensations of springing, sliding or flying that they communicate. In gymnastics or sport, along with admiration of superior skill in strength and aim, we are affected by the good form of the players.

Dancers have available infinitely more variations in motion sensation than athletes, who are, after all, constantly limited by the demands of scoring and competition. Since the goal of classical ballet is to present dancers

OPPOSITE: **Charlene Gehm and Tyler Walters in the Joffrey Ballet of Chicago's** *L'Après-Midi d'Un Faune*. **Photograph © MIGDOLL 1998.**

moving in effortless grace, it is left mainly to modern choreographers (both of present-day ballet and of modern dance) to exploit the full possibilities of the effort scale. These range from a mimicry of lifelessness—the way Juliet appeared after swallowing the friar's potion—all the way to the pounding, punching violence that Jerome Robbins set for rival battling gangs in the musical *West Side Story* (composer Leonard Bernstein).

In the context of human drama, some movements from *Giselle* are worth looking at. Giselle's theme is the *pas ballonné*, a step of elevation in which one leg jumps while the other points out and then bends to point in towards the jumping foot. The village girl does this step lightly with a gay elastic spring, when she first dances with her beloved Albrecht. In the mad scene she almost parodies herself, marking the step with a heavy uncoordinated dragging, leaving the trajectory incomplete. Finally, near the close of the second act, as a Wili, Giselle dances her theme again with Albrecht, this time in concentrated precision that has a frenzied tension.

Mark Morris stresses the weightedness of movement. He trains his own company not only in ballet and modern dance, but folk styles as well. His approach is opposite to the approach of ballet, which makes dancing look effortless. In their almost awkward, very human motion, Morris dancers stand out from many slickly facile contemporary dancers. As biographer Joan Acocella put it, his dancers "are always thudding, falling, smacking the floor."[19]

Animals are a great source for effort patterns. Swans flutter and glide in *Swan Lake* (Petipa, Tchaikovsky, 1895). In *Life of the Bee* (1929, accompanied by offstage humming) Doris Humphrey had her dancers move like insects, quivering their arms (wings) and running (flying) frantically in all directions. She used the battle of a young queen bee displacing an aging queen, to express the eternal life struggle of new generation against old. Paul Taylor took off on this idea in *Insects and Heroes*.

As with the use of animal likenesses, images taken from our environment stand for, or symbolize a human state or emotion. For example water continually fascinates choreographers. When Frederick Ashton made *Ondine* (1958), a full length ballet about a water sprite who falls in love with a mortal, he said: "I spent hours watching water move and have tried to give the choreography the surge and swell of waves."[20]

The creative process is a mysterious one. A dance may express things of which the choreographer is completely unaware. Balanchine's *Davids-bÜndlertänze* follows 18 piano pieces that Robert Schumann composed over a century earlier to deal with his personal problems: his furious inner battles with the smugly stupid critics of his day; his marital problems with Clara; and his suicidal descent into madness. (Schumann died in a mental asylum.) Balanchine's choreography employs as a point of departure this

Paul Taylor dancers (de Jong, Blair, Taylor, Walton, Wagoner, Mathis) in Taylor's *Insects and Heroes*. Photograph by Nicolas Tikhomiroff, courtesy Paul Taylor.

famous composer's life, reflected in his music that flows with emotional contrasts. In essence, the ballet contains Balanchine's own inner view of romantic turbulence.

It is interesting that critics spoke of this Balanchine ballet as weaving together strands of the choreographer's creative life in a kind of farewell. The choreographer himself denied this, insisting that the ballet was about atmosphere. He said it was better not to analyze, lest you miss the dancing. But ironically, the dance was made shortly before Balanchine succumbed to a brain illness that killed him in 1983.

It also happens that a given dance may turn out to be very different from its original impetus. Frederick Ashton's masterwork *Symphonic Variations* (1946) is named after the César Franck score that accompanies it. The dance has no story, "only a mood created by the setting and costume, the music, and the dancers' response to it." But it started out with an elaborate scenario of a marriage, including scenes of "rapture caused by spark of love" and "the heart's joy in union." Further, the marriage was to be symbolic of mystical absorption in divine love, woven into a theme of the seasons. Ashton meant the opening to be winter with the women "moving alone coldly, unfertilized"; a man's dance would introduce the spring; at the end the corps would celebrate the "fullness of summer and plenty of harvest."

As he worked, however, Ashton first eliminated the corps de ballet, leaving only six dancing figures. Then he set about stripping away the mystical content until, in the words of British critic A.V. Coton, we were left with "six living bodies within a prescribed area of space which, throughout the duration of the music, move in splendour and heroism, creating solo, duet, and ensemble dances of a fascinating variety of shapes, emphases, and configurations. The disparity between these persons and the vast area of their action proposes an imagery of infinities … so that not too fantastically, we can catch the imagery either as planetary bodies moving with subtle rhythm against cosmic vastness, or as the geometric complexities revealed in watching the rapid formation of crystals under a microscope."[21] The reason that an "abstract" ballet can offer such splendid imagery is the richness of the original subject matter, which, even though it was eliminated per se, inevitably affected the result.

Subject matter in a given dance refers to its themes and ideas—which, as we have seen, can be almost anything. But the subject itself is certainly less important than the treatment of it. As Doris Humphrey put it: "The blunt fact is that subject matter is mostly of concern to the choreographer…. The enthusiasm for it and innate talent is what keeps it alive…. What audiences see is mostly the result in movement, which is exciting or not as the case may be."[22]

5

Compositional Engineering

Structure is the formal arrangement of a dance composition. Lacking the glamour of daring originality which often resides in theme and movement imagery, nonetheless it is a major preoccupation of the choreographer. Although the artist is by temperament a law breaker, his compositions adhere to an engineer's building code, no matter what flights of fancy they embody. In this respect choreography functions like architecture: Even when the designer has free rein, she or he is expected to design a structure that will stand up. A dance, like a building, falls down if it is not constructed according to fixed principles.

Organic Forms

In other words, a dance is composed only partially in response to a particular idea. The arrangement must also follow certain rules that apply to every work in the time arts, whether of music, drama, or dance. These rules are not arbitrary. They correspond to the way we experience the world through organic forms.

"Organic" refers to the fact that living beings and other physical phenomena fulfill certain necessary patterns. For example, a storm will be preceded by an oppressive stillness and followed by a freshening breeze; a plant will start as a tender shoot, flower in maturity and then wither and dry out; pressure building up inside a closed container will cause the container to swell and then burst; sexual tension mounts through stimulation, and releases in orgasm; people must sleep after hard work to regain the energy for more hard work; hunger drives animals to hunt food, eat, and then meander sluggishly while they digest. Under the influence of these natural organic forms, craftsmen structure their works.

Like life, all compositions in the time arts have a beginning, a middle and an end. Unlike life, a composition conveys a sense of order. In fact, most theories of art recognize that a major function of art is the achievement of form. Thus a composition does more than simply start and then go on until it stops. The beginning introduces the thematic idea and sets the tone. The middle section, or body of the work, develops the idea, sometimes along with contrasting material, and builds to a climax. The last part provides a satisfying resolution to the whole creation. The closing may be a spectacle or a quiet coming to rest. In either case, earlier motifs may be brought back in an altered form.

This three-part arrangement in both music and dance, the A-B-A form, is found so often in folk arts as well as in the most sophisticated expressions that it is virtually *the* basic model of choreographic structure.

Avant-garde choreographer Alwin Nikolais expressed impatience with

Murray Louis and Nikolais Dance Company in *Tensile Involvement* **by Alwin Nikolais. Photograph by Tom Caravaglia, courtesy Nikolais/Louis Foundation for Dance.**

the idea of an A-B-A form when he was asked in 1968 about its presence in *Tensile Involvement,* a piece that places its dance figures in an abstract field of elastic bands. It opens and closes with a group doing springs and turns, separated by a middle contrasting section where the dancers descend to the floor and do slow rocking movements. Nikolais said: "It isn't an 'A-B-A form'. It's a stand-up section followed by a down. I wouldn't think in terms of A-B-A form. That kind of thinking implies a formality which isn't the case. I work mostly organically—the continuity depends on the nature of the material. It doesn't go arbitrarily back to anything for the reason of form for its own sake."[1]

Of course it doesn't return "for the reason of form for its own sake." It departs and returns to provide contrast and resolution, for the sake of

interest in variety and of a human desire to come home. Forms have arisen because they satisfy human needs, not because they provide an arbitrary imposition of law and order. When forms petrify and become fixed in academic mannerisms, appreciated primarily by overeducated connoisseurs, then they need to be reinfused with life—modified. But their underlying principles do stand. Nikolais's disagreement really came down to a question of terminology.

Viewers and Choreographers

Structural factors directly affect an audience's overall reaction. They lead viewers to feel stimulated, bored, confused, let down, or fulfilled. For example, it is pretty well accepted that when an audience is exposed to a slow, heavy passage, they soon demand something more lively, lest they begin to creak in their chairs or engage in coughing fits as a relief from muscular tension. At the same time, the variation must not be so great as to leave the audience lost in chaos.

The element of structure is the point at which the needs of an audience and the needs of the choreographer coincide. Themes and ideas, stylistic approaches, the creation of movement—all these come from deep inside artists, a place to which the conscious mind may be denied access. Certainly viewers are not privy to the process. But when it comes to arranging structure, choreographers stand aside and themselves become sensitive, critical viewers.

Consider Jerome Robbins and his masterful *Dances at a Gathering* (1969). It opens with a youth who enters pensively, his back turned to the audience. Looking up at the sky, he begins to sway quietly. In an abrupt change of mood, he does a mazurka jump with the heels clicking and runs across the stage.

The dance proceeds in a series of appearances and meetings between friends in a bright, out-of-doors atmosphere. For over an hour, five girls in brief pastel chiffon dresses and five boys in muted tights and loose shirts spin out passage after passage of dance. While the technique is classical ballet, there are a number of steps based on ballroom dancing, along with gestures of familiarity and affection. There are also many folksy touches that relate to the Polish character of the Chopin mazurkas, preludes and waltzes that make up the accompaniment.

The emotional color changes in turn from lyrical to blithe, from languid

OPPOSITE: The final moment of *Dances at a Gathering* by Jerome Robbins. Photograph by Martha Swope, © Time Inc.

to flamboyant, from saucy to shy, from passionate to competitive, from pert to ecstatic. Each contrasting piece has its lightly sketched situation. There is a wind waltz, a walk waltz, three girls in the woods, two kites. There is a couples dance—but with five people, so that after each figure is formed, a different dancer is left apart. At the end, following a restless scherzo with everyone running out of sight, the dancers walk back in and look up to the now starry sky. A girl kneels, the youth from the opening touches the ground, and all turn their heads slowly in unison, as though they are following the motion of a bird, an airplane, or a storm cloud.

Jerome Robbins launched into the choreography without a fixed structural plan. In fact, he started with the simple idea of making a *pas de deux* to music by Chopin. But as he worked he kept adding more dancers and more sections. Then, after he completed most of the dances, he spent two weeks trying to get them into the right order, "making the dance have some continuity, some structure." He tried one part first, one last, then another, then yet another. For the all-important ending, it seemed logical to finish with the scherzo, because this segment has a climactic excitement with everyone running off like an eruption of particles. But it didn't feel right to him, that those people just "went whoosh and disappeared…. They are a community." So he brought them back after the scherzo, as though to take a stroll in the evening, and had them all observe an unnamed appearance in the sky. Robbins was surprised and pleased by the final effect. "Something is there that I didn't know I was doing," he told critic Edwin Denby.[2] Without doubt, the structure that he finally decided upon played a large part in the tremendous reception given to this ballet.

Recurring Patterns

For proof of the theory that dance structure follows general rules that have little to do with specific styles and themes, we will look at three very dissimilar works: *Swan Lake* Act II (its origin credited to Lev Ivanov, it is often given as a ballet apart from the other scenes); *Night Journey* by Martha Graham; and Merce Cunningham's *Scramble*. *Swan Lake* is about a prince's desire for a beautiful princess, who has been transformed into a swan by a cruel magician. It is a vision of ideal love cast in the noble harmonious style of classical ballet. *Night Journey* is a grim tragedy of sexual compulsion. *Scramble* is a casual composition about dancers and brightly colored objects moving through space. Yet in studying these totally different masterpieces, one discovers that they are very similar to one another in structure.

Each work sets a mood at the beginning, gradually introducing the figures with their particular attitudes and relationships. Each work continues for about half an hour. Within that time span, interest builds as many things happen. There are at least fifteen parts, with changes in gesture, movement qualities, tempo, dynamics, the number of people performing, and spatial formations—although in all cases remaining within the overall style and mood of the introduction. A high point is reached, and the piece winds down to a conclusion in which motifs from the opening are recalled.

As the curtain rises on *Swan Lake*, a party of huntsmen enter. They see some swans, and courteously summon Prince Siegfried to shoot them. The graceful swan Odette appears and pleads in fright with the prince to spare her and the other swan maidens, telling of her own enchantment by the wicked Rothbart, who suddenly appears as an owl. The swans dance. After the quiet mimed statement that opens *Swan Lake*, there is the pulling together of the wing-beating *port de bras* (arm patterns) of the swan maidens in their ensemble waltz; then the close-up of the adagio *pas de deux* with the ballerina's melting fall into Siegfried's arms and her quivering foot flutters, backed up with occasional accents by the orchestrated corps. This is a high point of Romantic idealization and yielding. Next the four cygnets offer their pert little diversion. Here, as noted by Cyril Beaumont, the requirements of the structure take precedence over pure artistic conviction: "The 'Pas de Quatre' is, I think, intended to afford contrast to the preceding love scene between Odette and Siegfried. It is bright, gay and theatrically effective, although it always seems alien to the general mood."[3]

Unity is maintained throughout with the underlying ballet technique, the universal noble bearing, the symmetrical harmonious groupings around and behind the soloists, and the occasional bits of mime. The coda is made up of phrases danced by the corps, Odette, the prince, and the prince's high-born friend Benno, ending with the swans flitting away, leaving the now lonely lakeside glen to the men. Thus the ballet winds down to a sparse ending, unifying the piece with the same figures who began the action, but now in an uncertain, minor mode.

In *Night Journey* there is a strong dramatic shape. It begins at the journey's end, with Jocasta staring at the rope that symbolizes both her umbilical ties to Oedipus and her fate in the circle of a hanging noose, while the Prophet walks by with ponderous steps, ominously banging his staff on the ground, marking the heartbeat of inexorable doom. His warning is amplified by the agitated arrival of an apprehensive Chorus that bewails the fate of the characters. The dance continues as memory of past events. The climactic section presents the mother and son in solo expressions of lust and aggression and in their dual entwining, interrupted and counterpointed by the writhing Prophet and the furious Chorus, who first anticipate the mating with symbolic flowering branches and then mourn the fateful yielding to temptation. The resolution offers the self-strangling Jocasta and the all-

seeing Prophet—the same figures who open the dance. Although variation abounds, there is unity in the overall approach as well as in the contractions, slide falls, and spread jumps of the basic technical vocabulary.

As for *Scramble*, the beginning reveals several motionless figures watched by a group of dancers standing at ease "off-stage" on one side, in full view of the audience, waiting their turn to enter the action. First one, then another, then a third dancer start to move, almost in place, intently, slowly extending a leg, or twisting the whole body around, or progressing with deliberate restraint across a stage that is everywhere set with colorful fencelike barriers. Gradually they are joined by others, until six figures engage in the seemingly random action, each fixedly pursuing measured motion.

After the sporadic sequences of the beginning, a single dancer does a fast, lively movement in which the group joins one by one until they are all involved. There follow a short men's unison trio; a man's solo; a circle around a single figure; a longer, restless, leaping men's trio; a swooping, waving female solo; a duet; six dancers in the same sequence done at different times; a duet by a second couple.

Something happens in the solos, in the duets, and perhaps most of all in the group passage just before the close, when five dancers form a tight knot pushing, touching and bending around each other, while all move quickly and abruptly in the same sideward direction. Still going fast, they cascade outward and then move slowly in unison. Exactly what happens can't be put in terms of a situation as in *Swan Lake* or the Graham dance. Yet the mounting energy released and expressed in the accumulation of dancers, the fast small movements, then the fast bigger movement events, and then the unison motion all give a sense of climax and even of significance. They thus prepare for a resolution with everyone walking about slowly pushing the fencelike props, reminiscent of the casual opening. Like the other two pieces, *Scramble* starts and ends in a muted manner.

We have surely stumbled upon a pattern that follows basic laws, when three such diverse compositions can share so many characteristics. There is no argument about *Swan Lake* purposely adhering to rules of sound theatrical entertainment (or experience, if one prefers not to use the word "entertainment" about serious art). And there is not too much question about Martha Graham's structuring of her dance plays according to these time-tested principles. But there might well be a question about *Scramble*, since Merce Cunningham steadfastly ignores so many traditional concerns of dance artists.

OPPOSITE: Martha Graham and Bertram Ross in Graham's *Night Journey.* **Photograph by Martha Swope, © Time Inc.**

It is well known that Cunningham has experimented with chance methods for working out the order and arrangement of the dance elements—in other words, the structure. Fortunately for his audience, however, he was flexible in this matter. Calvin Tompkins reported at length on the composition of *Scramble*: "It appeared that deliberate choice had been a far more important factor than chance in the evolution of *Scramble*.... Cunningham kept experimenting on the order of its various parts.... Just a few days before the performance, did he settle on the order."[4]

The considerations that prompted him were obviously an appreciation of the effects of timing, development, unity, surprise and interest that Marius Petipa, George Balanchine, Martha Graham, Jerome Robbins, Frederick Ashton and most other fine choreographers seem to share with Merce Cunningham.

Structure as Subject Matter

Added to the principles of development, variety and unity that apply to all the time arts, dance structure has special requirements. It must take into account the artistic qualities of the members of a performing company, as well as limits of human energy and the logistics of bringing dancers on and off stage or in position for the next step. Whether they are cast in starring roles or as anonymous members of a group, dancers need time to catch their breath. This fact affects the length, the location and the relative tempos of solos, duets, trios and ensemble dances that are the building blocks of choreography. It applies when the blocks are self-contained pieces as well as when they are parts of a larger work. To illustrate these factors, we could choose any work in the dance repertory. But we will proceed in an orderly fashion, and begin with small pieces, containing few figures.

Solos as Complete Dances

The rare solo in ballet that stands as a separate work is more often than not specially created as a showcase for an outstanding dancer. Fokine's *The Dying Swan* (1907), made for Anna Pavlova, comes to mind. The two-minute dance to music by Saint-Saëns didn't take much longer than that to compose, in an organic structure expressive of a waning spirit, through the lessening of energy and the constriction of space, broken by a brief climactic struggle. But the poetic image of the bird-dancer has lasted for decades in performance and in memory. She floats in a circle on tiptoe, her winged arms folded. She opens them out in a last attempt to fly before she sinks to the ground, her arms still fluttering. With peaceful finality, she bows her head before death.

In 1971, to take full advantage of Judith Jamison's mighty talent, Alvin Ailey choreographed *Cry*, a solo with a daunting sixteen-minute length. The dance, a tribute to the spirit of African American women in the face of humiliation and suffering, is built on few movement motifs, strikingly developed in pressured space and pulsing rhythm. The impossibly arched torso undulates with anguish and pride. The arms are almost wrenched from their sockets: straight up in the air, or stretched to the side and then bent at the elbow and forced back over the head. The legs dart outward, forward and back. The dancer moves along constrained paths, turning, bending, falling rising.

Solos as Pieces of a Dance

There are countless solos within larger works. These range from turbulent emotional displays in the main roles of *Romeo and Juliet*, through lighthearted buffoonery for characters in Frederick Ashton's *La Fille Mal Gardée*, to intangible images in an abstract mode like the figures in the work of Alwin Nikolais.

Once the choreographer settles on a sequence of actions appropriate to a given dance, the next step is building these movements into patterns. Now another basic principle applies: when a movement phrase is done once or twice, it doesn't make a full impression; but when it is repeated more than three or four times, it generally becomes monotonous. Thus three or four repetitions are the rule. From their classroom practice and their concert viewing, ballet students are quite familiar with the classical form that sends a dance step to the right, then repeats it to the left, once more to the right, and concludes the little passage with a turn or a leap and a final pose.

Similarly, early modern dances repeat movement sequences three or four times, sometimes making a slight change in the fourth. However, as dance works have grown increasingly more complex, this pattern becomes harder to spot. Subtle changes of direction and the way the body faces, rhythmic variations, and extra steps and movements interposed between repetitions are only some of the liberties taken with form. Nevertheless, the underlying pattern of three or four repetitions of a movement phrase, followed by a small coda, remains a choreographic constant. The principle applies not only to solos, but to duets, trios and larger groups.

Variations on the Pas de Deux

All-important in dance is the *pas de deux*, which contrasts the qualities of male and female dancers and provides an opportunity to exploit the virtuoso talents of a company's stars. In the chapter on style, we discussed Marius Petipa's *pas de deux* as a duet for the two main characters which comes at the climax of the ballet, generally near the end of the last act. Petipa set the classical ballet *pas de deux* in a fairly rigid mode that continues to influence choreographers over one hundred years later. It goes like this: 1) a duet in slow to moderate tempo in which the male supports the female and displays her to best advantage, as she assumes difficult poses (called the "supported adagio"); 2) the man's variation, in which he performs jumping, aerial steps; 3) the woman's variation of small, rapid combinations; 4) the man again in bigger, more flashy feats; 5) the woman now joining him in a succession of fast turns, creating a spectacular coda which closes with the woman caught by the man and held in a daring pose. *Pas de deux* in this form are frequently offered on programs apart from their full ballets, such as the one in *Le Corsair*, which has already been described. Modern ballets freely vary the *pas de deux*, but no matter how far they depart from Petipa's blueprint, they nevertheless construct a discernible structure.

Balanchine, endlessly fascinated by the supported adagio form that displayed the ballerina in all her glory, created dozens and dozens of *pas de deux*. In his 1956 *Divertimento No. 15*, named for its Mozart score, the final Andante section is one long supported adagio—despite the fact that it is danced by five women and three men. After an opening pose by all eight dancers, everyone exits save one ballerina and a partner. The ballerina goes through her lovely moves and poses, and her partner serves as her cavalier, finally carrying her offstage. A second woman enters with a partner and goes through her supported paces. She exits in the arms of her partner, to be replaced by the third, then the fourth, then the fifth ballerina. Because of the smaller number of males in the piece, two of the three men appear twice. The climax is reached in the last section, in which all eight dancers figure. Now two men each have a partner, one man supports two women, and one woman stands by herself in the center back. She isn't left alone for long, however, as everyone changes partners. Finally all the couples separate. The men cluster together, and the women do the same. Next, each group forms a line, the two sexes facing one another, and everybody bows graciously. In unison, all turn away and slowly exit.

The unequal numbers probably came less from choreographic vision than from the eternal shortage of first-rate male dancers. In 1977, when Balanchine composed the popular *Vienna Waltzes*, he featured Suzanne Farrell with an absent partner. Farrell decided that "my partner was relegated to a phantom existence ... because I was dancing once more with George" (the choreographer himself).[5] The reason Balanchine gave—that he was tired of running out of men—may have been closer to the truth.[6]

In a very different mode is Lester Horton's modern dance duet *The Beloved* (1948, score by Judith Hamilton). This is a short but complete piece that traces the deterioration of a man's sexual desire for his wife into rage at her imagined infidelity. The man and woman sit beside a table. The theme is stated when he abruptly shoots out a hand, the fingers splayed wide, summoning her to him. Her fingers move towards his in a nervous, fluttering response. The man and wife both rise. Several times he draws her to him, swings her to and fro, rolls over her body. He fights his lust and flings her away. His rigidly controlled reaching, pacing motions are countered by her softer circling, pleading, kneeling. He lifts her to his knee in a final swinging hold, and throws her down on the chair. At the end, his body shields her from our sight, until once more he flings his hand out, his fingers splayed, releasing her to fall dead across the table.

Structure in Ensemble Work

In ensemble works, structure may be interwoven with theme, as in Robbins's *Dances at a Gathering*, or it may enjoy a separate coexistence, as in Fokine's *Les Sylphides*, which is also a series of dances set to Chopin pieces. The opening of *Les Sylphides*, with the all-female ensemble and soloists grouped in a tableau around a poetic-looking male garbed in a flowing white shirt and black vest, introduces the mood. To the music of a *Prelude*, the male partners one sylph, then two, their arms intertwining with his, in the manner Balanchine was later to use so often.

The work continues with sections that vary one from another and yet maintain an overall unity. Solos and ensembles progress lightly and effortlessly from one pattern into another. The movement is classical ballet, but its lines are softened and rounded and balanced slightly off center. A female dances a gentle but joyous waltz, backed by the almost quiet ensemble. Then there is a buoyant solo mazurka, but this time the corps forms a three-sided background and echoes the soloist's *grand jeté*.

The mood continues to build in excitement with an exuberant mazurka through which the poet leaps eagerly, pausing before he exits the stage to kneel as though appealing to the clustered nymphs. Now there is a hush in the action, while the ensemble poses softly and a female does a dreamy waltz, and then the poet returns, this time to lead another sylph in a slow *pas de deux*. This reappearance of tranquility serves to heighten the tension before the dancers spring off once more to bring a climax to the action in a vivacious *Valse Brillante* with the poet and the female soloists bounding about, against the corps dancing in unison. As this waltz comes to an end, there is a rapid swoop of motion and the sylphs take their places to reform the picturesque tableau that opened the ballet, providing the fulfillment of a resolution. But we note that while the structure yields satisfaction, it is in no way tied to the theme of the romantic interplay between poet and sylphs, or the mood of misty nostalgia. The structure stands up simply because it adheres to sound engineering principles. One can think of other arrangements that would have served as well.

Types of Dance Structure

Although structures in dance devised according to the principles stated earlier are endlessly varied, it is worth looking at a few main types: 1) the form that follows music; 2) the composition that builds dramatically; 3) the form that is based on visual principles; 4) the framework structure; and 5) the flashback technique.

Musical Structure

Dance is usually accompanied by music, and frequently its structure is determined by the structure of the score. In music, a theme is a musical idea with melodic, rhythmic and harmonic elements. Themes are presented and developed with varying melodic, harmonic, tonal, rhythmic and dynamic patterns. The simplest structure is A-A-A, or constant repetition. The most common song form is A-B-A.

Other common structures are the rondo and the canon. From these easily grasped forms the musician proceeds to more and more complex forms like the sonata, the symphony, the fugue, the chorale prelude, and the polyphonic Mass. There are hundreds of examples of choreography composed according to its music.

José Limón's masterpiece *There Is a Time* (1956, music by dello Joio) is based on a poetic passage in Ecclesiastes that begins, "To everything there is a season, and a time to every purpose under the heaven." The passage arranges human existence into various segments, each assigned to its proper time. The dance, like the scripture, falls into the pattern of a theme and variations, each variation expressing another facet of life. "A time to laugh" has an open, shaking release; "a time to keep silence" has an imposed restraint; "a time for war" has flailing, hysterical gestures; "a time for peace" moves with serenity. The natural rhythm of life includes fighting, making peace, speaking, keeping silent, laughing and dancing.

Norman dello Joio's music was written first, and Limón followed its structure. While there are twenty-eight episodes mentioned in Ecclesiastes, the composer chose only twelve and reshuffled their order. For example, the original words read "A time to love, and a time to hate; a time of war, and a time of peace," the music and dance offer "a time of hate; a time of war; a time to love and a time of peace." Limón choreographed each phrase in appropriately shaped and timed gestures. The dance opens and closes with a full circle, representing the cycle of life and the people of a community continuing their appointed rounds.

Narrative and Dramatic Structures

Sometimes the structure of a work parallels the build-up, climax and resolution of a dramatic narrative. Agnes de Mille's *Fall River Legend* (1948, music by Gould), was based on the notorious historical episode of the unsolved murder of Lizzie Borden's parents, who were axed to death. The ballet introduces Lizzie, an ordinary girl in love with a man whom her parents drive away. Although in real life Lizzie was tried for the bloody double murder and acquitted for lack of evidence, de Mille took the liberty of presenting the girl's bitter resentment and turmoil as leading to the climactic violence of the dreadful dual murder. In the ballet, Lizzie is found guilty and hanged. A final resolution shows Lizzie reconciled with her dead mother, whose spirit calmly and compassionately accepts the deed and the doer. This artificially composed order is much more satisfying, at least to the observer, than the chaotic unjust world we really inhabit.

Visual Design

Dance sections may be repeated or contrasted according to visual form. Dissonant, jagged shapes can be resolved into orderly harmonious patterns. An "up" section may be contrasted with one down on the floor. When we speak of dance as kinetic sculpture, or pictures in motion, the governing principle is visual design.

Joffrey Ballet's Gerald Arpino used the flamboyance of Spanish dance to add piquancy to *Viva Vivaldi!* (1965). While the steps of *Viva Vivaldi!* are strictly balletic, the dancers' costumes, and their backs and arms arched in the manner of Spanish dance, impart an exotic accent to the piece.

In *Viva Vivaldi!* Gerald Arpino followed the musical structure of the *Concerto in D Major* by Vivaldi, which has four movements, the first and the third slow, the second and fourth fast. The opening movement has a couple performing a supported adagio that features high lifts, offset by a trio of men who take kneeling poses close to the floor. In the third

Jodie Gates of the Joffrey Ballet of Chicago in *Viva Vivaldi!* **choreographed by artistic director Gerald Arpino. Photograph © MIGDOLL 1998.**

movement, there is a reversal of the levels and sexes of the opening. Here an elegant couple moves on a low spatial plane, counterpoised by three females who float close together *en pointe* in high, airy graciousness. These slow parts provide a grave ballast to the effervescence and splash of both the second and fourth movements, each of which presents one sex: The second is exclusively female, the fourth exclusively male.

A detailed look at the choreography of the all-female lively movement shows a form that swells and contracts. It starts with a brisk step coming forward, done first by one dancer, then in unison with two more, then again two more, until five females are facing the audience in a wedge shape. Then the form diminishes, reversing to unravel the pattern bit by bit. Soon the group shifts to a wispy jump on the tips of their toes, their knees slightly bent, their arms held overhead behind the ears. This motif is continued by a diminishing number of dancers until only one is left. Two women enter for a brief dialogue in canon form, one doing a pose on one leg (*en attitude*) and an *entrechat quatre* and the other a standing pose in fourth position. They reverse roles four times, then do the phrase in unison and whirl off in opposite directions.

In the final movement, Arpino took advantage of his talented company soloists (as do many good choreographers). He staged a competition between Joffrey stars Luis Fuente and Robert Blankshine. Arpino had Fuente counterpoise his dignified Spanish swagger against Blankshine's light, balletic bounciness. In turn, the two men's splashy aerial movements were counterpoised by a group of men who knelt on the floor and formed patterns with their arms.

Dances in Frames

We come now to dances in which the overall form is used not just for general aesthetic reasons, but to communicate a point of view. *The Green Table* of Kurt Jooss, *Caprichos* by Herbert Ross, and Donald MacKayle's *Rainbow Round My Shoulder* all create structural frameworks that in some way comment on the dance action.

In *The Green Table* (1932, score by Fritz Cohen), Kurt Jooss created a modern dance with a number of striking vignettes featuring a cast of strongly differentiated characters. But his choreography is most persuasive and satisfying through its structural elements. A prologue and epilogue frame the piece with interchangeable international leaders gathered around a green conference table. These masked diplomats make ritual speeches and applaud one another's hypocrisy. Inevitably their deliberations break down and war is declared.

In the body of the piece, the figure of Death presides over the action.

His is a fearfully insistent motif: a grasping, implacable thumping that no one can escape. There are scenes of enthusiastic recruits gradually becoming dogged, plodding, exhausted soldiers who finally fall in battle. There are portraits of women bidding their men farewell, sad in the knowledge that many won't return. There are displaced refugees, pitifully huddled together. Death constantly reappears to claim a victim—or to serve as a fearful reminder of things to come. He is not always the enemy, as is shown when he tenderly carries off an old woman refugee who is comforted by his care. But that he is the undisputed champion is confirmed when he leads a funereal victory parade, a death march joined by all the characters. The return of the faceless diplomats in the epilogue not only rounds out the structure, it makes the point that they control everyman's destiny. It isn't important which particular individuals occupy the office: Diplomats see war as a game or a dance, and their machinations send others to the not always tender mercies of Death.

In 1950, Herbert Ross based a ballet on *Caprichos*, a series of etchings made by Goya in the 1790s to show the corruption and decadence of society. Ross, wishing to show that today's world also is seeped in degeneracy, brought four of the etchings to life with music by Bartók. To serve as a structural framework, Ross chose the picture of two girls in flimsy gowns who "have seats enough and nothing to do with them better than carry them on their heads," which was the comment that Goya made to accompany his cynical drawing. These useless, bored characters, who expose their bottoms and rub their legs together lustfully, become the titillated observers of three wicked incidents.

They are delighted when a bored woman courts rape by two men in a brief "bull-fight." The two gallants clap their hands sharply and fix the woman in position between them with toreador gestures. She runs around, careful to remain between them, never really trying to break out of the ring—a bull who wants to be gored. Then the girls are a giddy audience for a widower, who puts on a show of mourning his dead wife. His phoniness is apparent as he appeals to the girls with anguished gestures, meanwhile dragging his dead wife along the ground like a stuffed laundry bag. In the last episode, the girls stand on their chairs to get a better view of true horror: four hooded, sanctimonious figures burn an innocent woman to death, while she claws at herself in a vain attempt to escape. The two observers, excited by the victim's immolation, lift their gowns to warm their bottoms at the flames. Ross leaves the audience with the uneasy thought that they too, like the girls, are fascinated by the passing parade of obscene evil.

Thus *The Green Table* and *Caprichos* communicate a point of view in part through their structure. In both cases the point of view is ironic. Clearly the audience is not expected to empathize with the diplomats or Death, or with the voyeurism of the two girls.

Donald McKayle's *Rainbow Round My Shoulder* (1959) commented on the prison system in the American South by presenting all the dancers in dramatic opposition to a faceless establishment. Here the point of view is not ironic, but empathetic. The overall form is musical—a song of protest as a refrain, with the verses depicting the prisoners' memories and longings. The action consists of a chain-gang of convict laborers linked by ties of iron and sympathy, carrying out percussive, rock-beating tasks. The men violently twist and bend as though under the lash; they stretch their arms and slam them down repeatedly, as though toiling with sledge hammers. Against this angry background, each man stays alive through his memories of happier, freer times with female figures. For example, there is a duet in which a son keeps sneaking away to play, trying to avoid his mother who naggingly chastises him about chores. The bouncy tug of war, accompanied by a song in which the refrain is "Yes Ma'am," gives a charming picture of a moment in boyhood. In another duet, a man recalls making love to his sweetheart.

After each flight of fancy, there is a return to the fury of the convict-labor refrain. The tension of the men grows more extreme. Finally one of them bursts out of the line in a desperate attempt to escape, and is shot to death. The action and sound freeze in a climax that is musical, dramatic and organic. The piece ends in a mood of hopeless acceptance, as the men return to work, accompanied by the song "Another Man Done Gone."

Rainbow Round My Shoulder demonstrates the way masterworks combine a number of structural devices for maximum effect. In addition to a musical form and a framework, the piece offers flashbacks to contrast with the "present" grim reality.

The Flashback Technique

Martha Graham's *Night Journey*, Frederick Ashton's *Marguertite and Armand*, and Glen Tetley's *Alice* are all examples of the flashback technique, familiar to us from films. A work structured in this fashion begins at the end of a series of events or a lifetime, and presents the action as remembered by the central figure. The audience is thus led to see the world from that character's point of view. At the end of the work there is a return to the central figure as she or he appeared at the beginning.

Martha Graham's *Night Journey* is the drama of Jocasta and Oedipus, the most famous mother and son in literature and psychological tradition, originating with Greek theater, then picked up by Freud. The dance portrays incestuous desire that inexorably destroys the woman, along with the object of her sinful passion. As described earlier in this chapter, the beginning has Jocasta contemplating her fate in the circle of a noose. At the end, we see the same figure staring through the rope, revealing all the action to have been a flashback at her last moment of life.

Along with the flashback structure, Frederick Ashton's *Marguerite and Armand* includes the device of dividing the main character of Marguerite between two dancers. One Marguerite appears only in the Prologue, reclining on a chaise and gasping out her last days in the throes of consumption. The other—her young, glamorous self surrounded by admiring upper class French gentlemen, meeting and having a passionate love affair with Armand against the opposition of his father—is a figment of memory. It ends as it began, except now it is the second Marguerite on her death bed, in "real time." The still young woman clings with desperate passion to her lover, who has flown across the stage to be at her side, and she dies in his arms. As we watch Marguerite's animated flirtations and exultant love, we cannot help feeling the poignance of her wasted end.

Glen Tetley choreographed the ballet *Alice* in 1986, based on a combination of Lewis Carroll's *Alice in Wonderland* and the historically documented attraction between the thirty-year-old author, whose hobby was photographing naked young girls, and the ten-year-old Alice Liddell. The dance is framed at the beginning and the end by the appearance of Alice as an elderly woman. The action therefore takes place in Alice's memory, and the point of view is certainly hers. Tetley's *pas de deux* include familiar classical elements, modified and interrupted by both the fantasy characters and psychologically loaded images of real-life torments. Two simultaneous *pas de deux*—one between the child Alice and the adult author, which reveals her repressed pre-adolescent sexual feelings for him, and the other between the adult Alice and her husband, which reveals the confusing effects of the earlier ambiguous relationship—leave the audience to ponder all kinds of psychological ramifications. Near the end, child Alice is once again entwined with the author in a sensual supported adagio, interrupted by the entrance of the hurrying White Rabbit. At this point the girl joins the rabbit in a merrily springing *pas de deux*, to be interrupted by the adult Alice, now grown old. The White Rabbit hurries off, dropping behind him a single glove, which the old woman picks up as a treasured symbol of her fairy-tale childhood in Wonderland.

Structuring a Program

In the same way that a single work needs structure, so too does an entire concert program. To present a dance in the best light, attention must be paid to what comes before and after it. It is necessary to balance light and heavy pieces, short solos against large ensembles, premiers against well-known works, etc. Occasionally, an arbitrary theme ties a whole program together. In 1993, the Joffrey Ballet Company staged *Billboards*, a series of dances by different choreographers united only by the music of pop composer Prince Rogers Nelson. Balanchine created *Jewels* in 1967 for his New York City Ballet. The unifying theme here was the title, applied to three contrasting compositions: "Emeralds" was danced to music by Fauré, "Rubies" to Stravinsky, and "Diamonds" to Tchaikovsky.

The choreographic art has many options. Like music it has an underlying rhythmic pulse, and can create a mood; like painting and sculpture, it reveals visual designs and shapes. It can also, like narrative literature and drama, offer a situation, and mine it for riches of human emotion; or like poetry it can express ideas through association and analogy. In their compositions choreographers may lean towards one art form or another, but only at their peril do they neglect the structure of the building.

6

Music and Dance, Partners in Art

Along with kinesthetic reaction to movement, response to a dance event is clearly conditioned by the sound accompaniment, which can be produced by a composer's full score, by silence, by the taps and beats of a dancer's feet, by a drum, by words of a poem, by random utterances, or by any combination of these.

In this chapter we will look at various ways in which accompaniment affects choreography. We will consider the components of music; the dancer's need for music; the choreographic treatment of scores; available musical styles; composers in and out of fashion.

The Components of Music

To comprehend the components of music as a self-contained art, it is useful to consider, alternately, the thoughts of American composer Aaron Copland and Russian composer Igor Stravinsky.

Copland: "Every composer begins with a musical idea—a *musical idea* you understand, not a mental, literary, or extramusical idea.... The composer starts with his theme; and the theme is a gift from Heaven."[1]

Stravinsky: The tonal elements that comprise this theme "become music only by virtue of their being organized." Music is a chronologic art—an organization in time.[2]

Copland: Whatever its form, music must have a long line. "Every good piece of music must give us a sense of flow—a sense of continuity from first note to last."[3]

Stravinsky: "Time passes at a rate which varies according to the inner disposition of the subject.... Expectation, boredom, anguish, pleasure and pain, contemplation—each of these determines a special psychological process, a particular tempo."[4]

The Dancer's Need for Music

Some early modern dancers set out to prove that dance was an independent art, and could stand alone, without accompaniment. Doris Humphrey created superb works without music, like *Water Study* (1928). Eventually, most modern dancers decided that the two arts belong together. This was musician Louis Horst's explanation:

> Ideally, dance uses no music at all. But in practical terms this is trying on the audience, who hear only the feet and breathing of the dancers. Besides, music helps the dance by confining it, as a frame confines a painting. It provides a disciplinary measure for the choreographer, and it deepens the meaning of dance for the spectator.[5]

Even Doris Humphrey later went so far as to say that dance does not exist as an independent art. Rather, missing something when performed in silence, it needs a sympathetic association with music.[6] This does not rule out the creation of sections of dance without accompaniment. Martha Graham's *Dark Meadow* (1946), to a score by Chavez, opens with an unaccompanied ritualistic woman's circle. Here silence serves to emphasize this passage and to provide effective contrast to what follows.

An outstanding ballet created to silence is Jerome Robbins's *Moves* (1959), an image of relationships between individuals, couples, and groups. However, *Moves* really works a little like the passage in *Dark Meadow*, in the sense that it is not very long, and therefore stands in contrast to other numbers on the same program that would have music. Mark Morris's *Behemoth* (1990), a tribute to Merce Cunningham, was made to stand alone in silence. Eliot Feld's ballet *Endsong* (1991) was performed in silence—against the choreographer's wishes. The piece, which has a gentle, dreamlike quality, had been motivated by Feld's love for Richard Strauss's *Four Last Songs*. But Strauss's son had refused to allow the music to be used for dance. The choreographer urged the audience to protest to the score's publisher. Despite the lack of music, a critic found that the "ballet's sparseness and integrity of design echo the songs' elegant poignancy."[7] There is also an occasional choreographer like Dana Reitz who, as we shall see in the next chapter, works in an unaccompanied mode.

The above exceptions aside, why is almost every dance event accompanied by music? Is it because music, as the most abstract of the arts, is seen to soften dance, which is the most concrete of the arts (by virtue of the strong physical presence of the dancer)? Or is it that a performance that requires attention for a given period of time calls for the engagement of as many senses as possible? The ear abhors a vacuum and would strain to fill the void with sounds like chair creakings and coughing fits.

In any case, it seems that music is more than just accompaniment. For some choreographers, while the body is their medium, music is the heart and soul of their art. It motivates and inspires them.

Balanchine: "Whether a ballet has a story or not, the controlling image for me comes from the music.... In my choreographic creations I have always been dependent on music."[8]

Eliot Feld: "Music is a springboard. It crystallizes ideas. It gives rhythm and suggests line.... I choreograph a personal response to music."[9]

Robert Starer, who composed scores for a number of modern dancers like Martha Graham, Daniel Nagrin, Anna Sokolow and John Butler, expressed his respect for choreographic artists as follows: "So many jokes are told about the musicality of dancers that I would like to state at this point that I have never encountered more truly musical people than choreographers. They may not know the difference between F sharp and G flat, but they have an unfailing sense for what I would like to call musical 'gesture'."[10]

Music makes the listeners want to move, and their physiological changes can be measured. There is an increase in muscular tone; the respiratory rate fluctuates; blood pressure and heart rate rise.[11] If music doesn't actually make one want to dance, it causes restlessness, and sets feet or fingers tapping. One of the reasons people go to concerts rather than listen to recordings is that music lovers get something from the movements of instrumentalists and conductors.

Vivian Fine, who composed scores for piano, voice and orchestra, as well as for leading American modern dancers, saw the body as the common denominator in dance and music: "The body sensations that are the response to an idea ... are similar for dancer and musician. This underlying sense of movement is the first expression of a feeling we carry with us always."[12]

Composer Roger Sessions went so far as to claim that "the basic ingredient of music is not so much sound as movement.... Music is significant for us because ... it takes shape in the inner gestures which embody our deepest and most intimate responses."[13]

The continuity of time-flow is the main contribution of music to dance. According to Balanchine, it is from the music that dance receives its fundamental pulse:

> What I mainly expect from the composer ... is a steady and reassuring pulse which holds the work together and which one should feel even in the rests.... A choreographer can't invent rhythms, he only reflects them in the movement.... The body is his sole medium and, unaided, the body will improvise for a short breath. But the organizing of rhythm on a grand scale is a sustained process. It is a function of the musical mind.[14]

Gordon Boelzner, a musician who joined the New York City Ballet as Balanchine's rehearsal pianist in 1960, confessed that like many music students, he used to think that dancing was an unnecessary intrusion upon good music. His feelings changed completely to the point where, ten years later, he noted: "Now I feel disappointed when I go to a concert and don't see dancing."[15]

Treatment of Scores

Not every dance fits with every score. Music has a strong emotional component, and "there is widespread consensus between listeners about the emotional content of different pieces of music.... That is, whether a piece is considered poignant, wistful, elegiac, boisterous, rustic and so on, does *not* depend upon previous knowledge of the piece in question."[16] Aaron Copland wrote that although the sound elements vary with each composer, all music is expressive, that it has a certain meaning behind the notes, which constitutes "what the piece is saying, what the piece is about."[17] Of course one cannot state exactly what the meaning is, any more than one can say exactly what a dance means. Nevertheless, it is very unsatisfactory if the music is saying something entirely different from the dance. (Unless the choreographer does this deliberately, perhaps for irony or humor.)

Correspondences between dance and musical accompaniment vary. The partnership of dance and music is close in mood and structure taken as a whole. But an exact agreement, where each gesture is underlined with a musical note, is highly undesirable. This approach, known as "Mickey-Mousing," works well enough in the Disney cartoons from where the term arose, but in concert dance it quickly becomes obvious and boring. In other cases, a deliberate opposition of counterpoint or syncopation may be set up between music and dance. Stravinsky wrote of the pleasure that derives from contrast:

> Who of us, on hearing jazz music, has not felt an amusing sensa-tion approaching giddiness when a dancer or a solo musician, try-ing persistently to stress irregular accents, cannot succeed in turning our ear away from the regular pulsation of the meter drummed out by the percussion?[18]

"Music visualization" is the term used to describe a dance that sets out to mirror a musical score. Isadora Duncan wrote, "I was possessed by the idea of a school—a vast ensemble—dancing the 9th symphony of Bee-thoven."[19]

Balanchine noted that among others of his ballets *Symphony in C*, the *Brahms-Schonberg Quartet* and *Concerto Barocco* are dances with only musi-cal narrative. They have no subject matter beyond their scores.[20]

His *Concerto Barocco* (Bach) exemplifies the suite form with three move-ments: fast, slow, fast (Vivace, Largo, Allegro). But while the underlying pulse is the same for score and choreography, the dancers do not rise and fall with the melody; nor do their accents, holds, and fast steps mimic the rhythmic patterns and dynamics of the music.

In *Concerto Barocco* eight females are arranged in two opposing squares, where they shift rapidly in movements and positions. As the two violins take up their part in the music, two solo females arrive front and center. They move in unison, or echo each other in canon form, as the eight dancers behind them make an upstage frame, shifting into two straight lines, vertically or horizontally, or crossed, or two diagonal lines meeting in a V. In swiftly changing patterns the soloists and the group have leggy, angular movements, side-extensions, arabesques, *relevés*, and Balanchine's characteristic sassy lean into a pointed foot. In this typical Balanchine creation, the subject is at once the music and the elegant formalism of classical ballet.

Doris Humphrey also chose to choreograph to Bach, creating *Passacaglia in C Minor* (1938) to his music. A passacaglia is a form in which a theme that stretches over several metrical bars is continually repeated. The Bach music is based on an eight-bar theme that insistently repeats from beginning to end. Humphrey's dance opens with a group in pose, and movements start quietly. With each repetition, the musical theme varies slightly; and the dance keeps building up with bigger movements, wider spatial use, stronger rhythms and heightened accents. The dancers return to their opening positions as the Passacaglia music ends.

Those early modern dancers who chose music over silence took a cavalier approach to accompaniment. Louis Horst wrote that when he first became a musical director (in 1917, for Denishawn), "Dance music consisted of pieces selected from records—a bit of this and a bit of that."[21] Only gradually did the creation of musical accompaniment become a serious business. But choreographers continued the practice of cutting and pasting bits of great music to create a special arrangement suitable to a choreographic idea. A highly successful effort was Simon Sadoff's arrangements of Henry Purcell's dance suites for José Limón's *The Moor's Pavane* (1947).

Paul Taylor, feeling the need for strong music, has taken a different but still unconventional approach. He prefers to work to music of some kind, but it may not be the score he finally settles on. For example, he began the choreography of *Orbs* (1966) to Vivaldi's *Four Seasons* but ended up with several of Beethoven's late string quartets. Similarly, he rehearsed *Scudorama*, which was finally performed to a Charles Jackson score, to Stravinsky's *Sacre du Printemps* (Rite of Spring). Taylor also has something else in mind when he fiddles around with scores. He wrote: "*Not* following music is a major element in my search for musicality."[22]

Available Styles

Choreographers have roamed through the musical repertory of the past and present, finding almost any style of interest. Often they have chosen to dance to pieces from the existing musical repertory. This was not always accepted by musical purists who claimed it a desecration of great, self-contained music, to treat it as "mere" dance accompaniment. Cries of outrage greeted Isadora Duncan's use of scores by Beethoven, Bach, Gluck, Chopin, or Tchaikovsky. But the popular Duncan ignored their disapproval and continued to go her own way. There were also furious debates when Léonide Massine choreographed a series of ambitious ballets to symphonies like Tchaikovsky's Fifth and Brahms's Fourth.

Gradually, however, the practice was accepted. Balanchine used dozens of well known musical scores, beginning in 1934 with *Serenade*, about which the choreographer wrote:

> Named after its music—Tchaikovsky's *Serenade in C Major for String Orchestra*—the ballet tells its story musically and choreographically, without any extraneous narrative…. The score … contains many stories—it is many things to many listeners to the music, and many things to many people who see the ballet.[23]

But it is possible to reach back much farther, to find inspiration from early and primitive types of music. In tribal rituals, where dance movement is always accompanied by sounds, the drummer is the main music-maker. While body motions in tribal ritual tend to be simple and repetitive, the drumming accompaniment can be highly complex. Among African tribes, drumming is often polyrhythmic.

Pearl Primus, an African American woman who made her mark as a powerful modern dancer and then went on to research tribal forms in Africa, said:

> The good drummers, men who instead of playing the drum *are* the drum, are a rare breed indeed. In spite of popular belief, an African dancer doesn't dance to the beat. He spreads a carpet of movement around the beat. But the beat must be great.[24]

Religious Music

High culture in the Middle Ages was tied to the church. The great music of the period was written for the church mass, usually for voice, encouraged as a purely spiritual aid to religious worship. Dance was not in the picture; in fact, it was condemned by the church. Nevertheless, contemporary choreographers, who are sensitive to all music, have included great religious music in their repertory of dance ideas.

The year 1991 was the two hundredth anniversary of Mozart's death. John Neumeier was asked by the Salzburg Festival to choreograph Mozart's *Requiem*, a score that the composer died before completing. The enigmatic music, constructed for religious ritual, is at the same time abstract and intensely emotional, expressing both despair and resigned faith. The choreographer thought that the work would force both performers and audiences to confront and accept death. His vision required the presence of orchestra and singers onstage, along with the dancers, in order to communicate the depths of feeling in the music. Because of the anniversary, at least two other artists made dances to the Mozart *Requiem*: Edward Stierle for the Joffrey Ballet and Jean-Paul Comelin for the Ballet du Nord.

Mark Morris is another artist who has delved with zest into classical religious scores like Vivaldi's *Gloria* and Pergolesi's *Stabat Mater*. In 1993, Morris set a dance to Bach's *Jesu, Meine Freude*, using the composer's title. The dancers' movements express the fierce determination of finding and keeping faith. Critic Christine Temin wrote, "They sometimes seem to be shaking off sin with vigorous, literal motions—as if sin were something nasty and sticky on their hands." The reviewer noted that the choreographer honored the Bach motet, a religious choral composition, by following its spirit and structure, "and reached with it to offer a powerful, personal testament."[25] In connection with the same work, music critic Richard Dyer wrote that musicians want to perform with Morris's company because his choreography is so deeply musical in impulse; "he understands what they are up to better than their own audiences."[26]

With rare exceptions, Morris's repertory represents the idea that dance cannot stand alone—it needs music. His biographer Joan Acocella explained it this way, "Almost always, the idea for the dance is born from the music.... At the genesis of a Mark Morris work, he is listening to the music very hard ... but as he does so, an emotion is being born in his mind, an emotion that gradually eats the music, makes it his."[27] The choreographer often follows a score quite literally, mirroring not only its structure, but its melodic lines. Melodies go up, bodies go up; melodies go down, so the bodies. Critics have sometimes seen this as a virtue, as in the review above, and sometimes as a failing. Clive Barnes found in Morris's work "a literalness that I consider Disneyesque."[28]

Nineteenth Century

The nineteenth century, which saw a flowering of choreography, also saw a large number of composers of dance music who have since been dismissed as hacks. Nevertheless, those ballets which survived the 1800s to become the public's favorites up to the present day have fine scores—by composers like Adolphe Adam (*Giselle*), Léo Delibes (*Coppélia*), Alexander Glazounov (*Raymonda*) and, towering above them all, Pyotr Ilyich Tchaikovsky (*The Sleeping Beauty*, *The Nutcracker*, and *Swan Lake*.) These composers all wrote music on demand.

Nineteenth century composers in particular made use of an effective

Fokine's *Firebird*. Photograph by Martha Swope, © Time Inc.

device that relates music closely to a story dance: the leitmotif. The leitmotif is the use of a certain melodic theme, repeated in association with a particular character or situation. This device was Adolphe Adam's contribution to ballet music. In *Giselle,* Adam's score provides a theme repeated at every appearance of Hilarion, the robust peasant who loves the village girl; a theme for the flirtation scenes between Giselle and Albrecht, which is echoed during the girl's mad-death scene; and a theme for the Wilis, used prophetically in Act I and then for their entrance in Act II.

Or we have Stravinsky's music for Fokine's *Firebird,* based on Russian fairy tales about a prince who captures a firebird in the hunt. In return for releasing her, she gives him a magic feather. When he later sets out to rescue a maiden, imprisoned by a monster, the prince-hero is helped by the grateful firebird. A large part of the score for this ballet is constructed from a chromatic phrase of only four notes! Chromatic means that the melody progresses in a series of half-tones (adjacent notes on the piano keyboard.) The use of chromatic tones was a common device in Russian music for creating an exotic atmosphere. The four-note phrase in *Firebird* is repeated maybe thousands of times—yet so unobtrusively (it goes up or down, backward or forward) that, as one writer claimed, it is quite easy to see the ballet several times without noticing it at all.

A nineteenth century development of special interest to dancers was the rise of nationalism—pride in one's ethnic traditions and territory. While the primary focus of nationalism is political patriotism, the sentiment also infects artists. Specifically in music, national consciousness led to the incorporation of folk tunes and rhythms in classical works by a host of composers. In turn, the lively folk character of their music was and is an inspiration to choreographers. The Hungarian *czardas* in *Coppélia* and the Polish mazurka, the Neapolitan dance and the Spanish dance in *Swan Lake* are examples of this trend, which continued through the twentieth century.

Swan Lake is perhaps the most popular ballet of all time, in large part no doubt because of the music. Yet its composer, Tchaikovsky, died thinking *Swan Lake* was a failure. The history of both the music and the ballet is too complex to go into. Here it is sufficient to learn that the ballet, first performed in 1877 with choreography by Reisinger, was received indifferently. "The conductor said he had never in his life seen such complicated ballet music, while the choreographer thought it so unsuitable for dancing that he cut out about a third of the music, and replaced it with hack pieces of no musical interest. There had never been a ballet in Russia with good music; good music was not what people in the dance world wanted."[29]

Tchaikovsky's masterpiece, *The Sleeping Beauty*, is full of descriptive music. The English critic Robert Fiske gave much of the credit to choreographer Petipa, who knew how to find words to get the most out of his great composer. For the "cat" dance, Petipa asked for "repeated mewing. Caresses and blows. At the end, claws scratching and squawling. Start off three-four *amoroso*. End up in three-four with mewing, becoming quicker and quicker." For the Diamond Fairy he asked for "showers of diamonds, like electric sparks, two-four *vivo*."[30]

For *The Nutcracker*, Petipa again gave detailed instructions to Tchaikovsky: "The tree is lit up ... 8 bars of sparkling music. The children enter ... 24 bars of joyful animated music. A few bars of tremolo depicting surprise and admiration," and on and on. Composer Normal Lloyd commented, "That out of these instructions came the *Nutcracker Ballet* is a tribute to Tchaikovsky's genius."[31]

Although most of the *Nutcracker* music is excellent, its main interest for Tchaikovsky was his inclusion of one of the first celestes ever made. The new sound of this tinkling miniature piano made a big impression and ensured the popularity of the overture and march from Act I, the Sugar-plum Fairy's variation and the *Waltz of the Flowers*.

Although music grew in complexity from the middle ages on, the basic tonal system remained in force for centuries. Then, in the late 1800s, for all kinds of reasons in and out of music, composers broke down the accepted systems of tonality, harmony, structure and rhythm. Their modern music featured an extensive use of dissonance, devices like atonality and poly-tonality, and a wild freedom in metrical rhythm.

Most audiences found—and still find—much modern music unappe-tizing, calling it distasteful, even unmusical. However, the needs of chore-ographers are not the same as those of ordinary music lovers. Dance makers are wide-ranging in their search for sounds to suit their specific visions. Their works make appropriate partners for modern musical compositions. As a result, much modern and avant-garde music has been performed repeatedly as dance accompaniment, when it would not have received more than one hearing (if that) in the music concert hall. For examples, we look briefly at dances accompanied by Stravinsky and Webern scores.

Stravinsky holds a highly influential position in modern music and dance, and with good reason:

> *The Firebird* showed what Stravinsky could do under the influence of the Rimsky-Korsakoff-Ravel [orchestral] color scheme.... Stravinsky hit his stride in *Petrouchka*, which had no rivals for bril-liance and exhilaration of orchestral effect; and in *Le Sacre du Prin-temps* which remains ... the most astonishing orchestral achievement of the twentieth century. The pitting of energized strings and pierc-ing wood winds against the sharp cutting edge of brass, the whole determined by an explosive wallop.[32]

Today, when Stravinsky is played so frequently in the concert halls of music and dance, it is hard to believe that in 1913, his music, together with Nijinsky's choreography for *Rite of Spring*, not only elicited shouts and whistles of disapproval, but people actually hit each other in their violent outrage at the style. The composer had set out to create an image of pagan Russia in its annual reawakening from the frozen sleep of winter. Today, the music is regarded as a masterpiece. But nothing like the complex bro-ken meter and the bitonal sound had ever been heard before its premiere, and critics condemned it as "harsh," "brutal," "raw," "coarse," and "seriously ugly."

However, this very quality of rhythmical innovation made problems for some dance artists, particularly choreographer Fokine and the Ballets Russes company. As Fokine wrote:

> When I went to a rehearsal everything seemed clear. I remembered the music not only by heart, but I also retained in my head a visual image of the pages and the lines which contained the difficult passages for the dancers. However the dancers did not look at the music and had to remember everything by ear. It was necessary to stop continually and make excursions into mathematics.... The mistakes made by the dancers in counting retarded the progress of the work.[33]

Fokine also had a problem with the crowd scene in *Petrouchka*, because his concept diverged from the composer's: "If I had kept close [to the music], it would have resulted in my having a tediously static crowd on stage instead of a gay and merry one. Why? Because Stravinsky had all the described characters appear consecutively, while on stage I had them all appear simultaneously."[34]

In Stravinsky's *Les Noces* the chorus is accompanied by four pianos and a diversity of percussion instruments. As one critic has observed, "the abandonment of the strings as the backbone of the orchestra would have been unthinkable in the romantic orchestra."[35]

Later, writes Aaron Copland, "the neoclassic works emphasized the dry sonorities of wind ensembles." Still later, "in the ballets of *Apollo* and *Orpheus*, Stravinsky evinced renewed interest in the strings and gave them a texture all their own.... No other composer has ever shown greater awareness of the natural correlation of tonal image with expressive content."[36]

Agon (1957) was an historic occasion. Balanchine wrote extensively on this work.

> It was Stravinsky who hit upon the idea of a suite of dances based on a seventeenth century manual of French court dances—sarabandes, galliards, branles.... To have all the time in the world meant nothing to Stravinsky. "When I know how long a piece must take, then it excites me." His house in California is filled with beautiful clocks and watches, friends to his wish for precision.... And while the score of *Agon* was invented for dancing, it was not simple to devise dances of a comparable density, quality, metrical insistence, variety, formal master, or symmetrical asymmetry. As always in his ballet scores, the dance element of most force was the pulse.... As an organizer of rhythms, Stravinsky, I have always thought, has been more subtle and various than any single creator in history."[37]

Stravinsky has employed a type of meter comparable to the interpretation of the medieval *a capella* period or to the metrical technique of the Greeks. His melody, likewise, flows in strict allegiance to the accents of the language. This, in turn, is made possible by the employment of shorter, elastic, movable motifs in preference to the traditional type of four- or eight-measure themes that served the classicists. Stravinsky's measure consists of small units. His "phrasing now depends upon this rhythmical unit rather than upon the broad melody of the nineteenth century. This procedure takes the minimum unit instead of the maximum."[38]

Stravinsky "replaced the expressive power of music by its motor power." His work shows "a disdain for everything that charms or pleases, stinging brutalities—all of which were necessary for the destruction of sentiment and subjective emotion, and to make things act directly and by themselves."[39]

Turning from Stravinsky to Anton Webern, we find Webern wrote a passacaglia which, when contrasted with Bach's, would be a good object lesson in the difference between classical and modern music. While Webern's uses the continually repeated theme, the overall structure of the music emerges out of nothingness, develops into manifold forms, and sinks back into inaudible nothingness.

John Cranko used this modern passacaglia for his ballet *Opus 1* (1965). Just as the same basic melody underlies the various figure-variations in the music, a uniform set of steps and expressions runs through the choreography of the entire ballet. *Opus 1* opens with the hero curled up in fetal position, to the thin strains of the music. As the sound builds, he becomes upright, partly borne aloft on the hands of the group, partly asserting his own two-legged strength. At the high point, he encounters a female and communes with her while the group interweaves its presence. When the music begins to subside, the group separates the couple and he sinks to the ground, trying in vain to reach out to her. At the end the music fades away and he curls up again in the fetal position. Thus structure of the dance, like the music, follows the organic natural sequence of birth from the void, life, and final return to the void in death.

In 1959, George Balanchine and Martha Graham made a music-dance experiment, collaborating on *Episodes* with the idea of eventually choreographing all of Webern's orchestral pieces. Graham did the first part of the work, dramatizing the life and death of Mary Queen of Scots and her rivalry with Elizabeth. To *Opus 1*, the austere passacaglia of Cranko's ballet, Mary remembers her love for Bothwell. To *Six Pieces for Orchestra*, she vies with Elizabeth in a symbolic tennis game, loses, and kneels before the fateful axe.

Balanchine did the second part to stand by itself. To a number of Webern's pieces, his dancers in ensemble and in pairs reflect the dry careful music, which is the subject matter. Balanchine wrote: "The boy moves the girl as the composer moves his instruments."[40] The finale is a visualization of Webern's *Six Voices from Bach's Musical Offering*. Balanchine: "The dances here, as elsewhere in this work, praise the music. The further Webern goes, the more active and lean the music becomes. The energy it has is that of free polyphonic voices, each equally individual and expressive. They keep shifting in balance and so do the dances."[41]

The Balanchine section, which reviewers saw as a witty foray into modern dance, is still performed by the New York City Ballet and other companies. What a shame that the Graham piece is no longer coupled with it, as a demonstration of two such different but equally influential dance spirits.

We have already discussed at length the avant-garde movement led by musician and philosopher John Cage. Cage's approach to music was to include any sound—any noise—in a piece, beginning with his invention of the "prepared piano." (By placing pieces of metal and rubber hardware along the strings, he transformed the piano into a multi-voiced percussion instrument.) Then he extended his pursuit of noise variations to the use of electronic tape recorders and synthesizers, with which sounds can be modified indefinitely. Next, he set about removing conscious musical structure from his compositions by using chance methods (like throwing the dice to determine how many times a sound should be repeated).

With Merce Cunningham, he developed a relationship of simultaneity, having the dance and the music begin and end at the same time. To achieve this, Cunningham timed his movement phrases with a stop watch. After many repetitions, the dancers found that their muscles remembered exact durations. They also picked up cues from one another.

Because their sounds are so different from ordinary music, electronically manipulated scores are classified as difficult abstractions. Actually the sounds themselves may resemble literal noises like sirens wailing, trowels scraping, water bubbling, more than do the sounds of classical music. (Music made to present such sounds is sometimes referred to as *musique concrète*.) From the 1950s on, sound waves at dance concerts have often been agitated by electronically produced bloops and bleeps.

Jazz, Swing and Pop

In a class by itself, jazz music was a big hit with ordinary people long before it was ever accepted by the serious art world. Alvin Ailey was not the first to bring jazz music and dance into the concert hall. But because of the tremendous popularity of his company in and out of the United States, Ailey's work assured the solid acceptance of jazz as a concert art form.

Ailey made a number of works to music by Duke Ellington. He was not alone in his admiration for the Duke. The year 1993 saw tributes to the composer at the Smithsonian and the Museum of the City of New York among other sites. Duke (Edward Kennedy) Ellington was the first jazz

American Ballet Theater dancers perform *The River*, a collaboration between
Duke Ellington and Alvin Ailey. Photograph by Martha Swope, © Time Inc.

musician to have his works studied and analyzed as seriously as those of
white classicists. Called "something of an African Stravinsky," "the epitome
of elegance," "a genius beyond category," the Duke composed nearly 1500
energetic, full-bodied numbers that have graced nightclubs, the airwaves,
films, Broadway and concert dance stages. He lived and worked through
the Jazz Age, the swing era, the classical-folksy styles with their undertone
of rebellion that marked the 1940s and 1950s, and the rock-dominated
1960s.

In 1970 the American Ballet Theater commissioned *The River*, music
by Ellington and choreography by Ailey. For this work, Ellington composed one of his most ambitious scores. The music's sections had titles like
"The Spring," "The Giggling Rapids," "The Falls" and "The Lake." The
composer's program notes for the ballet said that the river starts as: "THE
SPRING, which is like a newborn baby. He's in his cradle ... spouting, spinning, wiggling, gurgling, squirming, squealing, making faces, reaching for
his nipple or bottle, turning, tossing, and tinkling all over the place."[42]

The section portraying "The Falls" includes glockenspiel and timpani, added to a rapid machine-gun beat of drums, while the band plays chords of extraordinary dissonance.

Later, Alvin Ailey made the dance *Night Creature* (1974) as a tribute to Ellington. As Ailey said, both he and Ellington were concerned with portrayals of "the life of their people."[43] The imagery in *Night Creature* presents American blacks who emerge like stars that come out (and come on) at night. They meet their social pleasures with a show-offy elegance.

Although the piece has a unity of theme and music not often found in postmodern works, in the respect of its movement combinations, it frolics on the edge of postmodernism. The choreographer had no hesitation in using ballet posturings as well as jazz. When Ailey put a trio of jazzy dancers pulsing percussively downstage center, he set as background for them a row of five "ballerinas" doing classical brisés and arabesque poses. The reason he combined such outwardly dissimilar styles is that the cultural heritage of the American black is composed of ballet and modern dance, right alongside of tap and jazz. Then too, Ellington's music has a Western classical aspect along with its syncopated swing. Finally, ballet as a system of movement expresses an elegance that is splashy and show-offy, making its use in this image completely appropriate.

Since the 1970s, a number of major dancers have delved into pop music. Balanchine's *Who Cares?* is set to Gershwin tunes. Twyla Tharp's *Deuce Coup* uses songs by the Beach Boys and her *Sue's Leg* piano bits by Fats Waller. Paul Taylor's *Company B* brings back World War II harmonies by the Andrews Sisters.

Led by these artists, many choreographers in recent years have routinely turned to jazz and pop vocals and instrumental music. Pop songs by Prince were used in *Billboards*, a 1993 evening-long Joffrey Ballet production that called on four choreographers to make separate pieces. The opening Laura Dean segment to "Sometimes It Snows in April" is the most balletic, with 18 dancers in gleaming white, exploding into turns and scissor leaps. Charles Moulton's "Thunder" has a group of troll-like characters in a take-off on MTV sexual gyrations. Margo Sappington did "Slide," in which Vogue-type figures vie with body-builders in sexual preening. Peter Pucci contributed the work's most talked-about moment in "Willing and Able": a female stands over a male and sticks the point of her red toe shoe into his open mouth.

Music and Text

Words have been used effectively as dance accompaniment. García Lorca's poem serves as the accompaniment as well as the scenario for Doris

Humphrey's *Lament for Ignacio Sanchez Mejías*. The woman who loves the noble bullfighter narrates the poem mourning Ignacio's death, as the danced action portrays the hero's brave and fatal confrontation with the bull. The finality of the bullfighter's death is evocatively underscored in the repetition of the poetic refrain: "At five in the afternoon." In this case, dance imagery is also complemented by music. For example, the drummed heartbeat in Norman Lloyd's score accents the bullfighter's fear as he uses his foot to beat an anxious tattoo against the ground. Lloyd described how, in the preparation of the score, he met constantly with Humphrey for about a year. "We tore the music apart, rearranged its sections.... Much as I hated to have my music lose its leisurely build-up, I had to admit that her theatrical sense was right."[44]

Custom-Tailored Accompaniment

When a score is commissioned to suit a choreographic vision, then the music creates an atmospheric setting as well a kind of prop for the characters, events, and emotions in a plotted ballet. In such a case, most theorists consider the dance primary. As Louis Horst wrote: "The dance should be the center of interest, the point of tension. The music should be transparent, open and spacious, so the audience can see the dance through it."[45]

Composer William Schuman wrote the score for *Undertow* (1945) according to Tudor's scenario, as Aaron Copland did for Graham's *Appalachian Spring* (1944). Copland's score is an example of commissioned music that perfectly suits the dance for which it was written. At the same time it is unusual in that it stands by itself as a fine piece of concert music. Dramatic artists like Graham, Birgit Cullberg and Ninette de Valois commissioned scores according to their own scenarios, then worked out the choreography, music in hand.

For *Job*, choreographed in 1931 by Ninette de Valois, composer Vaughan Williams wrote a score that contains color, atmosphere, clarity of theme and pulse.[46] The strongest musical influences are Palestrina, Bach, Holst and traditional English folk music. The opening pastoral dance to flutes, harps and violas expresses Job's prosperity. Satan's unperceived entrance begins almost from nothing and rises to a crescendo as he watches God. A "sublime Sarabande" describes the Godhead itself, with majesty and repose suggested by repetitive use of two chords traditionally used in the sixteenth century as the amen to psalms.

Later, Satan breaks into a triumphal leaping dance in counts of four, much syncopated in three time, with instruments like the xylophone to give harsh effects. Job's grim trials proceed, and he is comforted by "three wily hypocrites," whose true quality is revealed in their anger motif, which was part of Satan's earlier music. Then real comfort arrives as "the young and beautiful Elihu" performs a dance of youth and beauty to a violin solo that recalls the enchanted bird-song of *The Lark Ascending*.

When Satan prematurely claims victory, there is a triumphant galliard. But at its climax God banishes him, and Satan "falls out of heaven." A finale that shows dancing on earth and in heaven is accompanied by hints of the majestic Godhead theme.

Every choreographer has an individual approach to music. This is only right, according to Stravinsky: "Choreography as I conceive it must realize its own form, independent of the musical form though measured to the musical unit."[47] Stravinsky would have approved Doris Humphrey's treatment of existing scores.

While choreographing to Bach's *Passacaglia in C Minor*, Humphrey conceived of a dance processional. The musical theme ran for the traditional eight measures. Unfortunately, the right phrase for the dancers wouldn't fit properly into eight measures, but required nine—Bach or no Bach. The results were remarkably unshocking. Humphrey found that "of all the thousands of people who have seen this dance, including musical purists, not one has ever mentioned this discrepancy in phrasing."[48] In fact, she had to point it out before anyone noticed it at all.

Composers In and Out of Fashion

Philip Glass is a composer who has made a big impression on the dance world since the middle 1970s, beginning with his collaborations with Robert Wilson in the construction of experimental operas and "visual plays" like *Einstein on the Beach*. In their complex creations, lasting for hours, Glass and Wilson followed—indeed helped create—the postmodern approach that elevates concept above product. However, unlike John Cage, who had helped prepare the ground for Glass, the latter never lost his interest in musical structures and sounds, as well as theatrical forms. Glass discovered inspiration in centuries-old Indian rhythms which consist of small units strung together to make up large rhythmic cycles. In 1965, he wrote a piece in a reductive and repetitive style to go with Samuel Beckett's *Play*. Glass described the piece as "based on two lines, each played by soprano saxophone, having only two notes so that each line represented an alternating, pulsing interval. The result was a very static piece that was still full of rhythmic variety."[49]

Glass became sought after as a composer by choreographers like Kathryn Posin, David Gordon, Susan Marshall, Molissa Fenley, Twyla Tharp and Jerome Robbins, each of whom used the music very differently.

As Arlene Croce pointed out, Glass's music, which uses amplified electronic means to create an otherworldly atmosphere of mystical Asian sounds, is appealing in its simplicity, its formalism, its flow and its mystery. At the same time, in its neutrality, "the music has the capacity to reflect whatever the choreographer wants to do."[50]

Sometimes a composer who has fallen out of fashion becomes popular again. A good example is Stephen Foster (1826–1864), whose work suddenly became all the rage in the middle 1990s. This is not because choreographers copy one another but because artists are sensitive to currents in the air—in this case, looking back at America's past in a search for roots. Just as in their use of Philip Glass scores, their use of Stephen Foster varied widely according to each choreographer's vision.

Eliot Feld remembered Foster from his childhood. But as he pursued serious research, he was shocked by the racism implied in so many Foster pieces, written more than a century ago. So, deciding to avoid sentimentality as well as racism, in 1994 Feld made *Doo Dah Day (No Possum, No Sop, No Taters)* using a "contrapuntal antidote" to the long lyrical lines of well-loved songs like *Beautiful Dreamer*.[51]

Twyla Tharp met the sentimentality head on in *Americans We* (1995), in which Foster was only one of a number of composers she called on to "express optimism and idealism in the American character."[52] Tharp's interpretation set up a counterpoint between two groups: ordinary people doing square dances and grieving for men lost in the Civil War, and an ensemble of ballet dancers dressed in red, white and blue, performing bravura passages of classical technique.

What comes across in Mark Morris's *Somebody's Coming to See Me Tonight* (1995) "is sincerity and trust in honest lyrics and steps and choreography that is lyrical and true, gimmick-free."[53] Arlene Croce's comment about this piece is provocative: "When Morris makes a piece that shows how much music needs dance I am overjoyed.... In Morris's hands Foster is everything he is not by himself—original, charming, truly high-spirited, truly bardic, deeply evocative of his place and time.... The Foster ballet adds up—it leaves a residual impression, a feeling of objectivity, completion and unity."[54]

Thus while music is a mighty adjunct to dance, dance too can illuminate music. Balanchine's entire repertory illustrates this thesis. Although his methods are very different, Mark Morris has been hailed for a similar facility. Here is a review of his 1995 solo set to Mozart's *Rondo in A Minor*: "*Rondo* has a dreamy, doodling quality, but never strays far from the score. Morris lets different parts of his body articulate different aspects of the music, tracing the length and shape of a phrase or marking a rhythm with crisp steps. *Rondo* looks so simple only because it's so right."[55]

The conclusion seems to be that there are no hard and fast rules governing accompaniment. Only one thing is certain: A dance cannot be considered apart from its music, which has an effect on the audience that is as strong as, if not stronger than, the effect of the movement.

7

Designing
Artists

———

Imagery of a dance event is strongly affected by sets and costumes—the element of design. But the contribution of design is not a constant in a work. When confronted with a 1970 New York City Ballet production of *Firebird* that restored the Marc Chagall designs done for Ballet Theater in 1945, critic Robert Sealy was outraged. He vehemently declared that scenery and costumes are as transient as the performance of the dancers, as perishable as the viewer's ticket. "They are part of the production, not of the text. It is a disservice—indeed an insult—to our dancers" to tie them to famous past costumes and scenery that are impossible to restore.[1]

The relative importance of design in a dance event has changed radically through the years. We will discuss a few general thoughts on design practice in the first part of this chapter. In the second part we will take a survey of historical design. Finally, we will discuss highlights in scenery, lighting, and costumes during the last part of the twentieth century.

General Observations and Issues That Affect Design

How Stages Affect Dance

Scenery, lighting and costumes foretell an event, creating a crucial first impression, a context for a dance work. Different types of stages may also have noticeably different effects on a choreographed image. In 1946 when the British Royal Ballet moved from the Sadler's Wells Theater into the grander Royal Opera House at Covent Garden, the staff was dissatisfied with the way certain ballets looked and dropped them from the repertory. The ballets that did not survive the transfer were those whose drama and emotion were dissipated in a large space.[2]

Props

To make their imagery vivid, choreographers resort at times to symbolic props. The pineapple figures prominently in Santo Loquasto's set for Twyla Tharp's *The Catherine Wheel*, where it is first used traditionally as a symbol of hospitality; later, as personal relationships fly apart, the pineapple turns into a hand grenade and nuclear bomb. In David M. Chapman's design for *Rejoyce: A Pilobolus Finnegans Wake*, a balloon is picked out of the air to symbolize the moon fantasies of the characters. At the end of Balanchine's *Apollo*, the young deity and three muses climb a stairway, which symbolizes their ascent to the mountain home of the gods.

Lighting is used to affect tone and atmosphere. In fact, given the limitations on obstructive scenery, lighting is the most effective element in the dance designer's craft. It not only leaves the space free of threats to dancers, it can be changed as fast as dance movement. The degree of brightness and color both play their part. Emotionally, lighting provides tremendous range and subtlety. Appropriate diffuse lighting helps set the tone as gay, majestic or sombre. More obviously, lighting is used for visibility and highlighting specific characters and stage action. Raised or lowered lighting can also foreshadow a change in mood or emotion.

Costumes

The line of a costume has a visual influence on every dance movement shape. A costume may exist as a form in its own right, like the ballet tutu. Footwear is designed primarily for technique, as the pointshoe in ballet, the metal discs of tap dance, the sneaker in jazz. At every historical period, a search has been made for costuming that will please the viewer as well as reveal lines of the body in motion. Fashion plays a part as well as dance technique.

Cloaks have been used variously as costumes, as symbols, and as props in innumerable dances. Prince Albrecht in *Giselle* appears at the dead girl's graveside wearing a large cloak, which sets off his noble figure. But he also wields it as part of the action, to wrap himself defensively against the Wilis and to conceal his tears of mourning. In *Swan Lake*, the cruel magician Rothbart spreads his huge cape as though to spread his evil power over the scene. Many versions of *Dracula* have the fearsome count use a cloak to engulf an unsuspecting maiden, as a symbol of successful seduction.

In former periods, when dancers Marie Sallé, Isadora Duncan, or Ruth St. Denis wore diaphanous costumes or bared parts or all of the body, it was for an aesthetic effect, to enhance the imagery. Through the years, a number of serious dance artists have rediscovered nudity—the bare, unadorned body as a meaningful image in itself.

Nudity became an issue for choreographer Steve Paxton in 1970, when he planned to do *Satisfyin' Lover* at New York University. The piece was originally made in 1967 for a large group of people walking from stage right to stage left, stopping to stand or sit according to a written score. For the New York University concert date he planned a new version of the work, which was to include 42 naked red-haired performers, and notified the school of his intentions. At the last minute, the authorities ruled out the nudity. Now the issue was censorship. For the offending piece, Paxton substituted *Intravenous Lecture*. Ignoring the presence of a doctor who inserted an intravenous hookup in his arm, allowing the audience to see the medical procedure which sometimes caused blood to back up in the clear plastic tubing, Paxton talked about the problems of censorship. As Sally Banes wrote: "His performance made clear his conviction that censorship is more violent and more obscene than either the nudity would have been, or the medical attack actually was."[3]

When Mark Morris made *Striptease* in the 1980s, full frontal nudity was meant to shock, since this number was based on an essay by Roland Barthes, a postmodern French critic. Morris's dance embodied Barthes's statement: "Woman is desexualized at the very moment she is stripped naked. It is only the time taken in shedding clothes which makes voyeurs of the public." The tactic may have backfired, as critic Iris Fanger wrote: "Mark Morris's *Striptease* would be a shocker if frontal nudity were something new on the stage. But, ho-hum and alas, both dance and theater have been stripping since at least before World War I (and probably 3000 years before that)."[4]

Tradition and Spectacle

Ballet began in the Renaissance as an art of spectacle to which story, dancing and music were all subordinate. Both Raphael and Leonardo da Vinci were among the great artists whose costume designs and spectacular inventions contributed visual beauty and excitement to Renaissance festivals. Their scenes featured complicated machinery like floating clouds, rumbling chariots, flying harnesses, and larger-than-life animals, all involving platforms on wheels and rollers, hooks and pulleys, trap doors, and so forth. At that same period, theater architects introduced the use of permanent painted scenes, framed by solid arches and columns, and wings to accommodate surprising stage effects.

This emphasis on design continued through the seventeenth century, particularly under the reign of Louis XIV. Costumes were so elaborate that it was necessary to include manipulation of heavy fabrics as part of the courtiers' dance instruction. Performers were encased in gorgeous straitjackets of molded leather, metal cloth, heeled and laced high boots, masks, plumes, and gloves.[5] Once when he appeared as Apollo, Louis XIV wore fake violins on his arms and torso, and a large one as a hat. Gold and silver paint covered costumes, which also contained satin, egret feathers, precious stones, and huge animal likenesses.

Although the performers in these early court ballets were well taught and practiced their parts with great diligence, they were so burdened by costumes weighing up to 150 pounds that their movements were severely limited to simple steps—tracing symbols and patterns on the floor of the hall.

The closest thing to the Renaissance scenic contraptions that one is likely to see in contemporary productions is the Christmas tree in *The Nutcracker* that grows right before one's eyes. Renaissance and Baroque

spectacles are recalled today in ballets from the age of Petipa, set in palatial splendor. *The Sleeping Beauty*, with its vision of the world as fulfilling
an ideal of order and noble harmony, is an especially good example. Not
only is it based on a Mother Goose tale by Perrault, written during the reign
of Louis XIV, it demonstrates the similarity of outlook between the
courtiers of Louis XIV and those of the Russian tsar at the court of St.
Petersburg, which saw another high point of classical spectacle. In fact, in
the 1890 Petipa production, *The Sleeping Beauty* was set in a palace of Louis
XIV.

Romantic Era

The balletic image of a moonlit, misty forest possessed by spirit creatures and elusive, yearning dreams was created during the Romantic era in
France. The idea was conceived by producer Henri Duponchel and carried
out by painter Pierre Ciceri. The effective forest setting for lovesick melancholy created for *La Sylphide* and *Giselle* would not have been possible without the invention of the diorama. Louis Daguerre, a scene painter who is
best known for the early photographic print called the daguerreotype, developed the diorama, a method whereby breathtaking illusions are achieved by
projecting changing colored lights on partly translucent cloths.

Another innovation that designers of the Romantic period brought to
the stage was gaslight, which had recently been installed at the Paris opera
house. Before gaslight, stages were lit with torches, candles and oil lamps.
These were difficult to focus and localize, had to be raised or dimmed with
cumbersome metal shades, and frequently caused fires. Gaslight allowed
gradual variation in illumination without soiling the scenery.

As for costumes, the golden age of Romantic ballet gave us the full,
bell-shaped tutu that extends down to midcalf. In fact, Romantic ballets,
with their endless yards of white gauze drifting about the legs of ballerinas, are also called *ballets blancs* (white ballets) because of the popularity of
this costume. Later in the nineteenth century, the short tutu made its
appearance. To this day, for most laymen the tutu represents ballet. Designer
Rouben Ter-Arutunian wrote, "The tutu is still one of the most beautiful
and successful costumes ever devised."[6]

Early Modern Dance

We have already spoken about Isadora Duncan and Ruth St. Denis and
their use of costumes and props. In the last years of the nineteenth century
and the first decades of the twentieth, American-born Loie Fuller dazzled
audiences all over the world. Newspaper writers and poets raved about the

magical beauty of her work, beginning with her 1896 appearance in *Fire Dance*. The woman was a sensation through her revolutionary stagecraft. She had a heavy body and no expertise in dance technique. Her virtuosity actually consisted of undulating her body for the sole purpose of setting lighting and drapery in motion.[7]

Loie Fuller's rare artistry was that of an ingenious master technician: the manipulation of silken draperies, together with colored lights. By now gaslight had been replaced by limelight—originally produced by heating to incandescence lumps of lime (the grayish white solid derived from limestone)—and of course electricity. Fuller was intensely preoccupied with her technical inventions, which she kept secret. She used carbon arc lights and colored gelatins (made and combined with colors to her detailed specifications). She fitted large magic lanterns with slides of plain or frosted glass, which she painted with liquified gelatin. These were then projected (by her own trusted company electricians) in sequence and in combination on her own moving self, costumed in hundreds of yards of diaphanous silk. In this manner Fuller created mesmerizing visions of fire, fireflies, prisms, butterflies, a serpent, the sea, a moth, a lily, radium.

Diaghilev's Ballets Russes

Design was predominant in Sergei Diaghilev's Ballets Russes. Painter Léon Bakst's exotic treatment of Fokine's *Scheherazade* (1910), set in a sultan's court, precipitated a craze for orientalism in the fashion world of Paris and London. An emerald green curtain dominated a stage swirling with ornately patterned drapes, voluptuous cushions and lavish carpets, all in rich reds, blues and greens. The women of the harem, costumed in wild oranges and crimsons, added to the atmosphere of opulence, as did the hanging golden lamps and the perfumed wreaths of burning incense. The final coup was delivered by Nijinsky, darting about as the favorite slave, golden in flowing trousers, jeweled vest, careless turban and long earrings. The visual spectacle of *Scheherazade* made a lasting impression on the ballet world.[8]

Diaghilev delighted in presenting the work of the latest avant-garde artists, whose leader was Pablo Picasso. Picasso did the décor for *Parade* (1917). For the front curtain, he used a childlike representational style, depicting stage characters like a bullfighter, a harlequin and a sailor picnicking on a painted stage, and a sylphide figure on horseback. Behind this curtain he set a cubist street scene featuring characters in astonishing costumes that were towering constructions. One was an American "stage manager" who appeared as a robot. On his head was a hat that looked like a ship's funnel, complete with flags, and on his shoulders he bore tremendous cutouts of Manhattan skyscrapers. Completing the costume were a red-pleated shirt front and the cowboy leggings of Buffalo Bill, as well as a large megaphone that he carried. Another costume was that of a Paris show business manager wearing an eight-foot high construction of a dress suit, and a third manager rode on the old circus trick horse, made up of a performer at the head and a performer at the rear covered together by a horse costume. These managers introduced various acts of magic, acrobatics and hints of American movie scenes.

From then on, Ballets Russes productions were a running exhibition of new art movements like constructivism, cubism, surrealism, and social realism. To mention only a few examples: After *Parade*, Picasso did *Le Tricorn* (*The Three-Cornered Hat*, 1919). In 1944 Edwin Denby wrote that present standards for ballet decoration were set by Picasso, whose *Three-Cornered Hat* was still pictorially alive after twenty-five years.[9] In keeping with the folksy story located in Spain, Picasso designed scenery that was admirable for both its simplicity and the charm of its proportions. It was seen as a turning point in Picasso's work, helping him attain a synthesis between cubism and his concern for classical perspective. Before the dancers appeared, while the orchestra played a prelude, a gray drop-curtain picturing a group of spectators in a box watching a bullfight was displayed. (Originally, de Falla's music had no prelude, but he hastily wrote one at Diaghilev's request, to achieve a striking effect.) This curtain was raised to reveal a landscape of gleaming whitewashed village houses, a gorge, a wooden cage holding two birds, a well, a deep blue sky—all aglow in the burning sunlight. The set had the quality of a master's easel painting, and therefore the ability to stand up under steady scrutiny.[10]

Picasso also did *Pulcinella* (1920). Andre Derain designed Massine's *La Boutique Fantasque* (1919). Henri Matisse did Massine's *Song of the Nightingale* (1920). For a 1923 gala held to raise money to restore the palace of Versailles, Juan Gris built a stage for the Ballets Russes in the Hall of Mirrors. Picasso and Henri Laurens designed Nijinska's *Le Train Bleu* (1924), and Georges Roualt designed Balanchine's *The Prodigal Son* (1929).

In addition to overseeing every aspect of creation and performance of the Ballets Russes, Diaghilev personally took care of the lighting. He spent long nights with technicians working out detailed lighting plans before a ballet's premiere, and did the job all over again on tour in important towns where the stage equipment was different. Not only was he a master of the craft of shaping the stage with bright and dark areas, and of showing scenery and costumes to their best advantage, he created unique, beautiful effects that long remained in viewers' memories. One was a bitter cold light in *Petrouchka*, just before snow fell, and the second a moonlit moment in *Firebird* when the golden apples on the magic tree shimmered with an ethereal glow.[11]

It must be noted that the designs did not always work out from the choreographer's viewpoint. Fokine wrote that while he was happy with the production of *Firebird*, there were numerous shortcomings from the start. According to his original plan, after the monster Kostchei was destroyed in his evil-looking kingdom, there should have been a change of scenic colors to cheerful lighting, more in keeping with the happy choreographed ending. But designer Golovine made no such accommodation, and so the lively action and the gloomy set worked at cross purposes for the finale.[12]

In 1926, Diaghilev had *Firebird* redesigned by Gontcharova, after the Golovine scenery had been destroyed by dampness. By that date, because of personal conflicts, Fokine and Diaghilev were outright enemies, and the choreographer was not consulted. Fokine complained bitterly in his memoirs that the design changes made the dance plot meaningless. For example, when the princesses did the dance of their long tresses, Fokine reported: "All the movements remained the way I staged them in the original production. They threw their long hair back, loosened their braids, ran their fingers through their hair. The only thing missing was the hair—all the princesses had short bobs!"[13]

The Bauhaus School (1920s)

Contemporaneous with Diaghilev, Oskar Schlemmer, too, sought to create a kind of total theater. Schlemmer's interest, as part of the Bauhaus School which featured names like Kandinsky and Klee in painting and Gropius in architecture, was the interplay of abstract colored forms, in motion through space. He was as fascinated by oversize puppets as he was by human dancers, whom he encased in stiff, weighty constructions, and whose limbs he sometimes extended with long sticks. He created a number of dances featuring technical materials as indicated by the titles: *Metal Dance, Glass Dance, Hoop Dance*. For accompaniment, Schlemmer used whirring sounds, thumps, animal noises and unusual scores by composers like Hindemith.

In *The Triadic Ballet*, Schlemmer's most famous work, staged in 1922, two males and one female were the human engines for propelling eighteen costumes around the stage. The first section, framed by curtains of lemon yellow, was in a burlesque scherzo mood; the second was a solemn but festive pink; the third was monumentally heroic, draped in an atmosphere of mystical black. The female's clothing was always based on the ballerina tutu silhouette of flared wire at times fashioned from spheres, or layered circles, or triangular fans. The men appeared in robotlike cubes or cone shapes. Grotesque masks were worn, and figures were topped by coverings that were not so much hats as constructions that totally enclosed the head in an abstract form. Costume materials were padded cloth or stiff, painted papier-mâché, sometimes coated with metallic paint, or wire spirals. The figures conveyed various moods as they paced, trotted, stopped abruptly, turned grandly and otherwise moved along geometrical paths: straight lines, diagonals, circles. Like the costumes for Baroque spectacles, Schlemmer's were so heavy that performers became terribly tired just from trying to maneuver them.

Although Oskar Schlemmer is today only a footnote to dance design, *The Triadic Ballet* was restored and filmed under the supervision of Schlemmer's widow in the late 1960s and was staged in 1977 as part of the New York City Museum of Modern Art exhibition on geometric abstractions. In 1986, Schlemmer's *The Triadic Ballet* was shown in a New York theater, and it was still able to startle its viewers.[14]

Design Trends Since the 1950s

Ballet Classics

In the spring of 1987, Kenneth MacMillan produced *The Sleeping Beauty* for American Ballet Theater. Nicholas Georgiadis created wonderfully imaginative costumes. Colors for the fairies reminded one reviewer of marbled paper. For the evil Carabosse, the costume was a throwback to Queen Elizabeth, with a hideous, glistening scaly texture. Geordiadis's sets relied on hanging things: angels, lamps, drapes that when the palace fell into ruins literally fell on courtiers, "turning them into Halloween ghosts."[15] Vines covered the sleeping castle like green spaghetti. Not only did the sets achieve an airy, dreamlike effect, they also had the practical advantage of being easily packed for touring.

In addition to many luxurious productions of *The Sleeping Beauty* in the repertory of various companies, a number of other ballets follow the tradition of spectacular palace settings. These include *Swan Lake*, *Cinderella*, *Raymonda*, and *Don Quixote*.

Esteban Francés designed hundreds of costumes for Balanchine's *Don Quixote* (1965), to create "a sumptuous spectacle, the handsomest in international repertory."[16] There were elegantly stiff outfits of black and gold for the nobility at the court of a sixteenth century Spanish duke. There were flowing, Grecian-style tunics for the female figures in a dream scene, and gaily colored flounces on the skirts of gypsy dancers. There were goblins in grotesque masks to plague the puny Don Quixote, and a steely suit of armor for a giant (thirty-foot high) knight who cut him down. The style of the Francés costumes harked back to the Renaissance spectacles mentioned

The title character in Balanchine's *Don Quixote* is rescued in front of windmills designed by Esteban Frances. Photograph by Martha Swope, © Time Inc.

above, although the originals were a hundred times more elaborate. Of course while the Esteban Francés costume designs were less lavish, as executed by Madame Karinska they allowed the dancers complete freedom of movement.

The setting is an important part of the updating of ballet classics. Consider Rudolf Nureyev's 1987 production of *Cinderella* for the Paris Opéra Ballet. He departed completely from the time-honored approach to the familiar fairy tale, transposing it into a fantasy of Hollywood stardom. The scenario gave Romanian designer Petrika Ionesco plenty of opportunity to use his impressive imagination. The work opened in a glass-cold structure that could be a railway station, with the two stepsisters leaving for Los Angeles to compete for a screen test. The action switched to a Hollywood landscape dominated by three proscenium-high cutouts of movie star Betty Grable in a bathing suit and high heels. Cinderella's pumpkin inflated into a Cadillac. The second act took place on a "soundstage" where scenes referred playfully to favorite movie themes like the French Foreign Legion, Keystone cops, Tahitians in grass skirts, a huge King Kong, and American Indians. The Japanese *haute couturière* Hanae Mori had wide scope to show off with her more than 150 extravagant costumes, beginning with Cinderella's fairy godmother, who entered as a motorist in leather jacket and goggles and turned out to be a producer.[17]

Or take *Coppélia*, which presents a lighthearted village tale of Franz, mooning over the unattainable Coppélia who sits all day at the window, immersed in her private world. The lad doesn't know that Coppélia is a doll, created by the old wizard Dr. Coppélius. Fortunately the spirited Swanilda sets about exposing her wooden rival and wins Franz for herself.

Maguy Marin mounted a revolutionary production of *Coppélia* in 1993 in Lyons, France. Marin's updated version changed Dr. Coppélius from an ingenious toymaker to a filmmaker. Renaud Gaulot's décor placed apartment blocks of a suburban housing development on each side of the stage, flanking a large area where film was projected. The folksy villagers were now members of rival gangs who danced roughly in the street, while Dr. Coppélius spent his time in a studio, photographing the model doll Coppélia, who wore a sexy red suit and a peroxide-blonde wig, the work of costumer Montserrat Casanova. Coppélia danced both onstage and in larger-than-life filmed images. At the climax of the work, two dozen "live" Coppélia dolls invaded the studio to dance and flirt with Franz, who was watching the films with old Dr. Coppélius. Swanilda, the village heroine, arrived in time to destroy the illusions of the multiple dolls, half of whom were danced by men. In cases like these, designing artists may be as important as choreographers and composers.[18]

Balanchine

A 1993 celebration of George Balanchine's repertory, showed how the master had moved increasingly towards abstraction not only in his choreography, but also in décor. In works like *Apollo* (1928), *Concerto Barocco* (1940) and *Four Temperaments* (1946) that were originally set and costumed lavishly, Balanchine gradually omitted the backdrops and replaced the costumes with black tights and white T-shirts for the men, and simple, short tunics for the women. By the time he did *Agon* (1958), he had the women as well as the men dancing in tights. His ballets in the grand classical manner also got a new look, aided by his longtime collaboration with Barbara Karinska. In 1950, for *Symphony in C*, they developed the "powder puff" tutu, which did away with hoops. The new tutu was constructed with multiple layers of gathered net "that fell in a natural slope to the tops of the thighs, revealing the full line of the leg. Waists were dropped or cut in a diagonal.... The result was softer, lighter and more flattering."[19]

On the other hand, Balanchine mounted a number of spectacular story ballets: *The Nutcracker* (1954) with sets by Horace Armistead, costumes by Karinska; *A Midsummer Night's Dream* (1962) with scenery by David Hays and costumes by Karinska; and *Don Quixote*, as described above. As late as 1980 Balanchine used a romantically elaborate design by Rouben Ter-Arutunian for Robert Schumann's "*DavidsbÜndlertänze.*"

Graham

We noted earlier that Martha Graham's work relies heavily on symbolism. Her stage becomes a landscape of memory and emotion. She commissioned décor from a host of designers, notably Isamu Noguchi. Noguchi always included movable pieces that became part of the action, adding symbolic and visual interest. For *Appalachian Spring* (1944), he designed a stripped-down pioneer landscape for a bride and groom, allowing all properties to be used in the action: the farmer gazing over a section of fence rail; the bride exploring an entrance and one wall of a clapboard house; a revivalist preacher using a tree stump as a pulpit; an older pioneer woman calmly nodding her acceptance on a rocking chair. For *Clytemnestra* (1958), Noguchi provided large crossed spears which at one moment became a platform to transport a triumphant warrior, and later a litter to carry a corpse.

From 1944 on, Graham's lighting was done by Jean Rosenthal, who was a genius at enhancing the choreography by the constant shifting of colors, intensities and areas of light. As insane jealousy possessed the Medea figure in *Cave of the Heart*, Rosenthal unforgettably bathed the stage in blood

The malevolent sorceress in Martha Graham's *Cave of the Heart*. Photograph by Martha Swope, © Time Inc.

red. For *Herodiade*, a duet for two women based on a Mallarmé poem in which the title character confronts her past and her future in a mirror, Rosenthal had the curtain rise on a black stage. For a full minute, Hindemith's music accompanied only the movement of light as it revealed different areas of the stage, which seemed to be waiting for events to happen. After the mood was set, the Herodiade figure entered.

Martha Graham wields props designed by Isamu Noguchi for *Clytemnestra*. Photograph by Martha Swope, © Time Inc.

Jean Rosenthal described the way she used patterns of light to produce different emotional values. She found that long diagonal shafts of side light-ing created an impression of moonlight or sunlight, suggesting a feeling of aspiration. Low horizontal patterns seemed to create a mood of earthbound mystery. Long shafts of light projected directly down onto the stage gave an impression of depth, as if the dancer were moving in planes beyond the realistic plane of the stage level.[20]

In 1974, Graham commissioned the Dani Karavan to do a set for

Dream, her version of Jacob's ladder. Karavan designed a ladder that extended up and out of sight, on which near-nude angels could entwine and climb, and which Jacob mounted at the end with his angel of destiny, as a sign of ascent to God's grace. He also supplied a doorlike structure to open, close, and frame a pagan goddess, symbol of what the Israelites must finally reject.

In her heyday, Graham herself designed the costumes. Rouben Ter-Arutunian, himself a noted designer, wrote: "Martha Graham has found an ingenious way of costuming her girls. The kind of skirt/harem-pants idea she has devised for them is so simple and so intelligent and so useful. The covered part of the body becomes almost more visible. It is like a veil that reveals and accentuates the legs."[21]

Gradually, Graham's costumes became more complex and dramatically symbolic. In *Cave of the Heart*, Medea first pulled out of her mouth a long red ribbon, a symbol of her burning jealousy, and then she placed a poisoned cape on her young rival and watched her writhing death agony. As Clytemnestra she welcomed Agamemnon home with a cape twenty feet long and five feet wide. In the course of the action, the cloak turned into curtains, which Clytemnestra parted to reveal her murder victims, and then into drapery for the victims' funeral cart. Queen Clytemnestra herself donned an enormous red cloak to conceal the murder of her unfaithful king. In *A Time of Snow* (1968), the old, cold Heloise tried to warm herself in a cloak, as she recalls the love for Abelard felt by her youthful self. Again in *Dream* there was a cloak which Jacob's mother removed from his body, to unite it with the angels' totem of Israel.

Other Choreographers and Designers of the Twentieth Century

Doris Humphrey devised a group of blocks and platforms of different sizes (influenced by the abstract sets of Gordon Craig) which she used in many dances for both spatial dynamism and dramatic excitement. For *Story of Mankind* (composed for José Limón in 1946), she had Michael Czaja design an ingenious box to be used in a circular history of man from the primitive cave to a cave in the atomic age: "In the Greek scene it was a couch; in the medieval scene it looked like a banquet table; in the brownstone age with the addition of some small benches, it somehow seemed like a small parlor; and finally, in the end, Limón lifted the box, with his partner on it, to a vertical position and it became a penthouse with a terrace."[22]

From then on, modern dance continued Humphrey's tradition of spare, abstract sets that emphasized massed volumes, broken areas and varying

horizontal levels. A 1993 production that also used a setting as part of the choreography was Kathryn Posin's *Stepping Stones* for the Milwaukee Ballet, about the steps women must take to gain power and recognition. The point made in the title was graphically present in Carol Vollet Kingston's set: Spaced diagonally across the stage were six small platforms, each a step higher than the one before it. On each platform, equipped with rails that symbolize banisters, barres and barriers, a female dancer struggled up to the next level.

Reminiscent of Oskar Schlemmer was Alwin Nikolais, a wizard who used every technical device around and developed some of his own. His works were multimedia images. Costumes, on which he painted designs, altered or blurred body lines. Light patterns projected by slides further transformed the appearance of bodies and backdrops. Dance figures changed color when they stepped from one area to another, and lost their identity behind the masks, helmets, tubes, and yards of fluid material that covered them.

In *Imago* (1963) Nikolais organized each section around a theme. "Mantis" extended the arms with bonelike appendages and explored slow, sinuous patterns. "Fence" broke the stage space with parallel elastic lines along which the figures draped themselves. "Boulevard" sent a crowd of figures in ballooning fabrics careening about.

In the final scene of *Somniloquy* (1967) the dancers moved through a projection of white dots like a snowstorm, freezing in place as the projection went out of focus and moving again as it cleared. Finally the bodies disappeared and the snowstorm was left in possession of the stage. *Cross Fade* (1974) drenched the dancers and curtains with gorgeous red, yellow and green spirals. *Persons and Structures* (1984) had human figures in nude-colored tights forming geometrical angles, balanced against other figures who were posed on different levels in a cubed structure.

These fantastic mixed media scenes might demand 200 light cues within a half hour. Nikolais was fully involved in every performance, pushing buttons at the controls of his sophisticated equipment. He also created the electronic scores that accompanied his visions.

We saw in the previous chapter that John Cage, the dominant influence on Cunningham in accompaniment, was also a leading figure in the world of avant-garde music. In the same way two prominent avant-garde painters, Robert Rauschenberg and Jasper Johns, were closely involved with Cunningham's work. From 1954 to 1964, Rauschenberg designed décor and costumes for the company stage manager. His most famous design was a

OPPOSITE: Rauschenberg designed the décor for Merce Cunningham's *Summerspace*. Photograph by Martha Swope, © Time Inc.

pointillist backdrop for *Summerspace*. For the costumes, he had leotards and tights similarly painted with dots, creating a startling merge effect.

Rauschenberg's décor and lighting for *Winterbranch* (1964) assaulted the audience. Brilliant lights flashed on and off at irregular intervals, sometimes turned right into the eyes of the spectators. This was in response to Cunningham's asking him to think of light at night: "I don't mean night as referred to in romantic pieces, but night as it is in our time with automobiles on highways, and flashlights in faces, and the eyes being deceived about shapes by the way light hits them."[23]

In 1967 Jasper Johns became artistic advisor for Cunningham. He worked true to his minimalist philosophy of not placing objects to interfere with what was happening on the stage during a dance.[24] The major exception was *Walkaround Time*, for which he designed a setting based on *The Large Glass*, an avant-garde concept that Marcel Duchamp worked on in the 1920s. Johns had Andy Warhol design Cunningham's *Rainforest* (1968). Warhol created clusters of inflated silver pillow shapes, some of which were tossed casually around the floor. Others were helium filled so that they would float in the air.

Trisha Brown is a dancer whose ideas were formed during that period. In a 1993 retrospective of her work, she presented *Glacial Decoy*, with a scene design by Rauschenberg. Black and white photographs of mundane scenes, with a dull black and matte white surface, were projected onto some panels. A "deeply satisfying textural interplay" was created by the live dancing figures wearing capacious white dresses against the comparative dullness of the photos—an effect of brilliant white light coming from the dancers' bodies.[25]

In October 1966, Rauschenberg participated in what was "probably the most elaborate and expensive presentation of avant-garde performances ever attempted in this country."[26] *Nine Evenings: Theater and Engineering* took place at an armory on Twenty-fifth Street in New York City. To the armory series, Rauschenberg contributed *Open Score*, in which 300 people were directed to make simple gestures in complete darkness while infrared television cameras photographed them and projected their images on three large screens. The accompaniment was a tape recording on which one person after another said "My name is—" giving their names.[27]

Jennifer Tipton is a leading dance lighter of Twyla Tharp, Jerome Robbins, Eliot Feld, American Ballet Theater, Joffrey Ballet and the Limón Company. She says her work is all about "making beautiful dance beautiful.... In essence I compose the picture, carving the air—the space—away from solid things, leaving only the dancers or actors."[28]

Tipton has worked with experimental dancers like Dana Reitz and Sara Rudner. The three created *Necessary Weather* (1994), featuring two

women in white doing pure movement patterns, in relation to a third partner: pools of light. An unexpectedly emotional atmosphere resulted from
changes in the light's color, intensity and shape—the way the changing
weather affects us.[29]

In 1995, collaboration between Tipton and Reitz produced *Unspoken
Territory*, a solo for Mikhail Baryshnikov performed in silence. "There is a
sense of urgency about the work, suggesting that Mr. Baryshnikov was
making an expedition through a wilderness of light and darkness.... Like
a moth drawn to a flame, he looked as if he was simultaneously lured by
and wary of the patches of light that kept brightening and vanishing.... A
cascade of light poured down upon his head in a moment of heroic glory.
The triumph was short-lived, for darkness descended."[30]

For Taylor's *Spindrift* (1993), about a man awash in the memories of
his life, Santo Loquasto created a garish, spectacular seaside scene, with
swirling clouds, boardwalk and beach umbrella. The painted backdrop
responded to a remarkable lighting pattern that made parts of the scene fade
in and out of sight, and the clouds change from orange sunset to indigo
storm—synchronizing with moods of the dance. Loquasto said his goal in
designing is appropriateness. "You try to find a visual line comparable to
the emotional line the dancers portray."[31]

To sum up: Dance is a theater art, and the elements of sets, costumes
and lighting all play their part. As we have seen, however, design is not tied
to the essence of a work as are choreography and music. Rather it changes
according to state-of-the art technologies and the dictates of fashion.

8

Gods and Goddesses: Performers on Stage

A dancer in full flight recalls the mythical powers of Olympian gods and goddesses. He or she appears before us as a human ideal who embodies vigor, eternal youth, strength, freedom, and beauty.

This ideal is hard to pin down, since it differs according to dance style and is further complicated by the dualism of being both a passive instrument of company and choreographer, and an active interpretive artist. While there are similar problems with the role of the performing musician or actor, the dancer's case is extreme. Nothing objective is interposed between performer and audience the way a violin is in music, or speech is in drama. The "tones," "melodies" and "words" of movement are not only interpreted by the dancer, they are fashioned from her or his own body. The dancer is the instrument, producing movements that are intimately bound up with the kind of instrument she or he is.

In this chapter we will look at selection and training of dancers, interpretive artistry, Nureyev and male dancing, outstanding stars of the 1990s, partnerships, and stages of a dancer's life.

Selection and Training of Dancers

A few youngsters from an early age want, more than anything in the world, to dance. Others aspire to the adjoining arts of music or acting, from which they slip into dance. Some are implanted with an unforgettable image of a particular dancer. As she toured the world, Anna Pavlova did this for Agnes de Mille and Frederick Ashton, along with countless other children. Ruth St. Denis had a similar effect on Martha Graham and Doris Humphrey. And who knows how many unsung teachers in the small private dance schools that are found everywhere (running the gamut from excellent to terrible), have inspired their pupils to enter the field?

A strong, focused drive among children is rare. Moira Shearer, delightful star of *The Red Shoes* (the original movie, 1948), scoffed at those who said they saw Pavlova when they were five, and knew from that moment they wanted to dance. "At five years old, what do you know about what you're going to do? It's crazy." She admitted however that when kids like her fall—or are pushed—into a class, a spark may be ignited. Ballet lessons were the idea of Shearer's mother. At first Moira disliked the daily grind of disciplined labor to which would-be dancers are condemned. Then pleasure arrived through the classes of Nicolai Legat, who arranged the routine exercises into dance-like sequences of steps. With Shearer's mastery of technical difficulties came motivation.[1]

Five-year-old Anthony Dowell, who rose to be the director of the British Royal Ballet, was also enrolled in a ballet school by a mother who loved dancing. He took to it immediately. Judith Jamison, brilliant Alvin Ailey dancer and later head of his company, was sent to ballet school by her mother to preserve her own sanity against a high-spirited daughter. From the start, six-year-old Jamison was not only fascinated with dance, she showed a natural ability in any movement style.

Physical structure is as important in the equipment of the future dancer as it is for the athlete or gymnast. Anatomy is the first consideration in selecting dance students. Needless to say, perfect anatomy is an idle dream. As far back as the eighteenth century, Noverre observed that most dancers' bodies reveal one of two principal faults: they are either knock-kneed (with short muscles and long tendons) or bow-legged (with long muscles and short tendons). However, good training can turn these defects into assets, allowing the former type to attain speed and elevation; and the latter, flowing lyrical motion.

Whatever the pre-set anatomy, a dancer usually reveals the inborn coordination and facility that we call grace. Other personal characteristics, although they may be as important to the dancer's success as the physical ones, are harder to identify. Innate emotional make-up, mental quickness, musicality and interpretive sensitivity are all significant. Hardest to recognize at an unformed stage, but most important, is the capacity for sustained, persistent effort.

A talented dancer with a strong drive, can overcome anatomical limitations. Judith Jamison's back is not very supple, but she learned to use her strong middle and long thighs to give an impression of flexibility. "Part of the magic of dance is that it can be illusory," she said.[2] Edward Villella agreed. Audiences were always surprised at how short he was in person— not only because the stage enlarges all performers, but because Villella understood how to lift up and out, to project classical stature. Movement can even be used to deceive about weight. Gelsey Kirkland said she can make herself appear heavy or light, "adding or losing pounds" by changing posture and accents.[3]

The first criterion of selection for the Royal Danish Ballet School (in the early 1950s, when Peter Martins auditioned) was a small foot with a big arch and a big instep. Teachers looked for a pleasing, well-proportioned appearance, as well as grace, musicality, intelligence and demeanor. Eight-year-old Martins was accepted despite his large feet and insolent manner. Talent worked strongly in his favor, as did a shortage of boys.

It has always been the goal of companies to have their own school. In this way, they are assured of a continuing source of new talent. This is obviously necessary in a modern dance company, which grows and develops in synchronization with the unique creativity of the founder.

However, it is also true that although the classical ballet technique taught anywhere in the world has the same roots, it has different branches shaped by various artists like Auguste Bournonville, Fokine and Balanchine. Each company tends to develop its own technical standards and its own style, which comes down to the neat precision of the British Royal Ballet, or the bounding élan of the Royal Danish, or the dramatic flamboyance of the Bolshoi.

A wider, more comprehensive approach to techniques, is found at colleges and a few specialized secondary schools. Putting professional dance training into public education has proved to be highly successful, at least in the case of New York City's High School for Performing Arts. Opened in 1948, the school was the catalyst for a number of young men choosing dance careers. Bruce Marks (currently director of the Boston Ballet Company) auditioned for the school without really knowing why. He started out performing in modern dance, and went from there into ballet. Miguel Goudreau, a self-described "hillbilly from Puerto Rico," applied to enter the school as an accomplished violinist. Enchanted by the dance classes, the talented performer switched allegiance and after graduation moved from spots on Broadway to a triumphant career with Alvin Ailey. William Louther's interest in acting led him to the school, where halfway through his freshman year he altered his course to dance. Louther has been a commanding presence in the companies of Martha Graham, Alvin Ailey, and Donald MacKayle.

"Schooling" is a cold word for what the dancer often receives from a man or woman who is totally dedicated to passing along a lifetime of knowledge and experience. Good teachers are a prize beyond price. Once Peter Martins got into the Royal Danish Ballet school, luck kept him there—in the person of a great teacher. Stanley Williams was known not only for teaching technical skills, but also for the sympathy and understanding he showed his students. After years of helping hundreds of Danes to master their craft, Stanley Williams joined the staff of Balanchine's School of American Ballet. There he left his mark on many, including Edward Villella, *the* male ballet star of the United States in the 1960s. Another great teacher was Alexander Pushkin at the Kirov. Both Nureyev and Baryshnikov credited Pushkin's classes for their own understanding of how to perform with classical artistry.

How to perform with a company is another lesson altogether. For many dancers it is a shock to discover that acceptance into a company is not the "be all and end all" of their dreams, but only the beginning of a new set of difficult situations. They are now confronted with personalities in the art world, notorious for high-handed, unconventional behavior.

Sad tales are told at all the world's major ballet companies, where students and lowly corps members wait in vain to be tapped for solo parts. Some remain dependable foot soldiers in the ranks. Some, facing the truth that they will never soar, resign the field to join the rest of us in our mundane daily rounds. A fortunate few rise to the top. Others achieve a degree of fame but, never finding exactly the right spot, move around from place to place.

Sylvie Guillem received her early training in gymnastics and at the Paris Opéra Ballet, which she joined. A young corps member, she was promoted to a principal soloist when Rudolf Nureyev became the company's revolutionary artistic director. She had the lead in *Swan Lake* and in Nureyev's modernistic *Cinderella* (described in the previous chapter). Reviewers found her to be a dancer of tremendous skill, bordering on the acrobatic, with an impressive performing manner of verve and flexibility. In 1988, partnered by Nureyev, she danced the lead in a British Royal Ballet production of *Giselle* before ecstatic audiences, who had never seen such vitality in their staid old company. Sometime later, Sylvie Guillem became a permanent guest artist with the Royal Ballet. However, because she did not heed directions and insisted on doing their repertory in her own way, she offended the Royal Ballet's conservative management, and lost the "permanence" of her guest status.[4]

Modern dancers have by no means been free of such problems. Paul Taylor spent some time in Merce Cunningham's company. For a piece called *Dime a Dance*, everybody had to rehearse all the parts. Only after the curtain went up did they know who was to do what, by picking papers from a basket. Since Taylor's symbol was never drawn, he didn't get to perform. When the disappointed dancer confronted the "chance" choreographer, Cunningham said that his company was not the place for someone who disapproved of his methods. Taylor, who didn't lack other job opportunities, resigned, but with misgivings.[5]

Interpretive Artistry

Once in a company, for the dancer in the ranks, there is very little freedom. Ensemble dancing is carefully planned and dictated in minute detail, so that each member of the group conforms to the wishes of the rehearsal director (or of the choreographer, if it is a new piece). No matter how talented the individual, it is more disturbing than helpful when she or he stands out in a supposedly unison passage. This is not because precise military drill is a major goal in dance, but because the unison passage often has a deliberately anonymous, if not an abstract function in even the most literal choreography, and a dancer who calls attention to herself or himself breaks up the atmosphere. It is as if a single violinist lingered in a romantic ritard while the other violinists were briskly sawing away. Hardly permissible! Peter Martins was never a good corps dancer; he was always out of step and bumping into the other boys, worrying about whether he was doing the steps precisely like them. Fortunately, in recognition of his extraordinary ability, he was soon given solo roles.[6]

The soloist, whether in a brief entrance or a lead role, is no longer merely an instrument. She or he is also a player of the instrument—an interpretive artist. Today, the great majority of performers, whether soloists or corps members, exhibit a technical command that was the property only of the stars of previous generations. Thus it is a given that a soloist can execute the movements, steps and positions of a role accurately. Interpretation communicates the artistic qualities of a part. It involves timing, attack, musicality and emotion, and is the true test of a good dancer.

There are two schools of thought concerning dance interpretation. One school holds that motivation is the key. Erik Bruhn, a brilliant classical dancer, known for his powerful interpretations, wrote that we have forgotten that these steps came in the first place, to express reality. To dance a role properly, even in abstract ballets, one must search for meaning in a character, and then adjust the muscles to the idea.[7] The other school holds that the dancer must focus on the movements and the music, and the rest will take care of itself. Balanchine, the leading exponent of this school, never spoke about feelings or character. He would tell his dancers, "Don't act!" Or he might say something like, "Present yourself. Present your feet."[8] Which school holds sway in a particular performance depends partly on choreographic and directorial decisions, and partly on the temperamental qualities of individual dancers. A soloist learns a role while it is being choreographed, or from someone who used to dance it. Inexperienced soloists copy their interpretations from veteran coaches. Later, they find their own way.

Ballet principals continue to be judged primarily by their performances in *Swan Lake*, *The Sleeping Beauty*, and *Giselle*, as well as in works like *Romeo and Juliet* and *Manon*. Natalia Makarova remembers that her teenage approach to the swan maiden Odette in *Swan Lake* was that of a twittery, birdlike maiden. Later, she did the part as an emotional human female. Finally she developed the aspect of an enchanted bird-maiden, whose human love can only end in failure. In a B.B.C. broadcast Makarova, now a mature artist, coaches Raffaella Renzi, a novice Odette, in her first encounter with the huntsman prince: "Seek him. You are frightened... Keep your eyes on him, maybe he shoot you... Don't forget to use neck... What do you want to say here?... [The prince has captured Odette in his arms.] You want to fly and you can't... Don't dance abruptly, connect..."[9]

Partnerships

Partnering skills are very important, since the *pas de deux* is often the high point of a ballet. The female needs a sure and reliable partner. The male must know exactly whether she is on or off balance for a particular performance, whether she requires a firm support or a light one. The male dancer must learn not only the various forms of supporting—the holding of the hand, the wrist, the arms and the waist—but also how to walk with a noble demeanor, and even how to stand still. While there are different ways to lift the ballerina, there is only one way to place her back down on the floor: lightly. It not only destroys all illusion, it is certainly most uncomfortable for the ballerina if she is let down with a heavy thump. Most important of all, the cavalier must concentrate on the ballerina. As Anton Dolin, who formed a great partnership with Alicia Markova, pointed out, "Nothing looks worse than to see the male dancer looking everywhere else but at his partner."[10] All these principles apply whether the ballet is classical or modern, regardless of the intricacy of the lifts and turns and the female's positions. Exceptions occur only when the choreographer intends the effort to be shown for a comic or emotional effect.

Fine partnerships are found in any decent ballet company, like Patricia McBride and Edward Villella, or Suzanne Farrell and Peter Martins at the New York City Ballet (in the 1960s and 1970s). But the most exciting, popular "team" of their day—perhaps the greatest partnership of the twentieth century—was formed by Rudolf Nureyev and the British Royal Ballet's Margot Fonteyn, although she was almost twenty years his senior.

Each one alone was a charismatic dancer. Reviewers and audiences cherished Fonteyn. They regarded her physical proportions as perfect, and they raved about her beauty, her musical phrasing, her fresh simplicity, her magical sparkle.

As for Rudolf Nureyev, the year he was twenty, he caught the attention of the Russian ballet world with a splendid performance at his Kirov Academy graduation. During the next few years he built up an adoring public as a leading dancer in the Kirov Company. But at the same time, his refusal to follow the rules of the secret police made him many enemies in the bureaucracy.

When Nureyev's friends told him that after his 1961 appearance with the company in Paris he would not be allowed to leave the Soviet Union, he decided to defect. His bold actions in eluding the Russian secret police made headlines all over the free world. The affair thrilled Western ballet audiences, and they came in droves to see him. In short order, however, his performances and personality became the attractions. His technique was not perfect in the clean, noble manner of Erik Bruhn's, but he thrust himself

into the air with such daring, and he projected such a full-out, almost demonic determination, that no one cared. His was a uniquely dramatic demeanor never before associated with traditional classics.

One explanation for the unprecedented success of the Fonteyn-Nureyev partnership was the contrast between Fonteyn's innately gracious English reserve, and Nureyev's Russian sensuality and fearlessness. The other was the warm personal relationship that infused their dancing and radiated from the stage.

Nureyev and Male Dancing

After Fonteyn retired, the Royal Ballet refused to tolerate Nureyev's rebellious arrogance any longer. Although the company's attitude embittered the superstar, it did not stop him from continuing to dance around the world, to enthusiastic audiences. (Note the similarities between Nureyev's situation and that of Sylvie Guillem.)

When he died in 1992, Nureyev left a legacy of improved male dancing. Before Nureyev, George Balanchine's attitude, "Ballet is woman," predominated. The superstar's message to fellow dancers was to fight back. He taught the freedom and power of letting go, and he prepared audiences to appreciate the male in his own right. After Nureyev, the male dancer took center stage no longer merely to support the ballerina, but as her equal.

From the Romantic era to Nureyev's day, women had always outjumped men because they had learned to extend their legs fully in flight. Women had also developed more flair in pirouettes and more elegance in poses. Nureyev carved a space for superior male dancers. Today, men's jumps, leaps, and turns are unbeatable—and in stage value, they often eclipse the women.

Outstanding Stars of the 1990s

It is hard to pick out the great stars of one's day, because it is impossible to predict who will grow and endure. Stars emerge rapidly, but some fall quickly out of sight, while others take on more brilliance with the passage of time. Out of dozens of companies and hundreds of stars worldwide, our focus will be narrowed to one ballet company and one modern dance group: The American Ballet Theater and the Paul Taylor Dance Company, respectively.

OPPOSITE: Nureyev personified the glories of the male animal in Nijinksy's *Afternoon of a Faun*. Photograph by Martha Swope, © Time Inc.

Like every company, the American Ballet Theater has had its ups and downs. In 1992, when Kevin McKenzie, himself a company *premier danseur*, was named director, American Ballet Theater was in a bad way: flat broke (a deficit of almost six million dollars) and completely demoralized. The reasons were partly economic recession and partly problems with previous management, which had converted from a system of importing stars like Baryshnikov and Makarova and guest visits from Nureyev, Fracci and Erik Bruhn to internal promotions from corps to soloist to principal. Although this new policy had created fine dancers like Amanda McKerrow, the house was full only for Julio Bocca, Alessandra Ferri and Nina Ananiashvili, whose Bolshoi bravura is so uplifting. McKenzie combined the two policies: He made full use of internal talent and at the same time hired gifted soloists like José Manuel Carreño and Angel Corella, both of whom combine fabulous technical brio with enormous charm.

Heading the list at Ballet Theater is Julio Bocca, a man who ranks with (or above) any contemporary performer. Reviews speak constantly of his soaring leaps, of how he sits in the air, of his whizzing, razor-sharp turns, of his exciting mime, which ranges from hot-blooded to witty to gallant. His partnership with Alessandra Ferri has been mentioned as the closest we have come so far to the Nureyev-Fonteyn ideal, although the brilliantly talented Ferri, of a passionately tempestuous disposition, is totally unlike Fonteyn. Ferri spoke of her rapport with Bocca: "Between us there is perfect understanding.... We rehearse very little.... The rest comes on stage. You can say we improvise with each show."[11] Their *Giselle* has been hailed as superb.

Bocca is a national hero in his Argentinean homeland, where he rose from miserable poverty to stardom. Although he guest dances all over the world, closest to his heart is Ballet Argentino, a troupe of finely trained young dancers whose goal is to showcase Argentine subjects, music and choreography. When Bocca appears with the company, he boosts their stock even though he deliberately plays himself down to avoid outshining the youngsters.

It is a pleasure for reviewers and other members of the audience that Ballet Theater boasts more than one cast able to satisfy the demands of a classical ballet. One enjoys seeing how each artist endows a role with a different quality. Bocca gives an interpretation of Basil that is both grand and unassuming in McKenzie's staging of *Don Quixote*, a fine contrast to Nina Ananiashvili's sweetly childlike Kitri. The accent on youth is represented by Paloma Herrera (born in 1975) and Angel Corella (born a year later), both technically fabulous, who project an innocent exhilaration as the lovers in *Don Quixote*. (It is a great delight for a dance fan to spot talented teenagers emerging from the corps, and going on to develop mature artistry.) José Manuel Carreño lets himself go as a roguish Basil to Susan Jaffe's saucy Kitri. Carreño and Jaffe make a beautiful pair in other ballets, like *The Sleeping Beauty*, where the earthy manliness of his prince is a perfect foil for her melting Aurora. Secondary roles are also filled with panache, like Angel Corella's hard-dancing gypsy boy in *Don Quixote*.

Reviewers write of Vladimir Malakhov's exotic, mercurial dancing, and the character of a brooding Byronic poet that he gives to Balanchine's *Ballet Imperial*. They describe in *La Bayadère* the contrast between Amanda McKerrow's touchingly delicate Nikiya and Paloma Herrera's sophisticated Gamzatti, the two women who love Solar, played by Bocca with fiery passion. With the help of all these stars, American Ballet Theater is regaining its former glory.

Directors of modern dance companies vary in their treatment of old works and new dancers. Some act the way Makarova did when she taught a traditional interpretation of Odette to a novice. Others encourage each performer to find his or her own way. Paul Taylor is definitely in the second mold. After the death of Christopher Gillis, who was "godlike when you saw him onstage," Paul asked Patrick Corbin to do Gillis's role in *Sacre du Printemps (The Rehearsal)*. "Paul is totally about evolution. He didn't want me to do Chris's part; he wanted to see Patrick doing the part."[12] Not all viewers agree with this push to see new personalities. Liking what they saw originally, they believe the works lose something when presented with fresh interpretations.

Paul's attitude, however, is so much a part of himself that it extends to creating new works. Thirty years ago, when he was first becoming well known, Paul Taylor wrote of his company: "More often than not, the kind of dance we work on together turns out to be dependent on these different dancers as individuals."[13]

Through thirty years of the Paul Taylor Company, which inevitably has seen a large number of dancers come and go, there have naturally been ups and downs. But the general picture is definitely up. A review of a 1993 performance mentioned "the vivifying powers of such newcomers as the statuesque Angela Vaillancourt and the ebullient Edward Talton-Jackson ... the compelling and accomplished Andrew Asnes ... the elation and dynamic brilliance of Thomas Patrick."[14] In a 1994 concert, a writer spoke of Patrick Corbin in *A Field of Grass*, whose ecstasy "is contagious, creating widening circles of Corbin fans."[15] For Corbin himself, who had a bad time at the School of American Ballet and then spent four years at the Joffrey Ballet getting worse and worse (he was thrown into paralyzing anxiety by the company's policy of posting corrections of dancers' faults on the bulletin board for everyone to see), the Taylor Company is pure joy.

In 1995, Mary Cochran was singled out as a bright Taylor star, with

her "distinctive blend of spunk and radiance ... her verve, charm and daring ... airy lightness" that take her effortlessly through Taylor's buoyant pieces. At the same time, she rises to the dramatic challenges of "the knotty, darker roles."[16]

In 1996, a reviewer summed up the Paul Taylor Company's appeal: "Each company member is unique in physicality and temperament. Each is a superb dancer. Together they create an ensemble which has seldom appeared stronger or more proportionately balanced. It would be unfair to say that no dancer stands out for, in fact, they all do."[17]

Superior dancers with charisma are the ideal of the ideal: rare beings whose stage presence brings in large audiences, regardless of style and choreography. Charisma cannot be measured like the height of a leg extension or the number of pirouettes, but most people agree on its presence. It is possible that "magnetic" performers literally emit a stronger magnetic field than the average person. Attitude is certainly a factor. Mikhail Baryshnikov, a sensation in the ballet world since the 1970s, sets audiences gasping and critics raving. Spectacular technique together with fine acting in roles of all styles partly explains his impact. Beyond these, one can cite his attitude towards dance, a philosophy that the essence of art is to have pleasure in giving pleasure.

Exciting dancers often inspire choreographers. José Limón, perhaps the finest male modern dancer of his generation, was a soloist in Doris Humphrey's company. When Humphrey could no longer create on her own body because of crippling arthritis, she used Limón as her choreographic instrument, for masterpieces beginning with *Lament for Ignacio Sanchez Mejías*. Humphrey would describe her ideas for each rhythmic phrase to Limón, who understood what she wanted and came up with complete movements.

Similarly Frederick Ashton, who shaped the core of the British Royal Ballet repertory, credited Margot Fonteyn with being his muse. She was a collaborator in his ballets as surely as the music composer and set designer.

A charismatic superstar may have a downside. For example, Nureyev's presence could interfere with the performance of a ballet. There is a passage in the Royal Ballet's *Swan Lake* where the evil motions of the villain Rothbart, raging aloft on a stairway, are played against the noble solo of Prince Siegfried, dancing on the ballroom floor below. When Nureyev played Siegfried, the audience stopped the ballet dead with wild cheers, destroying the dramatic interplay. Likewise, during a Royal Ballet visit to New York, Nureyev and Fonteyn proved so dazzling that audiences practically

OPPOSITE: Baryshnikov and Makarova thrilled audiences with their dancing in *Giselle*. Photograph by Martha Swope, © Time Inc.

overlooked the appearance of Antoinette Sibley and Anthony Dowell, a superb duo who shared a style of noble but restrained lyricism.[18]

Stages of a Dancer's Life

Once a person decides to be a dancer, it is not a question of embarking on a "career" but of making a life in dance. From that day forward, every action and every decision are related to the cloistered dance world. Faith in the future must be strong and the commitment total, because mentally and physically, the dancer becomes a battleground for unrelenting war. On the one side there are the relentless requirements of the art. Grouped against these are the obstacles of injury, illness, obesity, pregnancy, and old age, and all the distractions of pleasure that the flesh is heir to.

The dancer always runs the risk of permanent damage to knees, ankles, back, and other body parts brought on by physical toil under adverse conditions of bad stages, insufficient warm-ups, careless partnering, illness, and the tension of strenuous rehearsals. Miserable periods of cancelled performances, even career changes forced by injury, are part of every dancer's biography. Molissa Fenley had to cancel an entire New York season. Serious leg problems cut off both Balanchine's and Paul Taylor's chances of continuing to perform. Danish Ballet soloist Stanley Williams had to stop dancing at the age of 24 and Helgi Tomasson at 45 because of injuries. After Bruce Marks underwent a hip replacement, active dance was closed to him. However, the very talented aging or injured dancer has options like teaching (Williams), choreography (Balanchine), or direction (Taylor, Tomasson, Marks) and isn't forced to quit the field.

The maternal instinct is another issue. Moira Shearer left dance because she found it incompatible with demands of motherhood. Doris Humphrey, Maria Tallchief, Melissa Hayden, Carla Fracci, Natalia Makarova and Carmen de Lavallade are only a few of the female artists who had children and continued with their careers but were always subjected to guilty pressure. Many others, like Martha Graham, never even considered giving birth.

Dance resembles athletics in that its practitioners reach their peak of skill at a very early age. But unlike the athlete, a dance artist matures into the fifth decade. Interpretive power keeps growing—at the same time that technical prowess is declining. There is an optimum point for a dancer where physical ability, even if slightly declining, meets full-blown expressive beauty. After that point of intersection, we admire the fact that a dancer still goes on—an indomitable human spirit. But the dancer's appearances can be a depressing reminder of mortality. They can also be heartening, depending on the performer and the circumstances.

In 1939, Merce Cunningham had a remarkable quality of lightness. He would spring up from the floor with no visible preparation and seem to hang in the air. Martha Graham made full use of Cunningham's bouncing agility, in contrast to more solid, weighty men dancers in the company, and created major roles in her dance dramas on Cunningham's body. Still charismatic in 1992, Merce Cunningham in his middle seventies made a brief solo appearance in a composition, grinning and moving swiftly among his young, magnificent dancers. After the performance he was asked whether he could feel how much the audience loved his bit. Cunningham's answer was typical: He laughed. "Well, I was trying to keep my balance."[19]

In 1991 Jiri Kylian, director of the Netherlands Dance Theater, founded Netherlands Dance Theater 3, a branch for dancers over 40 (even into their 60s), to take advantage of the interpretive wisdom that comes only with years of performing in widely varied works. Their warmly received programs consist of specially commissioned works dealing with themes like the passage of time and love. In Hans van Manen's poignant *Evergreens* (1991), the man and the woman (Gérard Lemaitre and Sabine Kupferberg) portray a pair of lovers in the many ups and downs of a longtime relationship. Ohad Naharin's 1992 humorous treatment of the same situation has the man and the woman (Gary Chryst and Kupferberg) diving into embraces that shift suddenly "into a hilarious gymnastic battle, with feet in boots waving primly in the air," the couple having "a terrific time fighting everything out all over again on a white double bed."[20]

Martine van Hamel, who appears with the troupe, spoke of what a "mature" dancer can bring to a role. "It's the fact that you've lasted that long. You're pretty good.... There is a stage savvy or an intelligence to the way you move. Also a letting-go, a willingness to take chances."[21]

Then there is Maya Plisetskaya, one of this century's greatest ballerinas (with the Bolshoi since 1943). Plisetskaya danced several pieces at a 1996 New York City gala, including her signature solo Fokine's *The Dying Swan*, which elicited this review: "At 70, Ms. Plisetskaya, with torso only slightly stiff and legs in fabulous shape under a short white tutu, can only amaze. Her toe work is strong and centered; the power and lyricism of her classical style turn the solo, rightly, into an ode to the human spirit."[22]

Dancers keep going because by the time they are full-fledged professionals, they have made so many sacrifices, and their bodies and minds are so consumed with the business, that they are almost incapable of considering an alternative life style. Dancers love to dance. For the audience, this onstage magic is what counts. In the same way that people are drawn to athletes or pop musicians, an attraction to dancers is what turns a casual viewer into a devotee. Every dance fan hoards a rich collection of moving memories. Long after the stars have burned out, their light still reaches us in memory and tradition. The dance world will never forget Marie Taglioni, Isadora Duncan, Vaslav Nijinsky, Anna Pavlova, Rudolf Nureyev, and the list will continue to grow.

9

Thoughts About Repertory

Like the collections known as European and American literature or music, Western dance has a repertory, consisting of a basic body of known pieces and continuous new additions. In this chapter we will look at repertory in revival, creation of repertory by developing artists, works by old masters, and late twentieth century choreography.

Repertory in Revival

While there are often revivals of dance works, considerably more leeway is taken here than in drama and music. Some changes are clearly caused by the undependability of the method that has in the past transferred works directly from teacher to pupil, with a minimum of objective recording aids. Inaccuracy of memory accounts for continual variation. But even with a wide use of dance notation, film and video tape, even with a work that never goes out of the repertory, even with the best-known classics, new versions are deliberately being made all the time.

The art of choreography has something in it that is more flexible than playwriting or composing music, something that leads continually to revision. Movements are more concrete and tangible and at the same time less specifically expressive than words or musical sounds. Without doing violence to the original vision, many movement variations may be allowed within the framework of a title, a concept, and a musical accompaniment. In fact, since the eye tires faster and grasps sooner than the ear, dance imagery becomes old hat and clichéd, more quickly than musical or verbal imagery. Thus even in the "same" work, dance imagery must be freshened from one period to the next, from one place to another. As a result, the content (or scenario), the music, the décor, the choreographic patterns—one or all of these may be changed beyond recognition.

The question arises then: Does a work of choreography have an independent existence like the play *Hamlet* or Brahms' *First Symphony*, which exist to be learned and analyzed apart from performance? Can one discuss *Coppélia*, *Firebird*, *Night Journey*, *The Sleeping Beauty*, apart from a specific rendition? On the one hand, any particular version of a dance differs from any other to a much greater extent than would occur with *Hamlet* or the Brahms symphony. On the other hand, different versions of a dance have much in common—a wealth of specific imagery that is passed along by dance artists, students, historians, critics, and others.

Perhaps the best approach would be to look at a revived or restaged dance as a memorial to a tradition. That is, at some time in the past, one or more performances of a certain work took place. When at a later date someone decides to honor that memory with a production that corresponds in a number of ways to its antecedent, then we are entitled to speak of it as the same work.

The text of a work consists of the choreography and the music, but not the scenery and costume designs, nor the performing interpretation. A revival may attempt an accurate reconstruction, or the intent may be a major revision to suit a company director's taste or changing fashions.

The earliest ballet that is still in the repertory is *La Fille Mal Gardée* (1789). However, Dauberval's choreography and accompanying musical score have long since disappeared, leaving the village setting, the rough outlines of a comic plot, the idea of combining naturalistic pantomime with dance interludes, the mixture of folk dance and academic ballet steps, that today we call "caractère," and the use of music based on French folk tunes. Over the years many versions of *La Fille Mal Gardée* were made, but we now consider the standard to be Frederick Ashton's, created in 1960 to music by Lanchbery and currently in the repertory of several companies in the United States, England, and Denmark. Similarly, when we see *Giselle* today, we see it not in its 1841 version, but as reset completely by Petipa in the late nineteenth century and revised since by countless ballerinas and directors from memory, or deflected through their own temperamental bent.

In the interests of freshness and novelty, ingenious new versions of classics are constantly being staged. Amy Spencer and Richard Colton, alumni of Twyla Tharp's company, formed the Spencer/Colton dance company in 1995 from students at the Boston Conservatory. They created for their group a *La Fille Mal Gardée* set in 1930s America.

New ballets in the name of *Giselle* keep coming. There is an intriguing *Giselle* arranged by Frederic Franklin for Dance Theater of Harlem that remains true to the traditional choreography even though it takes place on a plantation in pre–Civil War Louisiana. Myra Kinch's hilarious *Giselle's Revenge* features a graveyard scene in which the ghostly nymph keeps floating right behind the near-sighted, unaware prince who can't find her.

In the 1970s, an exciting hour-long *Giselle* appeared in a Czechoslovakian arrangement designed specifically for television. By the use of appearing and disappearing camera tricks, the ballet was staged as a flashback in Giselle's mind. In her other-world sorority of wilis, she lived through memories of her meeting and love scenes with the prince. She switched back to her present with wilis who materialized from nowhere, one by one, in inventive rhythmic patterning to the traditional music. Neither Berthe nor Hilarion was introduced. The scenes flowed along in attractive unity, undisturbed by—to the modern eye—heavily mimed, melodramatic interruptions. It was pure dance, almost plotless, in the way Balanchine's *Scotch Symphony* uses *La Sylphide* merely as a point of departure.

Derek Deane's *Giselle* is set in a 1920s Austrian hotel. Giselle is a chambermaid and Count Albrecht a guest, arriving in a chauffeur-driven limousine. The second-act wilis are vampiric creatures, whose malevolent facial expressions and gestures are suitable for an ensemble of Dracula's followers. Evil also runs rampant in Christopher Gable's *Cinderella*, a spiced-up drama that features vicious brutality and a hint of psychological perversion.

Balanchine wrote of Petipa's *Raymonda* (1898) that the choreography was superb, "but his story was nonsense and difficult to follow." So Balanchine took part of the Glazounov score, which "contains some of the finest ballet music we have," and created *Raymonda Variations* (1961). The new version has a series of duets and solos framed by the opening and closing ensemble of fourteen dancers, but no literary idea. The dances are carried entirely by the "grand and generous manner" and the "joy and playfulness" of the music.[1]

Erik Bruhn's 1966 production of *Swan Lake* had the goal of beefing up the male dancing. He put "blood into the veins" of the originally paper-thin Prince Siegfried (along with a hint of Freudian attraction between Siegfried and his princess mother) and in general balanced Petipa's beautiful female dancing—solo and ensemble—with a long contemplative solo for the hero, and ebullient passages in the Bournonville manner for male courtiers.

When Baryshnikov staged *The Nutcracker* for the American Ballet Theater in 1976, instead of sticking close to the successful Bolshoi or New York City Ballet version, he chose to leave out the Sugar Plum Fairy, make the whole a tighter logical unit, and infuse it with a more lyrical style.

Mark Morris made a far more thoroughgoing revision, in 1991 transposing the classical Petipa-Ivanov *Nutcracker* to his postmodern *Hard Nut*. This is a piece of choreography that both uses and makes jokes about a widely known classic. Although Morris used the same well-loved Tchaikovsky music and a similar scenario, and even reverted to Ivanov and Petipa's original name for the "Clara" character (Marie), the choreographic combination of movement styles, the touches of sleazy modern life, and the dancers cast and costumed in unexpected ways resulted in a spicy, sugar-free version.

The Hard Nut presents a 1960s suburban party. The hostess, played by a large male, starts to drink even before the guests arrive, and proceeds to abuse the family maid, a black male dancer who stomps about the house in point shoes. The guests come to drink, flirt and do the twist, with much bumping of hips and shimmying of shoulders. Marie's sister sports go-go

OPPOSITE: *La Fille Mal Gardée*, **choreographed by Frederick Ashton. Photograph by Martha Swope, © Time Inc.**

boots and makes out with a moustachioed guy in bell bottoms. Their sassy teen-age brother is performed by a female. There is a purely classical *pas de deux* done with tender passion—by two males, Drosselmeier and the Nutcracker. At the premiere, Mark Morris himself appeared as a veiled, voluptuous Arabian harem dancer. A baby princess seated in a carriage has the head of a pig.

The action in *The Hard Nut* is carried forward with mimed gestures of sloppy, everyday behavior, set alongside formal pantomimic gestures of classical ballet. Whole pieces of the work are choreographed in disco movements (the house party); others in modern idiom (the waltzing flowers roll about freely on the ground); still others in classical ballet.

In the forest snow scene, for example, Morris designed leaping steps and circular, whirling spatial patterns for the human snowflakes that follow familiar lines. But the casting and costuming of the dancers are startling: not just girls, but male and female; not just Caucasian, but also people of color; not first rate ballet technicians, but performers trained primarily in modern dance. Males and females alike are costumed in white bodices with bare midriffs, tutus with white and dark layers of tulle, and white wigs that sit on their heads like ice cream cones. Some dancers go barefoot while others (both male and female) wear toe shoes. Finally, it is the dancers themselves rather than unseen stagehands who toss around the confetti snow.

As for its structure, *The Hard Nut* is "framed" by a TV screen, used to construct a "play within a play." The heroine's bratty brother and sister watch TV until they are forced to mingle with the party guests. At the finale of the ballet, Marie and the Nutcracker have a loving, lilting *pas de deux* in a never-never land of fantasy. The whole cast breaks into their tender duet with a showy display of split leaps and acrobatic turns. The action winds down to leave the couple kissing alone on a stage, which is then transformed back into a family room. The brother and sister are once more in place in front of the TV screen. It is an awesome moment for them when Marie's face appears in close-up—and turns out to be their own sister! At that moment the maid, who has functioned as a kind of chorus, abruptly switches off the box and sends the kids to bed.

Thus *The Hard Nut* questions seriously—or in mockery—conventional attitudes towards homosexuality, cross-dressing, the dominant position of Caucasian males in Western culture, and the etiquette of social relations. It also takes a somewhat skeptical attitude towards the venerable technique of classic dance and *The Nutcracker* itself.

OPPOSITE: *The Hard Nut*, **choreographed by Mark Morris. Photograph by Martha Swope, © Time Inc.**

One reason for revision may be to conform to the special abilities of stars or ensembles, as in the Bolshoi production of *Romeo and Juliet*. Maya Plisetskaya worked on the role of Juliet for more than five years before she danced it in 1961, creating a new portrayal—individual and utterly different from the original Juliet. Can you imagine the uproar if melodic passages were inserted into the Brahms symphony by a first violinist, or if Hamlet's soliloquies were changed to expound the theories of a socialist actor? Yet such things go on all the time in dance.

At times, historical accuracy is the guidepost for a revival, as it was for the Joffrey Ballet in their staging of Nijinsky's daring 1913 *Rite of Spring* and Massine's avant-garde 1917 *Parade*. In recent years, similar respect has also been shown to Doris Humphrey's *Shakers* (1931) and her *With My Red Fires* (1936), and to Alvin Ailey's *Revelations* (1960).

Accuracy, however, does not always guarantee satisfaction. Alwin Nikolais unfavorably compared a revival of Graham's *Primitive Mysteries* with his memory of the 1936 premiere performance, because of its lack of conviction.[2] And a critic noted that a 1995 performance of *Revelations* by the Alvin Ailey troupe could be faulted for a certain academic quality. "The blazing spontaneity of dancers of Judith Jamison's caliber wasn't to be seen."[3]

Creation of Repertory by Developing Artists

Good choreographers are a rare breed. It is therefore not unusual to find modern dance artists commissioned to make works for ballet companies, for example Twyla Tharp's *Deuce Coupe* for Joffrey and *Push Comes to Shove* for American Ballet Theater, and Laura Dean's "Sometimes It Snows in April" for Joffrey's *Billboards*.

Another case in point is David Parsons, originally a splendid member of the Paul Taylor Company, who went off on his own and arranged an entire repertory of sexy, virtuosic movement, much of it to jazzy music, for the Parsons Dance Company. His goal was to entertain the crowd. A high point in the repertory is *Caught* (1982), a strobe-lighted solo that he choreographed to give the illusion of a dancer walking on air. In 1996, the New York City Ballet commissioned him to create *Touch*, to a specially composed score by Richard Peaslee. The piece purports to be about various kinds of love, but its real theme is continuous, exuberant, joyful animation.

Peter Martins, who believes that the New York City Ballet should keep moving ahead and not be turned into "a Balanchine museum,"[4] has taken several steps to promote the creation of contemporary works. First, he conceived of the Diamond Project, a showcase for new works in the vocabulary of classical ballet, such as *Viola Alone* by Kevin O'Day. To the music of Hindemith, O'Day mixed colloquial and classical movements together with considerable imagination to provide the kind of concise, brash piece that brings out the best in New York City Ballet dancers.

Secondly, Martins himself has been creating steadily—in Balanchine's neoclassical mode, but with a stamp all his own. His 1994 *Mozart Piano Concerto* has "a bold, high-flying, kinetic approach to the music that was a pleasant surprise; the long central duet was worthy of Balanchine's eccentric duet in Stravinsky's *Symphony in Three Movements*."[5] His 1996 *Reliquary*, made to a Wuorinen score based on notes by Stravinsky, was the season's major premiere. Here as elsewhere, Martins created a cerebral dance in his own style that pioneers "a use of phenomenal speed in classical technique that extends that technique and says something about the world we live in."[6]

These works achieve various degrees of success. *Jazz: Six Syncopated Movements* came out of the collaboration between Martins and Wynton Marsalis. Ballet-trained Martins, dependent on fixed, counted sequences, had difficulty coping with the improvisational leeway that is taken by the best jazz groups. The moves of the dance ensemble don't involve the middle body and are classically cool and impersonal, in contrast to the soulful music. However, the solo roles have phrases that project the feelings of the score, and when danced by sensitive performers like Nikolaj Hubbe, Heather Watts and Wendy Whelan, they are wholly effective.[7]

Thirdly, Martins has encouraged some of his company members to try their hand at choreography. In 1994, brilliant dancer Damian Woetzel came up with a *pas de deux* set to music from Glazounov's *Ruses d'Amour* and a "tersely organized" *Stravinsky Ebony Concerto*, while Miriam Mahdaviani's *Correlazione* could be admired for the structural complexity of an overlong Corelli score.[8] Just as it is interesting for us to spot new dancing talent, it is also a pleasure to follow the development of a novice choreographer.

Works by Old Masters

The creations of time-honored choreographers are a different matter. During the 1990s, retrospective seasons have been staged of the repertory of a number of artists. George Balanchine, Martha Graham, Alvin Ailey, Frederick Ashton, Alwin Nikolais and Erick Hawkins, for example, have been honored in memory by their companies. Jerome Robbins, Merce Cunningham, Trisha Brown and Paul Taylor have presented their own summation of repertory. One sees on such occasions the strengths and weaknesses of an artist, and also how changes occur in a choreographer's style. The coming and going of company members and directors affects the interpretation of old works as well as new creations.

In 1990, to mark his retirement as a director of the New York City Ballet, Jerome Robbins staged 27 of his ballets, which ranged from the vigorously youthful *Fancy Free* (music by Leonard Bernstein), to the romantic *Dances at a Gathering* (Chopin), to the almost folkloric wedding celebration *Les Noces* (Stravinsky) to the musically formal *The Goldberg Variations* (Bach), to the archaic *Afternoon of a Faun* (Debussy), to the avant-garde *Watermill*, with its slow-motion meditation on life, echoed in the score of Japanese composer Teiji Ito. As different as the Robbins works are from one another, they all share an embodiment of human warmth.

At the same time, we see that choreographers who have been around for a while are as likely as not to change their styles. This is particularly true of artists like Twyla Tharp, Paul Taylor, and Trisha Brown, who began with minimalist creations and then gradually "reinvented" full theatrical productions.

Trisha Brown started out with "climbing the wall" experiments (see the chapter on style), to which she first added trained dancers, then a background set (Rauschenberg's slide projections). Music came in 1981 because, Brown said, she was tired of hearing the audience coughing.[9] Next she became interested in gender and partnering. However, her focus on conceptual dance has never really wavered. Brown's 1994 solo *If You Couldn't See Me* keeps her face and body's front facing away from the audience and consists of motion in contrasting shapes and dynamics: the torso undulates, while the legs, arms and feet form angles. A critic noted great sensuality in the performance: "Amazingly, what seems an exercise in restricted form turns into an ecstatic outburst."[10]

In 1992, Paul Taylor created *Oz*, a charming, bizarre, postmodern entertainment based on *The Wizard of Oz* and other novels by Frank Baum. At the same time, he revived nine of his old works, beginning with the minimalist *Epic* (1957). He also allowed company member Christopher Gillis to contribute *Andalusian Green*, an emotional piece to music by Granados. Taylor is continuing to include choreographic efforts by company members. In 1995 he solicited material from six dancers and edited the results for *Funny Papers* (to goofy American pop songs like "Itsy Bitsy Teenie Weenie Yellow Polka Dot Bikini").

More than any of the artists in this discussion of retrospectives, Merce Cunningham's dance view has remained consistent: objective movement patterns that take place haphazardly in a locale where a sound score happens to be heard at the same time. For years he has been producing a series of works that go by the title *Event*, which refers to a composition he creates from bits of old repertory. In 1995 he lifted large chunks of material from a number of his dances and combined them in *Minevent*. A critic spoke of his own solo as the centerpiece of the work: "He walks quietly onto the stage ... carrying a wooden folding chair.... White-haired and with feet crippled by arthritis, Mr. Cunningham knows how to share the stage comfortably with his younger, more agile company.... What is miraculous about the solo are its images of death and tenacious life, communicated with a daring, honesty and witty humor that are theater at its purest."[11]

Cunningham continues to explore media mixing. He has been experimenting with the combination of live dance and video, as well as with computer programs designed to make choreographic decisions. *Ocean*, premiered at 1994 arts festivals in Europe, is a standard Cunningham affair in its collaborative nature. The title is clearly realized in its two scores, one composed by Andrew Culver for a 112-piece orchestra, and one composed by David Tudor from electronically modified marine sounds of surf, seals and sonar pulses. Its costume and watery light designs by Marsha Skinner shimmer in cool blues, greens and purples. Two unusual features mark the work: It is performed in an arena, with the audience sitting around the dancers and themselves being surrounded by musicians; and the movements were created with an added collaborator, Thecla Schiphorst, operator of a computer software program called Life Forms. Schiphorst, a choreographer on the Life Forms design team, worked for hours with Cunningham. She told a reporter, "Merce is oriented to discovery."[12] Certainly this is not news to anyone familiar with his work.

Choreography of the 1990s

Throughout the previous chapters, examples have been given of recent repertory. Here, as representative of the 1990s, we add a John Neumeier, a Garth Fagan, a Donald McKayle, and a David Bintley.

John Neumeier's *Now and Then* (1993) traces developing human relationships through sheer movement, with no sign of a plot. A critic reported that *Now and Then* (to Ravel's "musical potpourri," the *Piano Concerto in G Major*) features a couple whose female runs in place, her arms "always reaching out for something that is not there." Her male partner tries to break through her defensive wall, but cannot. Another mysterious couple could be the same pair as they were in times past. Gradually the relationship of this couple "unravels, moving from carefree youth to tarnished adulthood." Five other couples mirror movements of the leads, but they also remain neutral "in a world where non-involvement is the key." In this anxiety-ridden view of men and women, classic ballet phrases are interrupted with flexed feet, angled arms. Unpredictable rhythmic patterns juxtapose upper bodies in slow-motion, with rapid and dizzying footwork. To touch his partner, a male doesn't use his hands but "crouches awkwardly to place his cheek against the outstretched palm" of the female.[13]

Garth Fagan's choreography expresses a more upbeat vision of relationships than Neumeier's. In *Griot* (1991), not only do women perform virtuoso phrases self-sufficiently alongside the men, they also pair off with men, their hands held trustingly. At one point a woman swings a man off the floor and turns him on her hip. This ferociously energetic work uses music by versatile jazz artist Wynton Marsalis, sculptures by Martin Duryear, and a company of dancers trained in Fagan's personal quirky but sometimes dazzling technique: spasmodically frantic leaps and jumps, whirring turns, back arches and leg extensions held in incredible off-center balances, slow wrung-out falls, wavelike torso gyrations, and pelvic thrusts that slant the upper body backward to a seemingly impossible degree.

Griot, a long dance, is broken into scenes. "Spring Yaounde" has an almost nude couple move in sensuous, tender embraces, their bodies folding over one another with chests, groins, chins, noses, and foreheads touching. "Sand Painting" presents the dancers as leggy stick figures, whose feet scrape the floor in shifting hieroglyphic postures. "The Disenfranchised" is a portrait of trapped, sloppily dressed, despairing men and women in torn clothing. Their hands and heads hang uselessly. They clutch at their own bodies. They are seized with spasms. They crawl along the ground and over one another. They run as though from hunters. The only hopeful note is one man cradling another, to comfort him. "High Rise Riff" has the air of a goodtime, mindless dance party. At the end, the couple of "Spring Yaounde" repeat their gentle duet.

Fagan's stated aim in the piece was to embrace the duality of ancient and contemporary African American life and thereby to provide an alternative to racism and sexism. Although the sexes are certainly equally balanced, the racial solution doesn't come across. But the wildly eccentric movement holds its own.[14]

Some works show signs that there are present-day dance artists who once again care deeply about issues, as they did in the 1930s and 1940s. But even if they take tried and true political positions, they present them in wholly unconventional dance forms. Donald McKayle's *House of Tears* (1993) was inspired by actual scenes in post–Perón Argentina, with women bearing witness to the appalling—but silent—disappearance and death of loved ones arrested by the new régime. Their testimony is also silent—the women walking in public processional, with white kerchiefs bound around their heads and photos of those who vanished tied to their necks. According to one reviewer, McKayle's choreography makes a universal statement against the victimization of innocent people, despite specific references in the powerful work. *House of Tears* is set to *Bandoneón Concerto* (composed by the late Argentine tango king Astor Piazolla). The backdrop bears a blown-up photograph of a child, and the dance features a cast of characters headed by a uniformed general and a passionate white-veiled Spirit of Argentina, whose dress bears a blood-red slash beneath her broken heart. McKayle's movement vocabulary integrates "the whipping legs of tango, the fiery hills of flamenco, the lyrical line of ballet, the angularity of modern dance, and the power of martial arts."[15]

David Bintley has a solid ballet background as one of the British Royal Ballet's directors. Nevertheless, his "*Still Life*" *at the Penguin Café* (1988, music of Simon Jeffes) includes modernistic movements in its presentation of high society as preening zebras, twitching chipmunks, sinuous lionesses, frisky monkeys, attended by sprightly waddling penguin waiters—all of which characters are delineated clearly by their masks and costumes, as well as by their dynamic gestures. The piece has a serious message about the animals and their human counterparts who disport themselves at a cabaret: All species on our planet are endangered. After the party comes the deluge, and, comforting one another, couples enter an ark, where they are preserved in memory.

The same names recur repeatedly in any discussion of repertory. Fresh names are constantly being added to the list, but if they seem to be played out after one or two efforts, they sink into oblivion. However, the chances are that once a person has turned out a number of fine works, she or he will continue to do so. Thus it is an event worth noting when a new work, or a revival of an old work by ___ (fill in any aforementioned familiar name) comes our way.

10

Moving Rituals

Up to this point we have treated separate elements of the dance art in isolation. Now our focus widens to consider the nature of the activity itself. Dance, which originated in prehistoric tribal ritual, appears to retain its ritual nature even in our sophisticated culture.

Tribal rituals were planned ceremonies, undertaken to acknowledge significant occasions of the individual's life (birth, puberty, marriage, death), significant occasions for the social community (agricultural seasons, hunting, war), or mystical forces in the universe.[1] Governments, religious institutions, the media and the arts have divided up many of these ritual functions in today's complex society. This brings us back to the art of dance, whose peculiar nature allows the embodiment of our innermost selves.

In this chapter, more than ever we will confront intangibles that fight analysis. Nevertheless, we will try to understand the way dance expresses basic themes of existence: the life force in the face of death, and sexual relations and identity.

If the implications of the topics in this chapter strike you as unresolved and amorphous, that's because they are. Yet what else have people been concerned with through the ages, if not questions of our connections to the universe, to one another, and to our own bodies?

The Life Force

The primary quality communicated by dance is a sense of energy—the life force, if you will. Certainly artists see it this way. Martha Graham declared: "My dancing is the affirmation of life through movement. Its only aim is to impart the sensation of living, to energize the spectator into keener awareness of the vigor, of the mystery, the humor, the variety and the wonder of life."[2]

Alwin Nikolais wrote that early man was compelled to dance, and for much the same reason that we do jazzy steps for recreation today. "At one time he must have lifted his arms and moved for the sole purpose of feeling his livingness—the sheer ecstasy of being imbued with life and ... feeling life coursing through him."[3]

Doris Humphrey said, "Dynamics is the lifeblood of the dance."[4]

Merce Cunningham maintained: "The disciplined energy of a dancer is the life-energy magnified and focused ... and thereby evokes the spirit of a god."[5] Furthermore, "dancing provides an amplification of energy that is not provided in any other way."[6]

Susanne Langer identified the primary illusion of dance as a virtual realm of power: "In watching a collective dance ... one does not see people running around; one sees the dance driving this way, drawn that way ...

and all the motion seems to spring from powers beyond the performers....
They are dance forces, virtual powers.... The subjective experience of voli-
tion and free agency, and of reluctance to alien, compelling wills ... the sense
of vital power ... is our most immediate self-consciousness."[7]

Historian Curt Sachs claimed that "the dance in its essence is simply
life on a higher level.... In the ecstasy of dance, man briefs the chasm
between this and the other world, the realm of demons, spirits, and God."[8]

For decades, artists have been consciously staging rituals in the name
of dance. We can trace this interest back at least to an early Martha Graham masterpiece, *Primitive Mysteries* (1931). The composer of the music was
Louis Horst, Graham's close associate during her formative years. Horst also
offered a course in modern dance composition that influenced the choreographic styles of hundreds of young dancers in the 1930s and 1940s. Two
of his assigned topics were an Earth Primitive and an Air Primitive. Horst
wrote:

> The pioneers in Modern Dance and their successors recaptured
> the relation that the primitive has to his body—an intimacy with
> the muscle tensions of daily movements which has been lost to
> modern man ... an inner sensitivity to every one of the body's
> parts, to the power of its whole, and to the space in which it carves
> designs.[9]

It is no longer acceptable (politically correct) to speak of "primitive"
culture. "Tribal" or some other word must be substituted. In any case, how
much there was of true primitivism in Graham's *Primitive Mysteries*, and
how much of Horst's description really applies to actual "primitives," are
not easy questions to answer. More germane to our subject is an examina-
tion of the moving figures in *Primitive Mysteries*, a religious mass to the Virgin.

The dance, to a score by Louis Horst, is in three sections, joined
together by silent, formal processions of women, who surround or precede
the Virgin figure. Agnes de Mille described the way the women stalk: "with
long, reaching legs, the foot brought to the earth with heavy forcefulness,
as though staking a claim to territory.... The configurations of dancers
looked wooden, childlike, drawn from ancient sources."

The first part of the dance is a hymn of praise to the Virgin. In the second part the soloist and the group are horrified witnesses to the crucifixion.
Here, writes de Mille, the chorus "is drawn up with waiting horror on one
side, breaking out at last ... one by one, bent double, their hands locked
behind their backs, like driven animals in a heavy-bodied circle."[10]

The third section is a joyful celebration. The movements were directly
inspired by American Indian and Mexican ceremonial dances that Graham

had seen with Horst on vacation trips to New Mexico. Thus the trilogy is clearly a prime example of a ritual. And although it holds allusions to the Virgin Mary and the crucifixion, it also evokes a general religious and mythic spirit universal in its implications. In fact, when it was restaged in 1964, Graham spoke about the virginal figure in white as the Sabbath queen of Jewish ritual.[11]

More recently, dancer Molissa Fenley was inspired by the Joffrey Ballet's reconstruction of Nijinsky's *Rite of Spring (Le Sacre du Printemps)* to make a solo titled *State of Darkness* (1988). Nijinsky's piece came from Stravinsky's music, which followed a scenario of Russian pagan folklore: Through the sacrifice of a virginal girl, the gods would ensure that the death-cold darkness of winter would once again give way to the warmth and fertility of spring.

Fenley's *State of Darkness* used the music to make a piece about fear, embodied in her bare-breasted self as the chosen sacrifice. The dancer explained, "I wanted to work with a lot of very subtle quivering movements such as a deer would make—this frightened, quivering thing—and I couldn't do that wearing a top." The *State of Darkness* was choreographed almost mystically. Fenley let the Stravinsky music wash over her as she did her warm-ups, and then "the piece just seemed to make itself."[12]

Fenley calls herself a postmodern dancer, one "who didn't come out of anybody." Yet isn't it significant that she chose to pay homage to both Nijinsky and Stravinsky, two giants in the dance tradition? Further, it is of more than passing interest that dozens of other choreographers, including Léonide Massine, Mary Wigman, Martha Graham, John Neumeier, Maurice Béjart and Paul Taylor, have made their own versions of *Rite of Spring*.

That Judith Jamison's gift for interpretation is matched by her choreographic ability is shown by *Divining*, the first of many fine Jamison compositions. *Divining* is danced to her own percussion score of thin, wailing reeds, pulsing drums and a warm strumming. It is a ritual whose themes—wandering, seeking, celebrating mystery, and strong female leadership—are close to the artist's heart. As Jamison described the action, four runners (two couples, absorbed in their mission) seek out a virgin space for their clan. With intensely proud strength and excruciatingly stretched-out limbs, the leader explores the space to make sure the ground and the air and the spirits are all right. She summons the group. Following her directions, they consecrate the space with forceful, tautly controlled gyrations. When the ceremony ends, with the power she has taken into herself, the leader readies her people for the next journey.[13]

OPPOSITE: Martha Graham's *Primitive Mysteries*. Photograph by Martha Swope, © Time Inc.

Arlene Richards, a spectacular dancer in the National Dance Theater Company of Jamaica, choreographed *The Cocoon* (1994), accompanied by music of Richard Burma, David Arkenstone and Patrick O'Hearn, in which

> two men discover a pod filled with strange green creatures who gradually and gently enslave them. The seven pod people turn out to be extraterrestrials. But Miss Richards's choreography and staging encourage more generalized meditation on the fear of difference, and even prodded the viewer into seeing the spacelings' private rituals through the eyes of men.[14]

That same year, American audiences were treated to *Contrastes* and *Waterzooi*, pieces danced by Maguy Marin's French company. *Contrastes* (to a Bartók score) contrasts a pair of Chaplinesque "little people," who shuffle, slump and make the monotonous, repetitive gestures of assembly line workers, with an upper class couple in evening dress who dine at a table. When a butler lights the candles, a nude man and woman are revealed reclining on the table. With unflappable *savoir faire*, the diners ignore the naked pair. The workers return at the end, and as two of them embrace warmly, we see that ordinary life offers more of the pleasures of love than upper class sophistication.

Waterzooi (the name comes from a Belgian stew) is a ninety-minute work, by turns comic and deadly serious, that explores the complexity of human nature. It illustrates Descartes's treatise *The Passions of the Soul*, whose narration serves as accompaniment along with delightful music by Denis Mariotte. Love is portrayed by a man and woman entwining tortuously while whispering to one another. Anger is shown by a comic flare-up in which the narrator too gets hit. Hate has a man strip-searched by three thugs, but then his body recovers from its naked humiliation by assuming the shape of a classical sculpture, accomplished with ingenious stage-lighting. A frightening image is formed by faceless dancers, their backs to the audience, surging forward with measured steps, to the words: "People we don't know are those who are massacred in genocide. We count them on our fingers.... The truth is, people we don't know, we actually don't give a damn about." Thus the whole is a ritual view of basic emotions.[15]

Choreographer Eliot Feld delved into magic. In 1995 he made a solo named *Chi*, a Chinese word that means "the vital forces in the body." In *Chi*, to composer Steve Reich's *Six Marimbas*, female dancer Buffy Miller was "energy made visible," and "a radiant incarnation of universal life." A reviewer wrote, "In its unhurried progress, Feld's work can seem a hymn to life."[16]

In 1986 Twyla Tharp developed movement themes from an image of two women who guard and organize the stage. She had been building the strength for these "power women" (dancers Shelley Washington and Chris Uchida) to take on this work for more than a decade.[17] Tharp wanted Philip Glass to compose for her because she felt that his music, with its quality of constantly unwinding and evolving, was exactly right. For years, Tharp and Glass had talked about working on a Mass together. Now, while he composed, she listened to a recording of a hymn by Mahalia Jackson that "modulated relentlessly upward." When she realized that her dance was actually becoming a secular Mass, she suggested to Glass that they use *In the Upper Room*, the title of Jackson's hymn, for the title of her work.[18]

After the power women open the stage like huntsmen loosing an arrow from the bow of their bodies, *In the Upper Room* proceeds in nine sections, with a display of men and women in athletically driven, fierce, relentless movement. The women wear red toe shoes and are lifted high overhead. At one point the women's arms are linked as they are lifted, in Tharp's image of communities building barns. A critic found *The Upper Room* to be "a masterpiece for an apocalyptic time.... Hope resides in the sheer unquenchable energy of young superhumans who ... appear and disappear in waves through the smoke that fills the stage: spinning, leaping and jogging at the edge of the volcano."[19] Recently, Tharp has become more and more intent on creating pieces like *How Near Heaven* and *I Remember Clifford* (1995) and *The Elements* (1996), which can be seen as cosmic allegories and meditations on life and death. In all cases, the movement embodies Tharp's unique kinetic, contrapuntal style.

Still/Here is a 100-minute ceremony of confrontation with dying and death, by Bill T. Jones. The title, like every phase of the 1994 production, is poetically evocative. *Still*, the first part of the work, refers in movement images to the frozen shock and the final sense of being alone with the news about a terminal illness. *Here* means fully present—here and now. It is the determination to make the most of each moment. The overall message is survival: We are still here. This includes the choreographer, who has been H.I.V. positive for over six years but still has no AIDS symptoms. It includes the eleven dancers of Jones's marvelously trained group, some of whom experienced serious personal loss, and all of whom suffered the constant awareness of dread diseases through the work's two-year gestation. It includes those dead or dying, whose words and wasted selves are still here in videotaped images that move across large screens while the dance proceeds.

Still/Here was pulled together from masses of gut-wrenching raw material: survival workshops attended by people with life-threatening diseases like AIDS and breast cancer that Jones conducted in a number of cities. Jones's method was to ask people to speak about their feelings, their treatments and their prospects—and even to choreograph their own deaths! "I'm not a therapist," he would tell them. "I'm a man and an artist looking for material." The workshops were filmed, and films were also taken later of the members in hospital rooms and at home, as they got sicker and sicker. In the end however, the horror of the content is diffused by the abstraction and formality of dance technique, and by the profusion of stylized elements in the video images made by Gretchen Bender, in the songs by Kenneth Frazelle and Vernon Reid, in Liz Prince's costumes and Robert Wierzel's lighting. Like all of Jones's choreography, this piece combines literal gestures with formal dance patterns and images that disturb and challenge, even as they gratify. Jones claimed that the work has a generalized context of surviving any difficulty.[20]

In 1994, Susan Marshall choreographed scenes of death and loss in *Spectators at an Event* and *Fields of View*, both giving rise to thoughts of AIDS. *Spectators at an Event* focuses on the voyeuristic aspect of suffering, by using projections of blown-up photographs by Arthur Fellig (known as Weegee) that depict the faces of onlookers gaping at murder or accident victims. Its accompaniment includes a realistic crash noise and the foreboding sounds of a Henryk Gorecki string quartet. *Fields of View*, to a Philip Glass string quartet, features a central female figure continually parted from her male partner. He is finally led away by a female whom a critic saw as either a rival or the angel of death, and the woman is left to spin alone in a flurry of descending snow.[21]

Bizarre visions of the body on the edge of crisis are the stuff of *butoh*, a Japanese avant-garde movement. A person hangs upside-down, suspended under a bridge, his feet tied together. A writhing line of almost naked male and female bodies, their private parts emphasized with mirrored appendages, their arms pinioned over a long pole, emit howling, gasping sounds. A man in a white chiffon dress smashes a watermelon. Dancers carrying other bodies run in the rain, shrieking. Born in 1959 out of a form of protest theater, butoh celebrates the beauty of death, destruction and deformity, side by side with ancient Japanese legends and the blood-red and ghost-white makeup of kabuki. Its founder was Tatsumi Hijikata, a modern dance teacher who grew up in aching poverty and fell under the influence of Mary Wigman's mysticism. After Hijikata's death, the movement split into several troupes, but they all try to capture "the space between, where gods and spirits dwell, and souls speak to one another."[22]

Butoh is extreme in its mystical weirdness. Fascinatingly, Hijikata enacted his own death. Although his body was entangled in intravenous tubes, he wanted to die while performing to applause. Bill T. Jones had similarly staged a performance at the deathbed of Arnie Zane. As Jones told a writer, he ritualized Zane's death with songs by Jones's sisters, with a rabbi's words about the Book of Genesis, with Yiddish songs, and with the members of his and Zane's dance troupe.[23]

Sexual Relations and Identity

Stemming from the fact that the body is the instrument of our art form, every dance work expresses a male-female attitude. This may go by the name of romance, love, mating, courtship, male dominance, women's lib, or just human relationships. Specific types of sexual behavior arise jointly from the choreographer's instructions and the performers' attitudes. Even in a solo work, the dance figure takes a sexual position—sex meant here as gender.

This sexual element lends a special intimacy to the dance situation. Needless to say, the intimacy is not one of direct contact, either dancer-to-dancer or with the audience. Among the performers, when their bodies touch in the closest, most suggestive ways, there is seldom any explicit sexual feeling. Similarly, as involved as the viewers may be in the dance performance, they do not become so sexually excited that they rush onto the stage and have it off with the dancers. That's because the choreographer never provides a sexual experience, but an image of one.

Balletic Attitudes

Male-female relationships in dance have constantly undergone changes in response to changing cultures. Classical ballets always feature a *pas de deux* for the lead couple, and as Balanchine has said, a duet is a love story. "People in love all over the world have a certain attitude of sweetness and tenderness in the way they look and talk and touch. A choreographer notices this and finds movements to portray not the romance of A and B, but romance in general."[24]

Traditional ballets offer three main approaches to sex. One approach stems from the romantic ballet, which denies the existence of sexual qualities. The male, costumed in flowing cloaks and airy sleeves, bears a dreamy demeanor. His love, her pelvis concealed by yards of tulle and her bosom flattened into a decorated bodice, acts like a sprite, a sylph, a doll—never a woman.

A second approach is Balanchine's contribution. His New York City Ballet, which excels in technical brilliance, also plays down sexuality. Whether the work is *Concerto Barocco* or *Stravinsky's Violin Concerto* or *Agon*, animal passion is never the issue. But his ballets don't play "let's pretend." Rather do Balanchine's males and females engage in rapidly changing, convoluted patterns that distill sexuality into a love of formal beauty.

A third approach is the traditional stance of noble perfection, as represented by Igor Youskevitch, who had much to say about the proper balance of masculinity and femininity:

> It is my belief that certain properties of physical motion are specifically feminine ... woman's walk, the gestures of her arms ... the conscious effort to please the opposite sex ... The inborn feminine tendency to show herself physically, combined with the natural feminine movements that are the cornerstone of her dance vocabulary, is to me the golden key to feminine dance.... Man does not possess any equivalent of the female's basic motion; consequently, his dance derives from external motivations.[25]

From the first step of a *pas de deux* we are aware of how the male looks at and treats the female, and vice versa. Does he lift her tenderly, or worshipfully, or merely as a 100-pound weight? Does she respond to him with abandon, or reserve, or not at all? Because the luggage that Bolshoi dancer Nikolai Fadeyechev had to transport (in a film of the *Black Swan pas de deux*) was the magnificent ballerina Maya Plisetskaya, he assumed a lovesick facial countenance as he carried her across the stage. However, his body, with its laborer's stance, belied his facial expression, and the effect was slightly ridiculous.

Nureyev's partnering of Fonteyn was more seemly. In the British Royal Ballet's film *Les Sylphides*, he floated her through space while himself maintaining a lightness and grace appropriate to the romantic theme and music. Yet the body attitude of both stars was romantic only within a limited, conventional framework, and the restrained bearing of the couple held little hint of surges of feeling or abandonment to emotion that have elsewhere gone under the label of "romantic."

Although the courtly classical tradition is very much alive today, male and female ballet roles are constantly changing. Antony Tudor and Agnes de Mille both made works that present men and women equally as strong, weak, tormented or fulfilled. His *Pillar of Fire, Undertow, Romeo and Juliet, Dark Elegies*, and her *Rodeo* and *Three Virgins and a Devil*, form portraits of people whose sexual orientation is modified by characteristics like awkwardness, or by the demands of their life situation.

All the choreography of Jerome Robbins dwells on youth and beauty in males and females, together and apart. With the exception of extreme cases like *The Cage* (described in the first chapter), the overall spirit of relationships is friendly, open and balanced.

Although most sexual relationships in dance are treated seriously, there are works of lightness and humor as well. In Frederick Ashton's cartoonlike *La Fille Mal Gardée*, village youngsters play tricks on an elderly widow who is trying to force her daughter Lisette, who loves Colin, into marriage with the foolish Alain. After much merriment, the happy couple is united with a kiss, and the widow too gets a man. A similar tone characterizes the love interest in Arthur Saint-Léon's *Coppélia* (described in the chapter on design).

New York City Ballet dancers in *The Cage* by Jerome Robbins. Photograph by Martha Swope, © Time Inc.

John Cranko used the *pas de deux* in *The Taming of the Shrew* to mark changes in Katherine's and Petruchio's relationship, from her spiteful fishwifery and his mean, domineering swagger to their mutual graciousness and affectionate love. In early duets he clutches and whips around her stiffly resistant, flex-footed, round-shouldered, twisting body, always depositing her with unceremonious thumps. In the middle of the ballet a similar type of lift-and-fall continues, giving way at unexpected moments to a looser, rollicking gaiety as they grow to like and appreciate each other's humor. In the final scenes he supports her with noble gentleness as she flies long-limbed, in graceful arcs above him—this more conventional balletic patterning alluding to their arrival at an accepted idealization of love.

Modern Dance Views

As for modern dance, from its very beginnings there has been a fairly equitable gender imagery. Isadora Duncan and the other early modern dancers (with the exception of Ted Shawn, all the modern dance pioneers were women) were not out to please men, but to express their own full involvement in life as strong, free and independent spirits.

Martha Graham's repertory presents the world almost entirely from the viewpoint of the powerful woman that she was. Her early works used only women, although this was less because of any principle than because men simply weren't available to her. In the late 1930s, when first Erick Hawkins and then other men, including the mercurial Merce Cunningham, joined her group, Graham was quick to make full use of their talents and their male qualities.

Graham wrote, "Desire is a lovely thing, and that is where the dance comes from, from desire."[26] But it is her desire. Men appear in a virile aspect. They battle with one another and sometimes pursue their own wishes. However, their primary function is to serve as catalysts for the emotional dramas of more complex women. Female qualities are presented as strength, self-assertion or ambivalence—rarely a trace of passivity. A woman may be subjugated by her own uncontrollable feelings, but never by a man. In her memoirs, Martha Graham wrote that she was baffled by women's liberation: "I never had the feeling I was inferior.... I always got whatever I wanted from men without asking."[27]

Doris Humphrey, whether in dramas like *Day on Earth* or musical visions like *Passacaglia*, portrayed a dignified equality of men and women. The same can be said of Hanya Holm, Tamiris, Anna Sokolow, Mary Wigman, and others. Their treatment of sexual love was sometimes sensual, but never licentious. In early modern dance choreography, the theme of conventional romance was often absent, or twisted, as in Lester Horton's *The Beloved*, described in an earlier chapter.

Both as the partner of Ruth St. Denis and as the director of his all-men's group, Shawn was an advocate for the principle of strong masculine dance. Shawn's group espoused a tribal approach to male gender, presenting a virile, self-sufficient world of stalwart warriors or tillers of the ground. Later, José Limón and others took up Shawn's position. In 1928, Limón chanced to attend a performance by the German Harold Kreutzberg. Limón was overwhelmed, and his direction in life was determined, when he saw that "a man could, with dignity and a towering majesty, dance. Not mince, prance, cavort, do 'fancy dancing' or 'show-off' steps. No. Dance as Michelangelo's visions dance and as the music of Bach dances."[28]

Dancing in his own compositions, José Limón had a fruitful partnership with a member of his group, Lukas Hoving. Limón used his own qualities in dramatic works, in opposition to Hoving's. Theirs was one of the first partnerships in Western theater dancing to feature a pair of contrasting men. According to one critic, the male duo worked like this:

As tall as Limón, Hoving was pale and Nordic where Limón was dark and Hispanic, coolly austere to Limón's passion.... Where Hoving was balletically vertical and rather brittle in his movement, Limón was tight and strong.... Limón chose these characters to represent situations or emotional struggles.... In *The Moor's Pavane*, a weak, shrewd man destroys his rival by finding out where he is vulnerable. In *La Malinche*, peasant overthrows tyrant.... *Emperor Jones* shows two outlaws from society seeking to gain control of a rogue empire.[29]

Both of these men, in their own way, were striking masculine figures.

Always, when he combined men with women, Limón clearly differentiated their movement styles. His convention of sexual love was an idealized human affection exemplified by his image of the first man and the first woman in *The Exiles*, where Adam and Eve are tenderly intimate, sharing a need for physical and emotional comfort—and in a flashback, a carefree partnership. Eve's gestures are more curving, softer than Adam's, out of respect for her femininity; yet they are equally desolate and mindful of the pain of banishment.

As modern dance developed through the 1950s, explicit sex scenes became the rule. Men and women were presented in tender, or passionate, or acrobatic, or flamboyantly sexual relations. Ted Shawn once bemoaned the fact that modern dancers, who had begun with such high purpose, were reduced to seeking ever new, ever more tortuous entanglements for love duets. He related one unforgettable *pas de deux* in which a female, borne aloft and spread-eagled on her partner's raised arm, slid down to his shoulder and slammed with her crotch against his jaw, causing his false teeth to emit a resounding clack in accompaniment. He chuckled, "Surely that was a novel percussion instrument!"[30]

Avant-Garde Sex, from 1960

When everything broke loose in the 1960s, not surprisingly there was inconsistent treatment of gender. Men and women were shown as ordinary people, as in Yvonne Rainer's *Connecticut Composite* (1969) in which lines of people walk back and forth along a wall, or in Jennifer Muller's *Lovers* (1978), in which males and females embrace one another or exchange angry looks. Echoes of Ted Shawn's all-male tribal approach are found in Gerald Arpino's *Olympics* (produced in 1966 by the Joffrey Ballet). A torchbearer, who spins around the stage in dazzling turns, presides over a display of physical prowess. Ten males wrestle, race and hurl themselves about in brilliant, athletically vivid dance passages.

John Butler used an abstract tribal approach in which the females are totally passive. Notably in *Carmina Burana* (1959), in *Catulli Carmina* (1964), and in *Moonfull,* he staged exotic lifts. But his males seem to drag, push, carry or otherwise support the weight of their females, who seldom get a chance to propel themselves independently through space. Butler's imagery is an updated version of the Olympian male, putting the female in her place. His pieces convey the coldness of a marble pavilion, littered with modish female statues. While the women aren't trophies of war, they are decorative appurtenances, displayed like embroidery on a satin vest. These works use females as graceful enhancements for a central male image.

The '60s also saw several sexual innovations, including attempts at erasing all sexual and gender references. In the dances that Alwin Nikolais choreographed, the performers' sex was indistinguishable. Such dance figures belong to a unisex race, proclaimed by their uniform body suits (skin tights and leotards), and more importantly by their neutral movement color. They are "creatures"—not animals, because much animal life is sex differentiated in conduct.

This sexual neutrality is probably the reason for the charge of "dehumanization" that often got Nikolais upset. He said, "I go psychotic everytime I hear the word. To most, it means no sex come-on."[31] Nikolais was right that his critics were troubled by lack of sex in his works—but not sex as come-on: sex as differentiated male and female human beings, which is the way most of us view people.

Merce Cunningham too was disinterested in gender as such. When he supported Carolyn Brown in *Scramble* (1967) he handled her with careful concentration on her balance and her safety. Sexual connotations did not enter the picture. Nor was it a case of a man displaying his partner, or lifting her onto a pedestal. A human male simply treated a human female with respect for her existence.

Less abstract but still "plotless," Paul Taylor's *Lento* (1967) features gender images of equilibrium. At the same time, there is a male-female *pas de deux* that conveys warm emotion. Women appear as graceful, lyrical, yet active figures; men are sturdy and dynamic, yet responsive and feeling.

Erick Hawkins, who like Limón had originally been inspired by Kreutzberg's manly dancing, changed completely after he left Martha Graham. He turned back to Isadora Duncan to recapture the plastic beauty of motion. In his pieces, men and women move in a fluid, undifferentiated serenity.

Another new twist made its appearance in the 1960s: the *pas de deux* with the tender, passionate image displayed by two men, rather than by a male-female pair. Rudi Dantzig's *Monument for a Dead Boy* is a clear homosexual statement; in other scenes, homosexuality is implicit. John Butler's *According to Eve*, which purported to be the tragedy of Cain and Abel as seen through the eyes of Eve, consists of several duets with Cain and Abel in slow-motion stroking that came across as an idealization of male affection. Paul Sanasardo's *Abandoned Prayer* is nothing more than the image of Judas consuming Jesus, the lover he betrayed. (At one point the Judas figure literally gnaws on the other's leg as though it were an ear of corn. If one is looking for a phallic symbol in a dance, here it is in that leg!)

In group choreography, one finds the all-male idea in pieces by Maurice Béjart for his *Ballet of the Twentieth Century*. John Neumeier followed suit in the first movement of his composition to Mahler's *Third Symphony*. Females are completely absent in this section, which features men cradling one another. Similarly, Neumeier's *Le Sacre* has a mass orgy with a group in the background; in the foreground there is an intimate, shuddering interlocking of two couples: on stage right, a male and female; on stage left, two ardent males.

Avant-garde choreographers also demonstrate that dancers of either sex may interpret roles which bear characteristics most often assigned to their opposite numbers. Take *Scheherazade*, originally choreographed in 1910 by Fokine to a score by Rimsky-Korsakov. In 1975, modern dancer Murray Louis created a new, two-hour version, accompanied by a collage of rock, electronic music, and Rimsky-Korsakov. He gave the title female role to male dancer Michael Ballard, because he wanted the part "to be sensual, not sexy."[32]

The piece is set in an East Village flat, where people meet to get stoned and dream. The Scheherazade figure moves in an arrogant, sinuous mode, taking many of the poses that photographs show us of Nijinsky himself. (Of course Nijinsky did not dance the role of Scheherazade, but the role of her golden slave. By copying the great dancer's poses, the choreographer set up echoes of Nijinsky's sexual crises.)

Twyla Tharp created *Fugue* in 1970 for herself, Sara Rudner and Rose Marie Wright. The three women, wearing boots and gaucho costumes, gave such an outstanding performance of quick, vigorous movements that are usually assigned to "macho" men that some thought it was a "feminist" dance. Ten years later, however, Tharp had Tom Rawe, Raymond Kurshals and John Carrafa do *Fugue*. A critic claimed that the men: "not only redefine the dance, they redefine male dancing.... Tharp is the only choreographer I can think of who gives her men their total physical potential.... She puts men and women on an equal footing. Sex is not an issue, which gives everybody's sexuality more scope."[33]

Another sexual image in dance is an androgynous one. *Last Night on Earth*, a 1993 solo, presented the muscular Bill T. Jones with shoulder-

Scheherazade, with Murray Louis Dance Company. Photograph by Tom Caravaglia, courtesy Nikolais/Louis Foundation for Dance. © Tom Caravaglia.

length hair and a flimsy white miniskirt that barely covered a sequined jockstrap, dancing and singing vehemently about love and loss, and concluding with his slowly lying down on a white rectangle that represented his deathbed. At times Mark Morris, himself with long curly hair, also clothes himself and other company males in chiffon skirts.

During the 1992 Jacob's Pillow season, there was an all-male concert to honor the centenary of Ted Shawn's birth. The man chosen to assemble the program was Robby Barnett of Pilobolus, a company that made its debut as an all-male quartet. (Later they included women in the group.) The memorial program featured *Kinetic Molpai*, premiered by Shawn's group in 1936 and restaged by Shawn in 1962. Its theme is death and resurrection, in the spirit of tribal ritual. A group leader is drawn down to the earth, and exits, leaving his men bereft. Then he returns—perhaps in spirit—to inspire and lift his fellows up once more.

A highlight of the 1992 concert honoring Shawn was José Limón's intensely moving *The Unsung*, a piece he had dedicated to Shawn in 1970. This too is a vision of tribal men. The sections were named for Native American heroes and nations, and the dancers' rhythmical foot stamping provided the only accompaniment. Along with other numbers, Stephen Petronio's *Surrender II* projected a straining sexuality, where two men entwine so completely that their physical boundaries blur.

As the 1992 concert demonstrated, since the era when Shawn's men's group was active in the 1930s, many changes have occurred in the male-female dance scene. Robby Barnett agreed that things could be said in the 1990s about male relationships that were taboo in Shawn's day. On the other hand, the dancer maintained that profound prejudices were still rampant.

In all versions of *Romeo and Juliet* and in *The Moor's Pavane*, José Limón's interpretation of Shakespeare's *Othello*, the inferior position of women is accepted as completely natural. It is a given that both Juliet and Desdemona will be totally submissive and obedient to the dictates of fathers, husbands and the society at large. From the late 1970s up to the present, however, in line with the women's movement, women have been seen and heard from in entirely new, sometimes startling ways.

Patricia Beatty choreographed *Mandala* (1993), in which five young women (one of them pregnant) are initiated by five older ones into the feminine mysteries. Beatty was part of a very serious group of dedicated artists who believed that unless a balance was achieved between feminine and masculine archetypes, the earth would be destroyed.[34]

A group calling itself Urban Bush Women, under the direction of Jawole Willa Jo Zollar, presented *Heat* in 1989, giving voice to black women's hopes and horrors. One scene has several disoriented street people dazedly move in the shadows while the enraged Zollar strips her upper body bare and crushes raw eggs against herself.

The Yellow Wallpaper (1993) is a strong indictment of society's attitudes towards females. The theatrically imaginative work by Paula Josa-Jones is based on a story by Charlotte Perkins Gilman. The dance traces the mental deterioration of women because of their repression at the hands of callous men. With the help of words, the dance shows how men use pious strategies like calling women "the fairer sex" to curb intellectual and physical freedom.

Among many artists that present feminist pieces, consider The Out-of-Towners 1990: "From Puerto Rico came Petra Bravo and Awilda Sterling.... The two, in negligees and mud masks, plump up their breasts and defiantly pinch the fat on their arms and legs, mocking male-imposed images of sleek feminine beauty."[35] Such specifically unpleasant images of women are designed not for an aesthetic experience, but to make the viewer think about their situation.

David Gordon created *Dorothy and Eileen* (1981) for two female dancers, Valda Setterfield and Margaret Hoeffel. The movement content is a restrained *pas de deux* which has the two women hold, caress and support one another. The accompaniment is verbal, each dancer relating autobiographical episodes about herself and her mother.

Nudity has also been used to shock audiences into awareness of sexual taboos for both genders. Thus Arnie Zane confronted his audience with *Continuous Replay* (1984). Throughout the piece, a naked male repeats the opening motif: a crouch with rounded back; a run; jabbing motions with cupped, pawlike hands; sudden turning and lowering of the head. Other males and females join in and split off at random, like a pack of primitive creatures, until the whole naked cast is assembled before the audience. Then the members of the herd wander in and out, unfolding their bodies and softening their motions, gradually donning undergarments: just a top, or a just bottom, then both. Meanwhile the key male faces us bare, continuously replaying his original phrase, challenging the audience with the basic nature of nudity and its cover-ups.

But for every sexual image calculated to instruct or shock, there are endless pieces that strive for passion and romance, whether dramatically representational, or coolly abstract.

Concluding Thoughts on Dance as Ritual

After this wide-ranging survey, perhaps you will agree that looking at dance is a ritual activity. Immersed in the flow of physical energy, the very element—the landscape—of our art form, the viewer becomes a communicant in a temple. He or she reacts kinaesthetically with nerves and muscles to the life energy of dance.

Planned dance events are unique in that they set up a dream field of poetic figures who put us in touch with the basic facets of being human: energy of body and spirit, life in the face of mortality, and sex. Choreographers may thus be regarded as priests and priestesses who lead their audiences through ritual services. There is, however, a major difference between our participation in contemporary dance events and the participation of our tribal forebears in their own rituals. Tribes are united in advance by their shared attitudes, whereas enormous variations on the basic themes of existence characterize our complex society. On the one hand, therefore, we attend dance events with diverse mind sets, and have to work at opening ourselves to different viewpoints. On the other hand, if we can suspend pre-judgment, we will come out of our dance experiences better able to understand our fellows.

11

Critical
Questions

Lastly we come to evaluation, a process of great interest in the dance world. We will look at audience response and the way company directors try to fill the house; then finally, we will discuss what makes a work good or bad according to critics and aestheticians.

Audiences and Directors

In places like New York City, the audience is really split into many audiences, each devoted to one type of dance or even a single artist. At any concert there is a snobbish élite who come to show off their own expertise as well as pay tribute to their idols. They may be few in number, but they tend to set the tone for the social ritual.

Although audiences play a reactive rather than an active role, their presence is as necessary to a dance performance as that of the dancers themselves. Responsive viewers lift performers to new heights, while bored and inattentive viewers literally throw dancers off balance. Even before they enter the theater, audiences are turned on by the appearance of big-name stars who easily become cult figures: Anna Pavlova, Vaslav Nijinsky, Rudolf Nureyev, Mikhail Baryshnikov in ballet; Isadora Duncan, Martha Graham, Merce Cunningham and Twyla Tharp in modern dance. Pina Bausch became a cult figure in the early 1990s, when she and her company were booked until the end of century.

Some dance events cater openly to audience preferences. About 200 American companies present *The Nutcracker* during the Christmas season. The New York City Ballet used to stage Balanchine's one-act *Swan Lake* when they wanted to bolster attendance. Director Bruce Marks of the Boston Ballet spoke of his "bookends" approach: opening and closing each season with a full-length story ballet, to pull people into the theater. Other directors try to win audience favor by doing something new. A case in point is the Joffrey Ballet's production of the show piece *Billboards* (to rock songs by Prince Rogers Nelson, known simply as Prince), which has elicited screams of pleasure from young audiences in towns across America.

But while audiences in general go for pop pieces like *Billboards*, there is one group of viewers who hold back: the critics. Martin Bernheimer of *The Los Angeles Times* sneered at *Billboards* as "tasteless, vapid and silly." Joffrey's director Gerald Arpino was incensed by criticism of its commercialism. He told a writer that the company was threatened with bankruptcy, and Prince's songs, which were donated and brought in full houses, were a gift from heaven. "I'm tired of begging!" he thundered.[1]

Arpino was responding to a most unaesthetic situation: the shortage of money, as ubiquitous and unpleasant a reality of the dance world as body sweat. Because dance productions are painfully expensive, artists continually find themselves up against hard budgetary facts. There is the cost of maintaining a building if one is lucky enough to own one, or else rental of theaters and rehearsal space. Fees are owed to composers, designers and choreographers. Materials and equipment must be bought and wages paid to specialists who construct scenery, set up lights, sew costumes, print and distribute programs and tickets, take photographs and videotape, get out publicity, usher in audiences. There are royalties on music, insurance payments, transportation costs for touring. Salaries must be paid to administrators and office help, musicians, and last—and often least—to dancers.

A number of companies count on *The Nutcracker* to pull them out of the red. These were expected yields for a recent Christmas season: San Francisco Ballet, $3.8 million; New York City Ballet, $5.5 million; Boston Ballet, $4.5 million; Houston Ballet, $2 million.[2]

Ticket prices alone can never support dance, and help has long been available from other sources. Private philanthropies like the Ford Foundation and the Lila Wallace–Reader's Digest Fund have made tremendous contributions to companies large and small. Individual impresarios like Harvey Lichtenstein of the Brooklyn Academy of Music and Jeremy Alliger of the Boston Dance Umbrella have raised money and provided stage space for avant-garde artists like Merce Cunningham and Mark Morris.

Government has also played a part through states' arts councils and the National Endowment for the Arts. Currently, however, the flow of American public money is subsiding. This is partly because of tight economic conditions and partly because of changing political and social values. Many American congressmen are arguing for severe curtailment of government spending on art. They say that subsidy is a luxury we cannot afford. Their cause is championed by vocal groups who attack the arts as leftist, or pornographic, or politically correct, or politically incorrect. In the light of the above facts, one can appreciate Arpino's impatience with critical disapproval of Joffrey's *Billboards*.

It is understandable for Arpino to ask why he should heed the judgments of critics when even at this "expert" level there is a wide divergence of opinions. Take *Still/Here*, the Bill T. Jones statement about death and survival. After its premiere performance in Lyons, France, a rapturous audience stomped its feet in appreciation for fifteen minutes. Critic Laura Shapiro called it a work so original and profound that "its place among the landmarks of 20th century dance seems ensured."[3] Yet Arlene Croce bitterly damned the work, which she refused to see, let alone review, calling it not art but "a kind of messianic traveling medicine show" and "intolerably voyeuristic," and "literally undiscussable—the most extreme case among

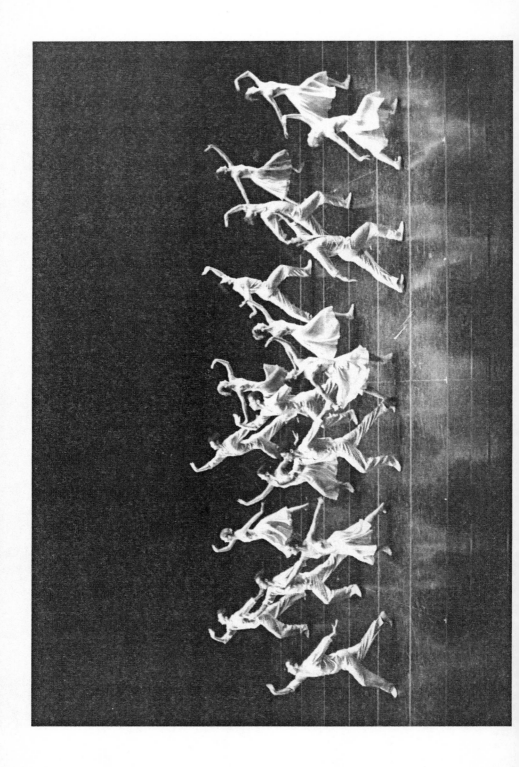

the distressingly many now representing themselves to the public not as artists, but as victims."[4]

Doris Hering, who did review *Still/Here*, complained that the dance added no fresh insight to the survival workshops that gave rise to the piece. She wrote that "Jones has yet to stare death in the face the way Kurt Jooss did in *The Green Table*."[5] In her reasonable tone, Anna Kisselgoff conceded that while the choreography has occasional blank spots and stop-and-go phrases that do not develop, "*Still/Here* succeeds because it evokes mixed feelings with an amazing blend of simplicity and sophistication."[6]

Many other examples of conflicting reviews could be cited, leading to the conclusion that no critic walks into a concert as an empty vessel, for the reception of an experience. Rather she or he is handicapped, aided, or at the very least influenced by personal taste and by aesthetic criteria that inevitably affect her or his reactions.

Dance Aesthetics and Critics

In one sense this whole book has been circling around questions of dance aesthetics, but its goal is not to formulate an aesthetic philosophy so much as to encourage what critic Edwin Denby called "aesthetic common sense."[7] After noting the ephemeral nature of dance and the consequent poverty of the dance-critical heritage, Denby went on to point out that it wasn't such a bad thing "that dance criticism is in a rudimentary or pioneering stage," because that makes it "more inviting to poets than to school teachers" and therefore for a century or so dance criticism should be "fun to write and to read."[8]

Each major dance style has had its advocates. Aesthetician Wilfried Hofmann touted classical ballet for a number of reasons. First of all, said Hofmann, its abstract movements have the most obvious mathematical-geometrical components, making them clearest in form. Secondly, it presents the best vision of "correct proportions" as well as the delight of asymmetry. Thirdly, in contrast to modern dance and jazz, it keeps a keen sense of the difference between the female body and the male, which "bespeaks its sophisticated human focus." Fourthly, because centrifugal (*en dehors*) motions are more extroverted, optimistic and healthy than centripetal (*en dedans*) motions, ballet, based on a turned-out posture, is a highly aesthetic form.[9]

Beginning in the 1930s, Lincoln Kirstein published articles, pamphlets

OPPOSITE: **Joffrey Ballet of Chicago dancers in** *Billboards*. **Photograph** © MIG-DOLL 1998.

and books making a case for the universality and timeless appeal of classical ballet. In one piece he wrote:

> Why do people like dancing, anyway?... [Because of its] denial of earthly gravity, an ultimate freedom of action, a super-human domination of flesh and earth. By definition, the dance is acrobatic.... Classic ballet training provides first of all substructure for acrobatic brilliance ... and the classic dance instructs us in something else which is even more necessary. This a classic style. High style ... is one of the few permanent visible signals of possible perfection in immediate human capacity.[10]

In contrast, modern dance advocates like Margaret Lloyd extolled the way modern dance continually opens "new paths for the expression of the human spirit ... the inner nature of man."[11] Susanne Langer's definition of art as feelings cast in expressive forms, and beauty as closely entwined with expressiveness, also struck a blow for modern dance. [12]

John Martin, perhaps the first fulltime dance critic in America, identified completely with modern dance. He was in the movement from the start "not as dancer nor dancewright but as spokesman and critic." He saw the works of the moderns from an ideological slant, to the extent that he frequently prescribed what modern dance should or should not do. For example, he said it was wrong to choreograph modern dance to a composer like Bach.[13] Doris Humphrey, who choreographed to Bach's *Passacaglia in C Minor* (described in the chapter on music), wrote in answer to Martin's decree that she had done so because Bach had "the greatest of all genius for these very qualities of variety held in unity, of grandeur of the human spirit, of grace for fallen man" that were so close to Humphrey's heart.[14]

George Beiswanger, a perceptive critic and aesthetician, was brought up on ballet, and discussed his first adverse reactions to modern dance:

> The writer has never forgotten his physical discomfort at the première of Martha Graham's *American Document,* a discomfort that failed to show up at any later performance. It was some time before I became aware of the reason: my perceptual insistence the first time around that the dance movement rise from, rather than dig into, the floor. Habits of seeing dance are not easy to change. It took more looking at Merce Cunningham's dances than I like to admit, to break out of the perceptual pattern by which movements had to be fitted to a regular rhythmic beat in order to go together.[15]

Cunningham's avant-garde work got a tremendous boost from his musical director John Cage, who was an enormously influential cult figure in his day. Cage characteristically liked only what was unfamiliar. One of his anecdotal comments was that when he heard Webern's short string quartet pieces some time in the 1940s, he was so excited he sat on the edge of his seat. But if forced to listen to that music twenty years later, he said, he would have walked out of the hall.

Susan Sontag defended the coming of the avant-garde:

> Art today is a new kind of instrument, an instrument for modifying consciousness and organizing new modes of sensibility.... Having one's sensorium challenged or stretched hurts.... But the purpose of art is always, ultimately, to give pleasure—though our sensibilities may take time to catch up with the forms of pleasure that art in a given time may offer.[16]

Critic Marcia Siegel reenforced the idea that the avant-garde was conceptual, an interesting mental exercise, and the more unusual it was, the more it required of the viewer. She wrote that the viewer was not courted by avant-garde artists, whose object was to keep one shocked and alert by the intensity of performance—never "lulled" into pleasure. The adventurous Siegel went so far as to participate in certain events. This was, she claimed, the best way of understanding postmodern dance.[17]

Others rejected the Cage Pied Piper. Paul Taylor wrote that the Cage mystique struck him as an example of the "emperor's new clothes."[18]

In 1970, when Cunningham staged his *Second Hand* in which dancers passed in and out of view as they moved behind large electric fans on long poles, this author found Cage's accompanying music highly irritating. He was meandering along the piano keys in wide intervals in the middle register without rhythmic pattern, accent or variation in dynamics. Taking advantage of a telephone interview with the choreographer the author complained that the music fought or even negated the movement. Cunningham's answer was fascinating: "But perhaps the two things worked together to support each other. Perhaps if the music would not have been what you call 'negating it' the dance would have seemed less interesting."[19]

Helped by the fact that they have some idea what to expect, experienced critics have the ability to size up the qualities of a dance on one viewing. An intelligent reader learns from critics "not what to think about a work, but how to think about it."[20] Critics are in a position to be the intellectual, philosophical specialists of the dance world. Their claim to expertise is based on knowledge about the repertory and the major technical systems of ballet, modern, ethnic dance and jazz. They have spoken to artists about their work and understand their varied choreographic approaches. They have a grounding in dance history, as well as knowledge about all the topics discussed in this book. The best ones have interesting minds and make stimulating companions for dance viewers. The best criticism provokes thought.

But we rely on critics first and foremost to supply us with another service. We want a judgment from the critics as to whether a dance event is worth the price of a ticket.

Aesthetic philosopher Bertram Jessup took a strong position on this aspect of a critic's job. He insisted that an essential ingredient of good criticism was evaluation.[21] According to Jessup we have every right to expect this service, and in practice, most reviewers do take on such a responsibility. To clarify the question of judgment, we will look at a number of reviews, paying less attention to the works and the choreographers discussed than to the way the critics evaluated them.

Bill T. Jones presented *Ursonate* and *Ballad*, both of them noteworthy for their accompaniment of verbal sounds. Anna Kisselgoff told her readers to "run, do not walk to see and (this is the operative word) hear *Ursonate*," a dance of structured disconnectedness choreographed together with Darla Villani to a rhythmic nonsense text by Kurt Schwitters, a founding artist of the Dada movement after World War I. To hear the stunning vocalist Christopher Butterfield "roll his r's, spew out grunts and syllables in an astonishing non-verbal display is to understand how the search for the 'transrational' acquires a meaning of its own." Although Butterfield provided strong competition, "Ms. Villani, lanky and loose-hipped, and Mr. Jones, coiled as a spring, held their own in duets or as part of a white-clad ensemble that rushed in and out."[22]

Then Jennifer Dunning commented that Jones took on a difficult task in *Ballad*, a loving response to Dylan Thomas's reading of his poetry. "His choreography seldom illustrates or overtly refers to the poetry. The pairing often works best if one thinks of the poems as word-music for the dance."[23] Thus in the Jones dances, the accompaniment was the interesting innovation, rather than the choreography.

About Kevin Wynn's *Of Sushi, Collard Greens and Salsa*, to music by David Lewitt, Dunning wrote that Wynn, with a highly impressive sense of full-stage patterning, "is as much an architect as a choreographer at heart." The piece has a "breathtaking formal beauty in the way the dancers seamlessly cluster and disperse." Unfortunately, the dance begins "to seem overly long and repetitious well before its end. And there is a sameness to all four pieces on the program."[24] Thus despite the strength in spatial design, the critic perceived faults in the structure of the piece, as well as in the development of movement rhythms and dynamics in the entire program.

Francis Patrelle offered his own new interpretation of Stravinsky's *Firebird*, subtitling it *A Passion Play*. He transformed the title character from a female to a male and pitted the forces of light against the forces of darkness. But, as Jack Anderson noted, the basic moral issues were presented so early in the action that the ballet became dramatically static, as the work proceeded with "a multitude of much too repetitive struggles." On the plus side, there were richly eerie spectacular elements—"symbolic prison bars, piles of skulls and mysterious caverns"—by Gilian Bradshaw-Smith, and strong performances by the dancers. "What was missing was a sturdy plot."[25] Again there were flaws in structural build-up, as well as weakness in unfolding the subject.

Antony Tudor's 1975 *The Leaves Are Fading* (to music by Dvorak) was an unqualified success. Dunning commented that the ballet, which "takes a lyrical, serene look back at youthful passion," was matched by American Ballet Theater's Julie Kent's perfect interpretation. Her "liquid phrasing and the lightness of her arms placed her character firmly in the past. Small, fleeting gestures established who that character was and why she was to be cared about, while Ms. Kent's quiet daring was very much of the present."[26]

According to Kisselgoff another Ballet Theater star made up for some generally bad choreography in *Voyage* (Mozart) by Renato Zanella, director of the Vienna Opera Ballet. "Vladimir Malakhov was nothing short of sensational ... moving with pantherine silkiness.... The choreography was trite in form and content. Yet Mr. Malakhov traveled so beautifully through this life journey of alienation that every movement was eye riveting."[27]

A self-defeating choreographer was the subject of Jack Anderson's review of Keely Garfield's *Paper Cuts*, which presented scenes of "love, grief, passion, madness and death." The production, which "mocked pop sentimentality, balletic Romanticism and operatic melodrama, revealed that Ms. Garfield had a real sense of humor." Nevertheless, after a short time the jokes in her 50-minute duet grew monotonous, because the two dancers, Garfield and Rachel Lynch-John, became obsessed with toilet paper. They "wore ball gowns and elaborate head-dresses made of toilet paper, immersed themselves in heaps of toilet paper, acted like cheerleaders waving toilet paper pompoms and pretended to be mothers giving birth to lumps of toilet paper."[28]

Garth Fagan's *Earth Eagle First Circle*, inspired by American Indian culture, was a stylistic mixture that came off badly in Jennifer Dunning's review, as indeed did the overall image. Although Dunning commented favorably on the smoothness of the dancers' movements, she found the work disappointing, mostly because of the score by Don Pullen (a jazz pianist and member of the Chief Cliff Singers). Dunning also objected to

> an unfortunate motif of whizzing à la seconde turns danced by a man wearing an Indian headdress with trailing feathers. And Mr. Fagan, not one for clichés, makes use of some fairly stereotypical elements of Indian dance and ceremony.[29]

Another matter entirely was a 1996 performance of *Intensities of Space, and Wind*, created by Erick Hawkins in 1991. Dunning praised its luminously radiant poetic image whose atmosphere of mystery "draws in the viewer." There was enhancement of the image by the "rich and vivid layering of sounds" composed by Katsuhisa Hattori and Meisha Tosha, and the "airy enclosure for dance created by Robert Engstrom's soft, clear lighting." Its ten dancers "cross and recross the stage space in pairs and on their own, running gently and traveling in cantering sideways jumps" in a ceaseless-seeming flow. The movement, punctuated by drops to the floor and a sensuous clinging, gradually grows more forceful and varied. Dunning found "the closing image of a man moving across a rapidly darkening stage" to be quietly stunning.[30]

In Conclusion

A great dance is one treated with imagination and fresh vision, in regard to each element discussed in this book: the overall image, the style and technique, the subject and its reflection in mimetic or abstract gesture, the development of the movement in its spatial design, rhythms and dynamics, the compositional structure, the sound accompaniment, the stage design and costumes, and finally the performance. Great dances don't come along too often. The best one can usually expect is a *good* dance, in which the strong points far outweigh the weaknesses.

Merce Cunningham said that dance is like water: "You know something is there, but it slips through your fingers."[31] In this book the author has tried to get a grasp on the fluid business of dance long enough to describe its nature. As each of you makes a journey of exploration through the dance world, with motives and experiences uniquely your own, the author hopes that the material presented in this study will add to your appreciation.

LIBRARY, UNIVERSITY OF CHESTER

Notes

Chapter 1. Life, Art and Dance

1. Paul Taylor, *Private Domain*, 31.
2. Susanne K. Langer, *Problems of Art*, 7.
3. John Cranko, 11.
4. Merce Cunningham, *Changes: Notes on Choreography*, unpaginated.
5. Marcia B. Siegel, *The Shapes of Change*, 303.
6. Judith Jamison, *Dancing Spirit*, 143.
7. Nancy V. Dalva, "Paul Taylor: A Very Appealing Genius," 40.
8. LeRoy Leatherman, *Martha Graham*, 38.
9. Walter Sorell, ed., "Martha Graham Speaks," 53.
10. Susanne K. Langer, *Feeling and Form*, 177.
11. Susanne K. Langer, *Problems of Art*, 26.
12. Martha Graham, *Blood Memory*, 231.
13. Michel Fokine, *Memoirs*, 222.
14. Vera Krasovskaya, "Marius Petipa and *The Sleeping Beauty*," 48.
15. Walter Sorell, ed., *The Dance Has Many Faces*, 39.
16. Michel Fokine, *Memoirs*, 183.
17. Richard Buckle, *Diaghilev*, 241.
18. Lee E. Stern, "Paul Taylor," 38.

Chapter 2. Styles in Review: Ethnic and Ballet

1. Meyer Schapiro, "Style," *Aesthetics Today*, 81–113.
2. Alan Lomax, *Filmmakers Newsletter*, vol. 4, no. 4.
3. Walter Sorell, ed., *The Dance Has Many Faces*, 9.
4. Jacqueline Kolmes in *Dance Magazine*, Dec. 1994, 34–36.
5. Review by Anna Kisselgoff, *New York Times*, Dec. 5, 1994.
6. La Meri, *Spanish Dancing*, 85.
7. Vicente García-Márquez, *Massine*, 136.
8. Cohen, *Dance as a Theater Art*, 1–10.
9. Joan Cass, *Dancing Through History*, 122–131.
10. Michael Fokine, *Memoirs*, 72.
11. Edwin Denby, *Dancers, Buildings and People in the Streets*, 79.
12. *Ibid.*, 85.

Chapter 3. Expressive Styles and Beyond

1. Victor Seroff, *The Real Isadora*, 357.
2. Ilya Ilyich Schneider, *Isadora Duncan*, 73.
3. David Vaughan, "Merce Cunningham," 82.
4. Merce Cunningham, *Changes*, unpaginated.
5. Quoted in John Cage, *Dancers on a Plane*, 29.
6. John Cage, Merce Cunningham, and Jasper Johns, *Dancers on a Plane*, 84.
7. Review by Jack Anderson, *New York Times*, Sept. 15, 1994.
8. Merce Cunningham, "The Function of a Technique for Dance," in Walter Sorell, ed., *The Dance Has Many Faces*, 257.
9. Sally Banes, *Terpsichore in Sneakers*, 42.
10. Michael Blackwood, *Making Dances*. Also see Sally R. Sommer, "Trisha Brown Making Dances," 9–11.
11. Sally Banes, *Terpsichore in Sneakers*, 61.
12. *Ibid.*, 65–70.
13. Sally Banes, *Terpsichore in Sneakers*, 189.
14. Pina Bausch, interview by Eva Hoffman, *New York Times*, Sept. 11, 1994.
15. Reviews by Anna Kisselgoff, *New York Times*, Nov. 19 and Dec. 11, 1994.
16. Robert Greskovic, "Smoke Got in Her Eyes," 88.
17. Review by Christine Temin, *Boston Globe*, July 7, 1995.
18. Review by Jack Anderson, *New York Times*, Apr. 18, 1996.
19. John Lahr, "King Tap," 90.
20. Nancy Reynolds, *In Performance*, 177.
21. George Balanchine, *New Complete Stories*, 261.
22. Marcia B. Siegel, *At the Vanishing Point*, 304.
23. *Ibid.*, 303.
24. Marcia B. Siegel, *The Shapes of Change*, 262–270.
25. Twyla Tharp, *Push Comes to Shove*, 273.
26. *Ibid.*, 209–223.
27. *Ibid.*, 337.

Chapter 4. Subject and Body Language

1. Review by Jack Anderson, *New York Times*, Feb. 7, 1994.
2. Nancy V. Dalva, "Paul Taylor: A Very Appealing Genius," 41.
3. Merle Armitage, ed., *Martha Graham*, 97.
4. George Balanchine, *New Complete Stories*, 465.
5. Vera Krasovskaya, "Marius Petipa and *The Sleeping Beauty*," 24.
6. George Balanchine, *New Complete Stories*, 121.
7. Agnes de Mille, *Martha*, 99.
8. Marilyn Hunt, "Antony Tudor," 40.
9. Michel Fokine, *Memoirs*, 131.
10. Iris Fanger, "Morris' Playful Persona," 38.
11. *Ibid.*, 62.
12. Joan Acocella, *Mark Morris*, 233.
13. *Ibid.*, 165.
14. Martha Graham, *Notebooks*, 157.
15. Marcia B. Siegel, *At the Vanishing Point*, 276.
16. Mary Wigman, *The Language of Dance*, 18.
17. *Ibid.*, 12.
18. Walter Sorrel, ed., *The Mary Wigman Book*, 56.
19. Joan Acocella, *Mark Morris*, 76.
20. David Vaughan, *Frederick Ashton*, 296.
21. *Ibid.*, 205–209.
22. Doris Humphrey, *The Art of Making Dances*, 26.

Chapter 5. Compositional Engineering

1. Alwin Nikolais, interview by Joan Cass, "Show Guide," *Boston Herald Traveler*, Jan. 29, 1967, 15.
2. Jerome Robbins, "Reflections and Conversations," 52–54.
3. Cyril Beaumont, *The Ballet Called Swan Lake*, 110.
4. Calvin Tompkins, "An Appetite for Motion," 97–111.
5. Suzanne Farrell with Toni Bentley, *Holding On to the Air*, 237.
6. *Ibid.*, 236.

Chapter 6. Music and Dance, Partners in Art

1. Aaron Copland, *What to Listen for in Music*, 20.
2. Igor Stravinsky, *Poetics of Music*, 24–29.
3. Aaron Copland, *What to Listen for in Music*, 24.
4. Igor Stravinsky, *Poetics of Music*, 32.
5. Selma Jeanne Cohen, ed., "Composer/Choreographer," 7.
6. Doris Humphrey, *The Art of Making Dances*, 132.
7. Review by Bill Deresiewicz, *Dance Magazine*, June 1992, 71.
8. Walter Sorell, ed., *The Dance Has Many Faces*, 39–40.
9. Eliot Feld, interview by Joan Cass, "Show Guide," *Boston Herald Traveler*, June 1, 1969, 14.

10. Robert Starer, quoted in *Dance Perspectives* no. 16, 12.
11. Anthony Storr, *Music and the Mind*, 25.
12. Vivian Fine, untitled, 8.
13. Anthony Storr, *Music and the Mind*, 184.
14. George Balanchine, *New Complete Stories*, 11.
15. *Ibid.*, 363.
16. Gordon Boelzner, "Music," 54.
17. *Ibid.*, 29.
18. Aaron Copland, *What to Listen for in Music*, 19.
19. Igor Stravinsky, *Poetics of Music*, 30.
20. Isadora Duncan, *My Life*, 213.
21. George Balanchine, *New Complete Stories*, 61, 93, 430.
22. Louis Horst, untitled, 6.
23. Paul Taylor, *Private Domain*, 164.
24. Ric Estrada, "3 Leading Negro Artists," 60.
25. Review by Christine Temin, *Boston Globe*, June 9, 1993.
26. Review by Richard Dyer, *Boston Globe*, June 9, 1993.
27. Paul Taylor, *Private Domain*, 169–171.
28. Joan Acocella, *Mark Morris*, 176.
29. Roger Fiske, *Ballet Music*, 37.
30. *Ibid.*, 50.
31. Walter Sorell, ed., *The Dance Has Many Faces*, 140.
32. Aaron Copland, *Music and Imagination*, 37.
33. Michel Fokine, *Memoirs*, 185–186.
34. *Ibid.*, 189.
35. Dorian, *The History of Music in Performance*, 325.
36. Aaron Copland, *Music and Imagination*, 38.
37. George Balanchine, *New Complete Stories*, 10–11.
38. Frederick Dorian, *The History of Music in Performance*, 326.
39. *Ibid.*, 327.
40. George Balanchine, *New Complete Stories*, 134.
41. *Ibid.*, 135.
42. Mercer Ellington, *Duke Ellington in Person*, 199.
43. Alvin Ailey, interview by Joan Cass, "Entertainment," *Jerusalem Post* (Israel), Nov. 23, 1976, 7.
44. Walter Sorell, ed., *The Dance Has Many Faces*, 142.
45. Louis Horst, untitled, 6.
46. Peggy Van Praagh and Peter Brinson, *The Choreographic Art*, 316–318.
47. Igor Stravinsky, quoted in *Dance Perspectives* no. 16, 35.
48. Doris Humphrey, *The Art of Making Dances*, 136.
49. Philip Glass, *Music by Philip Glass*, 19.
50. Arlene Croce, *Sight Lines*, 125, 213.
51. Robert Greskovic, *Dance Magazine* (June 1994): 59.
52. Anna Kisselgoff, *New York Times*, Apr. 30, 1995.
53. Review by Christine Temin, *Boston Globe*, June 8, 1995.
54. Arlene Croce, "Musical Offerings," *New Yorker*, Jan. 8, 1996.
55. Review by Christine Temin, *Boston Globe*, June 8, 1995.

Chapter 7. Designing Artists

1. Robert Sealy, "The 'New' Firebird," 5.
2. David Vaughan, *Frederick Ashton*, 203.
3. Sally Banes, "Steve Paxton," 14.
4. Review by Iris Fanger, *Boston Herald*, Feb. 28, 1986.
5. Lincoln Kirstein, *Movement and Metaphor*, 34.
6. Rouben Ter-Arutunian, "In Search of Design," unpaginated.
7. Sally R. Sommer, "The Stage Apprenticeship of Loie Fuller," 23–34.
8. Cyril Beaumont, *Complete Book of Ballets*, 576–578.
9. Edwin Denby, *Looking at the Dance*, 261.
10. Vincente García-Márquez, *Massine*, 130–136.
11. Peggy Van Praagh and Peter Brinson, *The Choreographic Art*, 256.
12. Michel Fokine, *Memoirs*, 170–171.
13. *Ibid.*, 175.
14. Lynn Garafola, "The Triadic Ballet," 28.
15. Joan Acocella, "Armies of Angels," 50.
16. Edwin Denby, "About *Don Quixote*," 33.
17. Margaret E. Willis, "*Cinderella* in Tinseltown," 58–63.
18. Brice Merrill, "Baby Doll," 86–88.
19. Lynn Garafola, "Designing Woman," *New York Times Book Review*, Nov. 19, 1995.
20. Saul Goodman, "Meet Jean Rosenthal," 21.
21. Rouben Ter-Arutunian, "In Search of Design," unpaginated.
22. Doris Humphrey, *The Art of Making Dances*, 145.
23. Merce Cunningham, *Changes*, unpaginated.
24. John Cage, Merce Cunningham, and Jasper Johns, *Dancers on a Plane*, 29.
25. Review by Jennifer Dunning, *New York Times*, May 10, 1993.
26. Michael Kirby, *The Art of Time*, 130.
27. Richard Kostelanetz, "The Artist as Playwright and Engineer," 109.
28. Hilary Ostlere, "Jennifer Tipton," 48.
29. Review by Anna Kisselgoff, *New York Times*, Mar. 9, 1994.
30. Review by Jack Anderson, *New York Times*, Aug. 20, 1995.
31. Nancy V. Dalva, "Paul Taylor, Santo Loquasto, and *Speaking in Tongues*," 37.

Chapter 8. Gods and Goddesses: Performers on Stage

1. Anna Kisselgoff, "The Original Red Shoes," *New York Times*, Jan. 9, 1993.
2. Judith Jamison, *Dancing Spirit*, 27.
3. Gelsey Kirkland with Greg Lawrence, *Dancing on My Grave*, 56.
4. *Sylvie Guillem*, video program directed by Nigel Wattis for London Weekend Television.
5. Paul Taylor, *Private Domain*, 48.
6. Peter Martins with Robert Cornfield, *Far from Denmark*, 22.
7. Erik Bruhn, "Beyond Technique," passim.
8. Francis Mason, ed., *I Remember Balanchine*, 458, 573, 592.

9. *Ballerina, Great Roles*, video program directed by Derek Bailey, produced by the B.B.C.

10. Anton Dolin, *Pas de Deux*, 12, 18, 19.

11. Maria Elisa Bucella, "Alessandra Ferri," 56.

12. Janice Berman, "Patrick Corbin," 33.

13. Paul Taylor, "Down with Choreography" in Selma Jeanne Cohen, ed., *The Modern Dance*, 91.

14. Review by Robert Greskovic, *Dance Magazine*, Feb. 1994, 139.

15. Janice Berman, "Patrick Corbin," 30.

16. Susan Reiter, "Mary Cochran," 62–64.

17. Review by Rose Anne Thom, *Dance Magazine*, Feb. 1996, 124.

18. Marcia B. Siegel, *At the Vanishing Point*, 48, 55.

19. Nancy Dalva, "Cunningham in New York," 45.

20. Review by Jennifer Dunning, *New York Times*, Aug. 20, 1994.

21. Review by Jennifer Dunning, *New York Times*, Aug. 15, 1994.

22. Review by Anna Kisselgoff, *New York Times*, May 13, 1994.

Chapter 9. Thoughts About Repertory

1. George Balanchine, *New Complete Stories*, 333.

2. Murray Louis, *Inside Dance*, 112.

3. Review by Christine Temin, *Boston Globe*, Apr. 29, 1995.

4. Lynn Garafola, "Peter Martins," 39.

5. Review by Anna Kisselgoff, *New York Times*, June 26, 1994.

6. Review by Anna Kisselgoff, *New York Times*, Mar. 3, 1996.

7. *Accent on the Offbeat*, video program from the *Dance in America* series.

8. Review by Kisselgoff, *New York Times*, June 26, 1994.

9. Roslyn Sulcas, "Trisha Brown," 45.

10. Review by Anna Kisselgoff, *New York Times*, May 5, 1994.

11. Review by Jennifer Dunning, *New York Times*, Mar. 9, 1995.

12. Emily Mitchell with Adrienne Jucius Navone, *A Mouse That Soars*, 1–2.

13. Paula Citron, "Now and Forever," 66.

14. *Garth Fagan's "Griot, New York,"* video program from the *Dance in America* series.

15. Wilma Salisbury, "Cleveland Ballet," 96.

Chapter 10. Moving Rituals

1. Joan Cass, *Dancing Through History*, 1–19.

2. Armitage, *Martha Graham*, 103.

3. Marcia B. Siegel, ed., "Nik: A Documentary," 24.

4. Doris Humphrey, *The Art of Making Dances*, 102.

5. Walter Sorell, ed., *The Dance Has Many Faces*, 250, 252.

6. Calvin Tompkins, "Appetite for Motion," 78.

7. Suzanne K. Langer, *Feeling and Form*, 175.

8. Curt Sachs, *World History of the Dance*, 4–5.

9. Louis Horst, *Modern Dance Forms*, 17.

10. Agnes de Mille, *Martha*, 177–179.

11. Don McDonagh, *Martha Graham*, 276.

12. John Gruen, "Molissa Fenley," 41.

13. *Alvin Ailey American Dance Theater*, video program produced and directed by Thomas Grimm.

14. Review by Jennifer Dunning, *New York Times*, Dec. 5, 1994.

15. Review by Anna Kisselgoff, *New York Times*, Aug. 7, 1994.

16. Review by Jack Anderson, *New York Times*, Mar. 10, 1995.

17. Twyla Tharp, *Push Comes to Shove*, 304.

18. *Great Performances: Twyla Tharp*, PBS video, 1994.

19. Review by Jennifer Dunning, *New York Times*, May 6, 1991.

20. Henry L. Gates, Jr., "The Body Politic," 122.

21. Review by Anna Kisselgoff, *New York Times*, Nov. 11, 1994.

22. Michael Blackwood, *Butoh*, videotape.

23. Henry L. Gates, Jr., "The Body Politic," 118.

24. George Balanchine, *New Complete Stories*, 557.

25. Selma Jeanne Cohen, ed., "The Male Image," 14–16.

26. Martha Graham, *Blood Memory*, 6.

27. *Ibid.*, 25.

28. Selma Jeanne Cohen, ed., *The Modern Dance*, 23.

29. Marcia B. Siegel, *The Shapes of Change*, 309.

30. Ted Shawn, interview by Joan Cass, "Show Guide" (Dance section), *Boston Herald Traveler*, July 20, 1969.

31. Alwin Nikolais, interview by Joan Cass, "Show Guide," *Boston Herald Traveler*, Jan. 29, 1967, 15.

32. Kitty Cunningham, "Michael Ballard," *Dance Magazine*, Dec. 1975, 40–45.

33. Marcia B. Siegel, *The Tail of the Dragon*, 104.

34. Paula Citron, "Dance and the Emerging Feminine Principle," 40.

35. Gus Solomons, Jr., "The Out-of-Towners 1990," 89.

Chapter 11. Critical Questions

1. Robert Plunkett, "*Billboards*," 1.

2. Christine Temin, "*The Nutcracker*," 16.

3. Henry L. Gates, Jr., "The Body Politic," 123.

4. Arlene Croce, "Discussing the Undiscussable," 54.

5. Doris Hering, "Bill T. Jones," 77.

6. Review by Anna Kisselgoff, *New York Times*, Dec. 2, 1994.

7. Edwin Denby, "Dance Criticism," in Chujoy, *Dance Encyclopedia*, 235.

8. *Ibid.*, 236.

9. Selma Jeanne Cohen, ed., "Three Essays in Dance Aesthetics," 22–26.

10. Lincoln Kirstein, "Blast at Ballet," 99–100.

11. Lloyd, *The Borzoi Book of Modern Dance*, Introduction.

12. Suzanne K. Langer, *Problems of Art*, 109, 119.

13. Selma Jeanne Cohen, ed., "Three Essays in Dance Aesthetics," 12.

14. Doris Humphrey, *An Artist First*, 256.

15. Selma Jeanne Cohen, ed., "Three Essays in Dance Aesthetics," 13.

16. Susan Sontag, *Against Interpretation*, 296–303.

17. Marcia B. Siegel, *The Tail of the Dragon*, 33.

18. Paul Taylor, *Private Domain*, 47.

19. Merce Cunningham, "I Begin with Moving," 14.

20. Denby, "Dance Criticism," in Chujoy's *Dance Encyclopedia*, 234.

21. Bertram Jessup, "Taste and Judgment in Aesthetic Experience," in Nadel, ed., *The Dance Experience*, 197.

22. Review by Anna Kisselgoff, *New York Times*, June 13, 1996.

23. Review by Jennifer Dunning, *New York Times*, June 18, 1996.

24. Review by Jennifer Dunning, *New York Times*, Jan. 9, 1996.

25. Review by Jack Anderson, *New York Times*, Mar. 16, 1996.

26. Review by Jennifer Dunning, *New York Times*, May 6, 1996.

27. Review by Anna Kisselgoff, *New York Times*, May 9, 1996.

28. Review by Jack Anderson, *New York Times*, Apr. 22, 1996.

29. Review by Jennifer Dunning, *New York Times*, Aug. 5, 1995.

30. Review by Jennifer Dunning, *New York Times*, Feb. 16, 1996.

31. *Cage/Cunningham*, a film by Elliot Caplan on videotape.

Bibliography

Accent on the Offbeat. Video program from the *Dance in America* series.

Acocella, Joan. "Armies of Angels." *Dance Magazine* (Sept. 1987): 48–53.

_____. *Mark Morris.* New York: Farrar, Straus, and Giroux, 1993.

Ailey, Alvin. Interview by Joan Cass. "Entertainment," *Jerusalem Post* (Nov. 23, 1976): 7.

Alvin Ailey American Dance Theater. Video program produced and directed by Thomas Grimm.

Armitage, Merle, ed. *Dance Memoranda.* New York: Duell, Sloan and Pierce, 1947.

_____. *Martha Graham.* Brooklyn, N.Y.: Dance Horizons, 1966.

Balanchine, George. *New Complete Stories of the Great Ballets.* Garden City, New York: Doubleday, 1968.

Ballerina, Great Roles. Video program directed by Derek Bailey, produced by the B.B.C.

Banes, Sally. "Steve Paxton: Physical Things." *Dance Scope* 13, nos. 2 and 3 (1979): 11–25.

_____. *Terpsichore in Sneakers.* Boston: Houghton Mifflin, 1980.

Beaumont, Cyril. *The Ballet Called Swan Lake.* London: C.W. Beaumont, 1952.

_____. *Complete Book of Ballets.* New York: Grosset and Dunlap, 1938.

Berman, Janice. "Patrick Corbin." *Dance Magazine* (June 1994): 30–33.

Blackwood, Michael. *Butoh: Body on the Edge of Crisis.* Videotape. New York: Michael Blackwood Productions.

_____. *Making Dances: Seven Postmodern Choreographers.* Videotape. New York: Michael Blackwood Productions.

_____. *Retracing Steps: American Dance Since Postmodernism.* Videotape. New York: Michael Blackwood Productions.

Boelzner, Gordon. "Music." *Ballet Review* 3, no. 4 (1970): 51–62.

Bruhn, Erik. "Beyond Technique." *Dance Perspectives* no. 36 (1968).

Bucella, Maria Elisa. "Alessandra Ferri." *Dance Magazine* (Apr. 1994): 54–56.

Buckle, Richard. *Diaghilev.* New York: Atheneum, 1979.

Cage, John, Merce Cunningham, and Jasper Johns. *Dancers on a Plane.* New York: Alfred A. Knopf, 1990.

Cage/Cunningham. Videotape. A film by Elliot Caplan.

Cass, Joan. *Dancing Through History.* Needham Heights, Mass.: Allyn and Bacon, 1993.

Chazin-Bennahum, Judith. *The Ballets of Antony Tudor.* New York: Oxford University Press, 1994.

Chujoy, Anatole, ed. *The Dance Encyclopedia.* New York: Simon and Schuster, 1967.

Citron, Paula. "Dance and the Emerging Feminine Principle." *Dance Magazine* (Sept. 1993): 40–43.

_____. "Now and Forever." *Dance Magazine* (July 1993): 66.

Clarke, Mary, and Clement Crisp. *Design for Ballet.* New York: Hawthorn, 1978.

Cohen, Selma Jeanne. "Antony Tudor, Part Two: The Years in America and After." *Dance Perspectives* no. 18 (1963).

_____. *Doris Humphrey: An Artist First.* Middletown, Conn.: Wesleyan University Press, 1972.

_____, ed. *Dance as a Theater Art: Source Readings in Dance History.* New York: Dodd, Mead, 1974.

_____. "The Male Image." *Dance Perspectives* no. 40 (1969).

_____. *The Modern Dance: Seven Statements of Belief.* Middletown, Conn.: Wesleyan University Press, 1966.

_____. "Three Essays in Dance Aesthetics." *Dance Perspectives* no. 55 (1973).

Cohen, Selma Jeanne, and A.J. Pischl, eds. "Composer/Choreographer." *Dance Perspectives* no. 16 (1963): 6–8.

Copland, Aaron. *Music and Imagination.* Cambridge, Mass.: Harvard University Press, 1952.

_____. *What to Listen for in Music.* New York: McGraw-Hill, 1957.

Cranko, John. "I'm Allowed to Be Nervous." Interview by Joan Cass. "Show Guide," *Boston Herald Traveler* (June 22, 1969): 11.

Croce, Arlene. "The Balanchine Show." *The New Yorker* (June 7, 1993): 99–103.

_____. "Discussing the Undiscussable." *The New Yorker* (Jan. 2, 1995): 54–60.

_____. *Sight Lines.* New York: Alfred A. Knopf, 1987.

Cunningham, Kitty. "Michael Ballard." *Dance Magazine* (Dec. 1975): 40–45.

Cunningham, Merce. *Changes: Notes on Choreography.* New York: Something Else, 1968.

_____. "I Begin with Moving." Interview by Joan Cass. "Show Guide," *Boston Herald Traveler* (Feb. 15, 1970): 14.

Dalva, Nancy V. "Cunningham in New York and Paris: Enter Merce Laughing." *Dance Magazine* (March 1993).

_____. "Paul Taylor: A Very Appealing Genius." *Dance Magazine* (October 1991): 38–42.

_____. "Paul Taylor, Santo Loquasto, and *Speaking in Tongues*: The Right Mix." *Dance Magazine* (Apr. 1989): 36–38.

Daniel, David. "In Mr. B's Steps." *The New Yorker* (May 17, 1993): 55–59.

de Mille, Agnes. *Martha.* New York: Random House, 1991.

Denby, Edwin. "About *Don Quixote.*" *Dance Magazine* (July 1965): 33–37.

_____. *Dancers, Buildings and People in the Streets.* New York: Horizon, 1965.

_____. *Looking at the Dance.* New York: Horizon, 1968.

Dolin, Anton. *Pas de Deux.* New York: Dover, 1969.

Dorian, Frederick. *The History of Music in Performance.* New York: W.W. Norton, 1966.

Duncan, Isadora. *My Life.* Garden City, N.Y.: Garden City Publishing, 1927.

Edwards, Jeffrey. "American Dancers Abroad." *Dance Magazine* (Mar. 1995): 67–71.

Ellington, Mercer. *Duke Ellington in Person: An Intimate Memoir.* Boston: Houghton Mifflin, 1978.

Estrada, Ric. "3 Leading Negro Artists and How They Feel About Dance in the Community." *Dance Magazine* (November 1968): 60.

Fanger, Iris. "Morris' Playful Persona Arises." *The Boston Herald* (June 10, 1992): 38.

Farrell, Suzanne, with Toni Bentley. *Holding on to the Air.* New York: Summit, 1990.

Fine, Vivian. Untitled article in "Composer/Choreographer," ed. by Selma Jeanne Cohen and A.J. Pischl. *Dance Perspectives* no. 16 (1963): 8–9.

Fiske, Roger. *Ballet Music.* London: George C. Harrap, 1958.

Fokine, Michel. *Memoirs of a Ballet Master.* London: Constable, 1961.

Fuente, Luis. "The Male Image." *Dance Perspectives* no. 40 (Winter 1969): 35–37.

Garafola, Lynn. "Designing Woman." *The New York Times Book Review* (Nov. 19, 1995).

_____. "Peter Martins." *Dance Magazine* (May 1993): 38–42.

_____. "*The Triadic Ballet.*" *Dance Magazine* (Feb. 1986): 28, 38–40.

García-Márquez, Vicente. *Massine.* New York: Alfred A. Knopf, 1995.

Garth Fagan's "Griot, New York." Video program from the *Dance in America* series.

Gates, Henry L., Jr. "The Body Politic." *The New Yorker* (Nov. 26, 1994): 111–124.

Glass, Philip. *Music by Philip Glass.* New York: Harper and Row, 1987.

Goodman, Saul. "Meet Jean Rosenthal." *Dance Magazine* (Feb. 1962): 19–23.

Graham, Martha. *Blood Memory.* New York: Doubleday, 1991.

_____. *The Notebooks of Martha Graham.* New York: Harcourt Brace Jovanovich, 1973.

Greskovic, Robert. "Smoke Got in Her Eyes." *Dance Magazine* (Mar. 1995): 88.

Gruen, John. "Molissa Fenley." *Dance Magazine* (May 1991): 38–41.

Hering, Doris. "Balance of Power." *Dance Magazine* (June 1991): 62.

_____. "Bill T. Jones." *Dance Magazine* (Apr. 1995): 77–78.

Horst, Louis. *Modern Dance Forms.* San Francisco: Impulse, 1961.

_____. Untitled article in "Composer/Choreographer," ed. by Selma Jeanne Cohen and A.J. Pischl. *Dance Perspectives* no. 16 (1963).

Humphrey, Doris. *The Art of Making Dances.* New York: Grove, 1959.

_____. *An Artist First.* Ed. by Selma Jeanne Cohen. Middletown, Conn.: Wesleyan University Press, 1972.

Hunt, Marilyn. "Antony Tudor: Master Provacateur." *Dance Magazine* (May 1987): 36–41.

Jamison, Judith. *Dancing Spirit.* New York: Doubleday, 1993.

Jessup, Bertram. "Taste and Judgment in Aesthetic Experience." In Nadel, Constance Gwen, and Myron Howard Nadel, eds., *The Dance Experience.* New York: Praeger, 1970.

Kirby, Michael. *The Art of Time.* New York: Dutton, 1969.

Kirkland, Gelsey, with Greg Lawrence. *Dancing on My Grave: An Autobiography.* Garden City, N.Y.: Doubleday, 1986.

Kirstein, Lincoln. "Blast at Ballet." *Three Pamphlets Collected.* Brooklyn, N.Y.: Dance Horizons, 1967.

———. *Movement and Metaphor.* New York: Praeger, 1970.

Kisselgoff, Anna. "The Original Red Shoes." *New York Times* (Jan. 9, 1993), Section II: 1.

Kolmes, Jacqueline. "Chandralekha Forges Feminist Abstractions." *Dance Magazine* (Dec. 1994): 34–36.

Kostelanetz, Richard. "The Artist as Playwright and Engineer." *The New York Times Magazine* (Oct. 9, 1966): 32, 109.

Krasovskaya, Vera. "Marius Petipa and *The Sleeping Beauty.*" *Dance Perspectives* no. 49 (Spring 1972): 6–56.

Lahr, John. "King Tap." *The New Yorker* (Oct. 30, 1995).

La Meri. *Spanish Dancing.* New York: A.S. Barnes, 1948.

Langer, Susanne K. *Feeling and Form.* New York: Charles Scribner's Sons, 1953.

———. *Problems of Art.* New York: Charles Scribner's Sons, 1957.

Leatherman, LeRoy. *Martha Graham: Portrait of the Lady as an Artist.* New York: Alfred A. Knopf, 1966.

Lloyd, Margaret. *The Borzoi Book of Modern Dance.* New York: Alfred A. Knopf, 1947.

Lomax, Alan. "Choreometrics and Ethnographic Filmmaking." *Filmmakers' Newsletter,* vol. 4, no. 4 (Feb. 1971): 26.

Louis, Murray. *Inside Dance.* New York: St. Martin's, 1980.

McDonagh, Don. *Martha Graham.* New York: Popular Library, 1975.

Marshall, Kathryn. "Life on Pointe." *Boston Globe Magazine* (Aug. 23, 1981): 11–23.

Martins, Peter, with Robert Cornfield. *Far from Denmark.* Boston: Little, Brown, 1982.

Mason, Francis, ed. *I Remember Balanchine.* New York: Doubleday, 1991.

Mazo, Joseph. *Dance Is a Contact Sport.* New York: Da Capo, 1974.

Merrill, Bruce. "Baby Doll." *Dance Magazine* (Sept. 1993): 86–88.

Mitchell, Emily, with Adrianne Jucius Navone. *A Mouse That Soars.* Time, Inc. 1994. America Online: Oldjericho, June 25, 1995.

Nikolais, Alwin. Interview by Joan Cass. "Show Guide," *Boston Herald Traveler* (Jan. 29, 1967): 15.

Ostlere, Hilary. "Jennifer Tipton." *Dance Magazine* (Apr. 1990): 46–49.

Percival, John. "Antony Tudor, Part One: The Years in England." *Dance Perspectives* no. 17 (1963).

Plunkett, Robert. "*Billboards.*" *New York Times* (Sept. 12, 1993), Section II: 24, 1.

Reimer, Susan. "Mary Cochran." *Dance Magazine* (Oct. 1995): 62–64.

Reynolds, Nancy, and Susan Reimer-Torn. *In Performance: A Companion to the Classics of the Dance.* New York: Harmony, 1980.

Robbins, Jerome. "Reflections and Conversations." *Dance Magazine* (July 1969): 47–55.

Sachs, Curt. *World History of the Dance*. (Trans. by Bessie Schoenberg.) New York: W.W. Norton, 1937.

Salisbury, Wilma. "Cleveland Ballet." *Dance Magazine* (Feb. 1993): 95–96.

Schapiro, Meyer. "Style." In Philipson, Morris, ed. *Aesthetics Today*. Cleveland and New York: World, 1961.

Schneider, Ilya Ilyich. *Isadora Duncan*. New York: Harcourt, Brace and World, 1969.

Sealy, Robert. "The 'New' Firebird." *Ballet Review* 3, no. 4 (1970): 3–8.

Seroff, Victor. *The Real Isadora*. New York: Avon, 1971.

Shawn, Ted. Interview by Joan Cass. "Show Guide," *Boston Herald Traveler* (July 20, 1969).

Siegel, Marcia B. *At the Vanishing Point*. New York: Saturday Review Press, 1972.

_____. *The Shapes of Change*. Boston: Houghton Mifflin, 1979.

_____. *The Tail of the Dragon: New Dance, 1976–1982*. Durham, N.C.: Duke University Press, 1991.

_____, ed., "Nik: A Documentary." *Dance Perspectives* (Winter 1971).

Solomons, Gus, Jr. "The Out-of-Towners 1990." *Dance Magazine* (Jan. 1991): 88–89.

Sommer, Sally R. "The Stage Apprenticeship of Loie Fuller." *Dance Scope* 12, no. 1 (Fall/Winter 1977–78): 23–34.

_____. "Trisha Brown Making Dances." *Dance Scope* 11, no. 2 (Spring/Summer 1977): 7–18.

Sontag, Susan. *Against Interpretation*. New York: Farrar, Straus and Giroux, 1966.

Sorell, Walter. *Hanya Holm, the Biography of an Artist*. Middletown, Conn.: Wesleyan University Press, 1969.

_____, ed. *The Dance Has Many Faces*. Cleveland: World, 1951.

_____. "Martha Graham Speaks." *Dance Observer* 30, no. 4 (Apr. 1963): 53–55.

_____. *The Mary Wigman Book*. Middletown, Conn.: Wesleyan University Press, 1975.

Stearns, Marshall, and Jean Stearns. *Jazz Dance*. New York: Macmillan, 1968.

Stern, Lee E. "Paul Taylor: Gentle Giant of Modern Dance." *Dance Magazine* (February 1976): 36–40.

Storr, Anthony. *Music and the Mind*. New York: Free Press, 1992.

Stravinsky, Igor. *Poetics of Music in the Form of Six Lessons*. New York: Random House, 1947.

Sulcas, Roslyn. "French Funding." *Dance Magazine* (Mar. 1995): 40.

_____. "Trisha Brown." *Dance Magazine* (Apr. 1995): 42–48.

Sylvie Guillem. Video program by Nigel Wattis for London Weekend Television.

Taylor, Paul. *Private Domain*. New York: Alfred A. Knopf, 1987.

Temin, Christine. "*The Nutcracker*." *The Boston Globe* (Nov. 29, 1992): 16.

_____. "San Francisco Ballet." *The Boston Globe* (Mar. 26, 1995): B22.

Ter-Arutunian, Rouben. "In Search of Design." *Dance Perspectives* no. 28 (Winter 1966): unpaginated.

Terry, Walter. *Miss Ruth: The "More Living Life" of Ruth St. Denis*. New York: Dodd, Mead, 1969.

Tharp, Twyla. *Push Comes to Shove*. New York: Bantam, 1992.

_____. "Questions and Answers." *Ballet Review* 4, no. 1 (1971): 41–49.

Thom, Rose Anne. "Cleveland Ballet/Dancing Wheels." *Dance Magazine* (June 1993): 63–64.

Tobias, Tobi. "Annabel Gamson." *Dance Magazine* (May 1995): 86–87.

_____. "Liz Lerman Dance Exchange." *Dance Magazine* (Apr. 1995): 76.

_____. "Twyla Tharp." *Dance Scope* 4, no. 2 (Spring 1970): 6–17.

Tompkins, Calvin. "An Appetite for Motion." *The New Yorker* (May 4, 1968): 52–126.

Van Praagh, Peggy, and Peter Brinson. *The Choreographic Art.* New York: Alfred A. Knopf, 1963.

Vaughan, David. "Cunningham, Cage and James Joyce." *Dance Magazine* (Oct. 1986): 54–55.

_____. *Frederic Ashton and His Ballets.* New York: Alfred A. Knopf, 1977.

_____. *Merce Cunningham: Fifty Years/Chronicle and Commentary.* New York: Aperture, 1997.

Villella, Edward, with Larry Kaplan. *Prodigal Son: Dancing for Balanchine in a World of Pain and Magic.* New York: Simon and Schuster, 1992.

Wigman, Mary. *The Language of Dance.* Middletown, Conn.: Wesleyan University Press, 1966.

Willis, Margaret E. "*Cinderella* in Tinseltown." *Dance Magazine* (February 1987): 58–63.

Sources for Information About Dance Films and Video Programs

Arc Video Dance
131 West 24th St.
5th floor
New York, N.Y. 10011

The Arts on Television 1976–1990
available from:
National Endowment for the Arts
1100 Pennsylvania Ave. N.W.
Washington, D.C. 20506.

Dance Film and Video Guide
available from:
Princeton Book Co.
P.O. Box 57
Pennington, N.J. 08534

Dance Film Archive
University of Rochester
Rochester, N.Y. 14627

Film and Video Catalogue
available from:
Cunningham Dance Foundation
55 Bethune St.
New York, N.Y. 10014

Kultur
121 Highway 36
West Long Branch, N.J. 07764

Michael Blackwood Productions, Inc.
251 West 57th St.
New York, N.Y. 10019

Video Artists International
158 Linwood Plaza
Suite 301
Fort Lee, N.J. 07024

Index

227